VEHICLE REFINISHING

PATRICK NORTH

OSPREY
AUTOMOTIVE

Every effort has been made to ensure that the procedures described in this book are correct. The Author and Publishers accept no responsibility for any loss or injury arising from any of the procedures and activities described.

Illustrations kindly provided by manufacturers and Chris Bennett, Colin Burnham, Jim Tyler, Duncan Wherrett and Andrew Yeadon.

Published in Great Britain in 1993 by Osprey, an imprint of Reed Consumer Books Limited, Michelin House, 81 Fulham Road, London SW3 6RB and Auckland, Melbourne, Singapore and Toronto

Cataloguing in Publication Data is available from the British Library upon request.

ISBN 185532 238 2

Project Editor Shaun Barrington
Editor Mike Darton
Page design by Gwyn Lewis

Film set by Tradespools Ltd., Frome, Somerset
Printed in England by BAS Printers,
Over Wallop, Hampshire

HALF TITLE Front wing of an MGB; the areas around the light clusters and beneath the chrome strip are common rust spots. The surface has been taken back to bare metal and given a coat of primer. (Photo: Jim Tyler)

TITLE PAGE Jaguar XK150 polished and buffed after the final coat. Six top coats have been applied with heat drying after each application and flatting with fine wet and dry paper. (Photo: Duncan Wherrett)

CONTENTS

ABOUT THE AUTHOR

I have had forty years' experience as a vehicle painter – I started as an apprentice and in time advanced all the way up to management. But it was during a two-year course in sign-writing at the College of Art in Bradford in 1965–67 that my career took an unexpected and, to me, highly pleasurable twist. The head of the department at the College, Mr Reg Wilson, asked me if I would like to teach a course on what I had already learned professionally, under the title Vehicle Painting and Industrial Finishing. No such course had been available anywhere on that subject before then – when I began painting vehicles there were not even textbooks on the subject – and I was delighted and stimulated to accept the challenge.

As a part-time lecturer, I taught students for City and Guilds examinations and at an advanced level for eleven more years thereafter. I enjoyed every minute of it, and I hope my pupils did too. The courses seemed to prove popular and useful; academically, they were pretty successful.

The long-term result of both my professional career and my lectureship is this book, something I regard as the virtual culmination of a lifelong commitment to my work. As a practical man, I like to think that I can hand the fruits of that practical experience on to others, and that it will once more prove of value, not just to the student this time but perhaps also to the craftsman who wants to know more about the materials with which he works.

Meanwhile I must acknowledge my eternal debt in relation to the help and guidance given me by two most knowledgeable gentlemen, Mr Reg Wilson and his successor Mr Charles Hartley.

Pat North

FOREWORD

Following the introduction of cellulose finishes now some 50 years or so ago, research chemists have combed the field of organic chemistry seeking further new media to give quick-drying and extra-durable finishes. The results have been the production of varnishes and enamels that possess properties which were simply unobtainable using natural gum and oil combinations.

The later advent of alkyds and other resins opened up vast scope for thermosetting and thermoplastic applications, and the recent addition of two-pack isocyanate enamels has increased the overall range of properties available in such a way that almost every imaginable application is now catered for.

In fact, the reader may well feel bewildered by the very wide choice of finishes on offer – yet each has its own special merits, its own advantages and disadvantages. And it is to impart such information that is the primary purpose of this book, combining not just the basics but also the latest trends in the industry.

Those latest trends include advances in applications that to some degree might appear peripheral to the overall subject – I mean in such fields as non-convertible coatings, which do nonetheless retain a position of importance in several industries (such as wood finishes, polyesters, acid-cured urea formaldehydes and polyurethanes) despite the competition of quick-drying or stoving convertible coatings. Or oxyacetylene welding. But the repair of damaged vehicles is an essential part of the refinishing operation, and I make no excuses for including such themes.

Finally, I hope the level of writing in the text will make it easily comprehensible both to students of and newcomers to the refinishing industry, and to the interested layperson.

INTRODUCTION

The annual world production of paint is approximately 12 to 13 million tonnes – enough to cover 30,000 square kilometres, or to create a painted swathe around the planet 1,100 metres wide seven and a half times over!

The greatest single consumer of the total world production of paint is without doubt the building and construction industry. After that the largest consumers are those industries that require paint for decorative purposes as much as protection – the finishing of cars, boats and furniture, for example.

So what is paint? As a material, paint has always been shrouded in mystery for the uninitiated, and is still so today – in some cases even to specialists in associated technologies. That the mystery continues is perhaps rather natural, for the paint industry has never been especially generous with information about the manufacture or testing of new products.

Even a specialist within the paint industry may face unexpected problems if he or she forgets to take into consideration any one or more of the essential aspects of paint application:
● the material on which the paint is to be applied (and its construction and purpose);
● the specific properties of the paint; and
● the method of application.
Only if these factors are compatible can the required **finish** be attained. For this reason, careful selection of an appropriate form of paint is utterly essential.

Ideally, a paint not only lends the desired optical or decorative effect but also produces an appropriate finish that requires little maintenance and provides fair protection to the surface it covers.

Paint research is still in its infancy as a science. Although for a few decades now research and development in the field have been extensive, resulting in today's enormous number of different products, much remains to be done. There are many questions that can so far only be answered in the light of practical experience – questions, for example, that appertain to the effects of additives, or the properties afforded by different methods of application, or the long-term influence of continuous solar radiation or low temperature. The paint industry is clearly a long way yet from being able to offer generally valid details on the behaviour of a paint in all conditions. In most cases a new paint is first formulated and produced, and only then tested to find out what practical properties it possesses.

In the future it is quite probable that today's many paint factories will in any case progressively combine to form new, larger manufacturing units, and that the remaining small paint factories will of necessity be obliged to specialize in the production of only a few types of paint. This development has already been discernible in Europe and elsewhere for a number of years, although the process has reached different stages in different areas. It must of course be regarded as an inevitable consequence of severe competition in the field.

COLOUR AND COLOUR PERCEPTION

The range of colours visible to the human eye correspond to the spectrum of colours into which white light can be broken by means of a prism, an effect also seen in the form of the rainbow.

Colour is perceived as rays of light pass through the cornea and lens of each eye and are focused on the retina at the back of the eyeball. Nerve endings on the retina channel the signals via the associated optic nerve to the brain, which interprets them partly in terms of black and white (for visual clarity) and partly in colour through sensors that are able to detect light frequencies corresponding roughly to red, green and blue. All the colours that we distinguish can be made up from combinations of these three frequencies. Red and green, for example, combine in order to produce yellow, and all three together combine to produce white. In terms of light, then, red, green and blue are the three primary colours, whereas in terms of pigments and paints, red, yellow and blue are the three primaries and together produce black.

In nature, human vision sees as colour the light that is reflected from an object. What light is absorbed by the object, and what light is reflected, depends on the object's surface and pigmentation. How it is perceived also depends upon the light in which the object is viewed. A white object appears violet when placed in violet light, blue in blue light, and so on; it reflects light of almost all colours, and absorbs almost none. But a violet object placed in violet light appears bright violet, and in light of any other colour (except white) appears black; it reflects only violet light and absorbs virtually all the other colours; a blue object appears blue only in blue (or white) light.

Ray of light passing through a prism and breaking up into coloured bands.

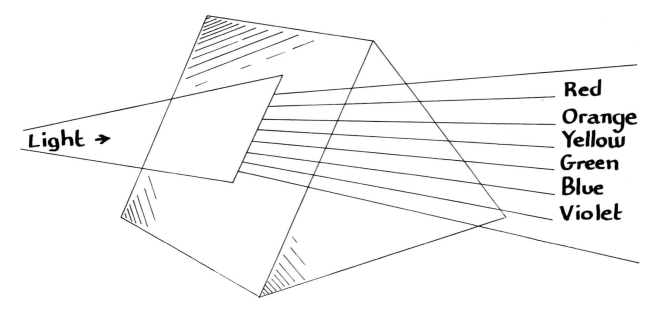

Light →

Red
Orange
Yellow
Green
Blue
Violet

Combinations of colours in light tend towards completing the spectrum and thus producing white light: this is known as additive mixing of colours. It is subtractive mixing that occurs when pigments are combined. The appearance of colour in this case depends on the absorption of some but not all of the illuminating light. For instance: yellow paint absorbs blue from illuminating white light, and reflects red and green which to the eye together appear yellow.

Short Glossary of Technical Terms: Colour

achromatic colourless
advancing colours colours that give the illusion of proximity to the observer
cast perceptible inclination of one colour towards another
chroma intensity of hue; brightness
complementary colours contrasting hues that go well together
cool colours hues in which blue predominates
deep colour intense hue with no apparent presence of black
fugitive colour colour tending to fade, especially in a combination
hue technical term for 'colour'
neutral dull; grey
nuance small gradation or difference between hues
receding colours colours that give the illusion of distance to the observer
shade lightness or darkness of hue
tinge slight trace of colour
tint pale/light value of colour
warm colours hues in which red or orange predominates
xanthic yellow

Many commercial products owe something of their popularity to the fact that the parts of which they are made up match in colour. The match (or less commonly, contrast) between a car's body paint and its upholstery is one good example. But how well the colours match may actually differ depending on the light under which the parts are illuminated.

The most usual forms of lighting are:
daylight – white light, useful for colour matching
tungsten – (light bulbs) red and yellow light
sodium – orange light
mercury – blue light
By the very nature of human vision, in that there are only three primary light colours, many different combinations of stimuli may together lead to exactly the same perceived colour. The stimuli of this kind are technically known as metamers, and the phenomenon is called metamerism. It is metamerism that may lead to poor colour constancy – a match that changes under different lighting conditions. Recognition and avoidance of metamerism plays a major role in the industrial coloration of materials.

There are other aspects of colour science related to metamerism. Colour rendering describes the ability

Metamerism *The stimulus perceived as colour is made up of the spectral power (or, as here, energy)*

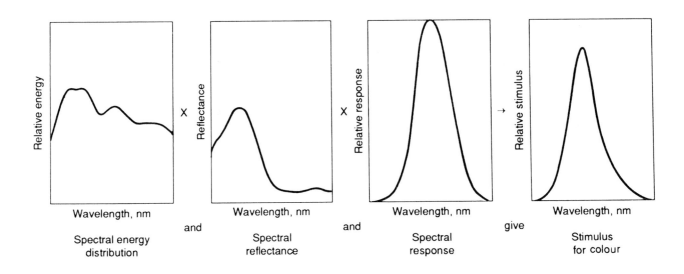

Relative energy Wavelength, nm Spectral energy distribution	and	Reflectance Wavelength, nm Spectral reflectance	and	Relative response Wavelength, nm Spectral response	give	Relative stimulus Wavelength, nm Stimulus for colour

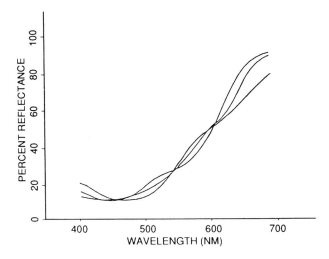

Spectral reflectance curves of three yellow materials that match in colour and lightness: paint, fabric and plastic roof of an automobile.

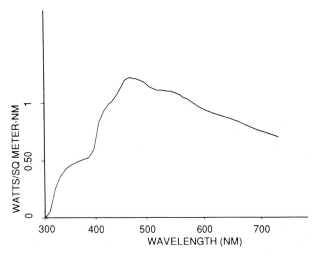

Spectral power distribution of average daylight. Irradiance per unit wavelength interval. (NM = Nanometer.)

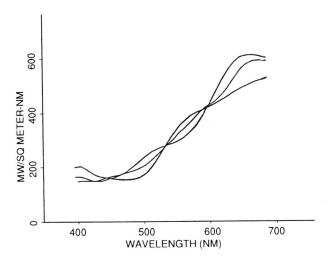

Spectral power distributions of the light reflected and entering the eye of the above materials when illuminated by average daylight.

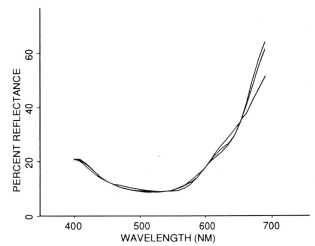

Spectral reflectance curves of three purplish materials that match in colour and lightness when illuminated by average daylight.

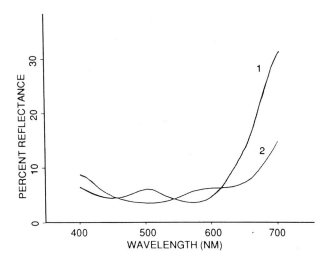

Spectral reflectance curves of two pinkish grey materials that match in colour and lightness when illuminated by average daylight.

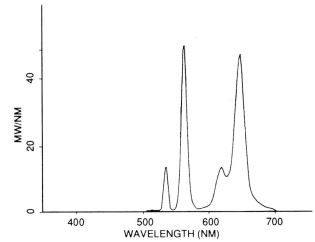

Spectral power distribution of a fluorescent lamp emitting primarily yellow light near 580nm and deep red light near 660nm.

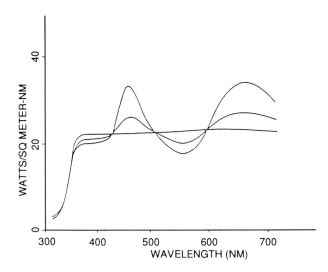

Spectral reflectance curves of three grey materials that match in colour and lightness.

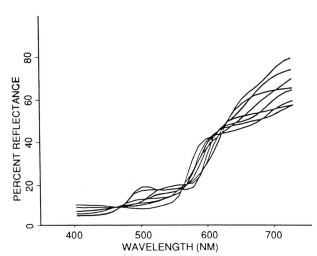

Spectral reflectance curves of eight orange materials that match in colour and lightness when illuminated by average daylight.

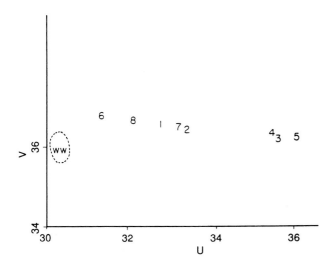

The 1960 CIE U, V uniform chromaticity diagram. Chromaticities of the eight materials below left when illuminated by the fluorescent lamp. (WW = warm white light; V = colour valence; U = wavelength.)

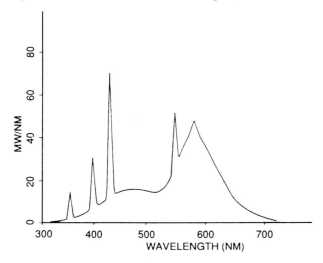

of a test illuminant to produce the same colour effects as a reference illuminant. Chromatic adaptation results when the responsivity of the eyes is altered so as to preserve the colours of objects viewed under specific conditions. But it has to be said that these are research aspects that are not yet fully documented. At the same time, the measurement and use of spectral reflectances of materials is a well established procedure in many industries.

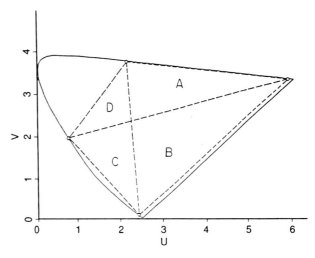

ABOVE *The 1960 CIE U, V uniform chromaticity diagram. Open circles: approximate chromaticities of the four components of an actual fluorescent lamp designed to reveal metamerism in samples matching under daylight.*

LEFT *Spectral power distribution of the commercial cool white fluorescent lamp.*

A SHORT HISTORY OF PAINTS AND PAINTING

Paint has influenced the human imagination ever since our earliest ancestors walked the earth. Drawings and decorations have been discovered in caves where once these ancestors lived, and dated to more than 20,000 years ago. The paints used then were probably produced by mixing different clays, with milk or the sap from trees as the binder (the medium by which the pigment is transferred as a layer to the surface).

Later, the ancient Egyptians added a knowledge of mineral colorants to the earth-based pigments – notably ultramarine, most likely derived from the semiprecious stone lapis lazuli. It was they who introduced the use of vegetable oils and glues as the binder, and who first utilized litharge (lead monoxide) as a siccative (the drying agent, allowing oils to dry rapidly).

The ancient Greeks used mostly red and yellow earth pigments but could also call upon soot for blacking and upon vermilion, a red form of mercury sulphide. Common binders for them were preparations of wax.

The Romans used pigments such as white lead, chalk, ochres, red iron impurities, vermilion, ultramarine, and bone- and smoke-black. Nut oils and linseed oil were the binders. Decorative paintings produced at this time were done with tempera, casein or chalk paints. The durability of these last was improved by burning the colours in with hot irons.

Well before medieval times in Europe, the countries of the Far East – notably India, China and Japan – developed a comparatively advanced technique in paint production. It was from India, and through the Hindi word loaned to most of the languages in Europe, that the organic form of paint known as lacquer (German *Lack*, French *laque*, Russian *lak*, Finnish *lakka*, Hungarian *lakk*, etc.)

derived. Originally lacquers were any of several alcohol solutions that contained the organic substance shellac produced as a glossy film by specific insects on trees in India, but later the term was in English extended to other resinous solutions, and later still to different coating materials altogether.

In Europe, the Dutch first began to import raw materials in order to produce paint for the prestigious painters of their artistic renaissance. The Germans quickly followed suit and themselves made great advances in technique and production methods. Some advances, on the other hand, came about through pure chance. It was probably at about this time that red lead was first discovered, when a barrel that had contained white lead was recovered from a storehouse that had been burned down. Similar presumably happenstance discoveries included the fact that linseed oil could be mixed with resin gum to form a varnish.

The eighteenth century was a period of tremendous progress, in which many innovations in the paint world were made public. To boil linseed oil before mixing it into paint was found to allow the paint to dry much faster. New copals (lustrous resins) and other resins were imported from Africa and mixed with linseed oil to produce paints with new and better qualities. Many new pigments were discovered.

But until the early twentieth century the production of paints was still on an individual basis – every painter bought his or her own materials and mixed them according to a favoured recipe. Gradually, industrial production became more common. One of the great breakthroughs in the development of the paint industry came about when the Germans successfully synthesized several different dyestuffs and colorant agents from coal and coal tars.

Synthetic materials have today by far replaced the natural materials, which are now both expensive and difficult to get hold of. Another tremendous step forward was the introduction of cellulose paints and dopes: their extremely short drying times forced the paint industry to search for new application techniques.

And so to the present. Developments are taking place in many fields and with various effects. Paints are now available for use in the most diverse conditions and under a multitude of circumstances. Nonetheless, the more that is discovered and produced, the more it becomes evident that the science of paint technology is incredibly complex and that much remains to be done.

The paint industry can still be regarded as a relatively young industry and the same can be said of research in this field. During the last 30 years, however, extremely rapid progress has been made and in several countries the technical standard of the paint industry has reached a very high level.

In the future it may be anticipated that the numerous paint factories currently in existence will be combined to form a few large production units and that any remaining small paint factories will, of necessity, have a specialized production. This development is naturally at different stages in different countries but has been discernible for many years and must be regarded as an essential consequence of the increasingly severe competition.

1 · PRIMARY CONSIDERATIONS

SAFETY

In the paint industry, the importance of guaranteed, continual safety in all locations, under every circumstance, and at all levels is paramount. The transport, storage, handling, mixing and application of paints have their own individual inherent dangers, precautions against some of which are regulated (in England and Wales, Scotland, and abroad) by law.

This section gives details about the maintenance of health and safety by taking general medical and practical precautions, including the initial design of workplaces and protective clothing and equipment; about the symptoms and signs of industrially-related ill-health, whether as an emergency or over a long period; about the symptoms and signs of poisoning by toxic chemicals used in the paint industry; about precautions against the risk of fire and measures to take in the event; about the general and English legal requirements for safety in the storage and handling of paints, solvents and other flammable substances; and finally, information is given about the disposal of potentially hazardous waste substances.

Health precautions

General
Anyone who handles or uses paints or thinners should wear overalls, and must wash the hands before eating, drinking, smoking, or using toilet facilities.

The skin
Many chemicals in the paint industry can cause skin irritation; repeated or prolonged contact with such chemicals may result in the unsightly skin condition dermatitis. A suitable barrier cream may help to protect exposed areas of skin.

Some solvents may not only irritate but pass through the skin into the body and into the circulation. Cleansing of the hands with solvents or thinners (such as white spirit) after using paints should therefore be prohibited. Splashes of paint on the skin should be removed promptly, if necessary with the assistance of a proprietary cleansing product, and the skin should then be washed with soap and water.

In particular, when cleaning small quantities of peroxide catalysts, acid catalysts or organic catalyst activators or accelerators from the skin, only soap and water should be used to wash the skin thoroughly. Paint thinners or solvents should never be used.

Medical attention should be sought if skin irritation persists or a rash develops.

The eyes
Whenever the risk of paint splashing up into the eyes is present (as when opening a tin of paint, or mixing), protective goggles – preferably of the chemical-resistant type conforming to British Standard 2092:1967 – should be worn. Contact lenses afford no protection to the eyes in these circumstances, and wearers should also wear goggles to avoid eye contamination.

Splashes of paint in the eye should be treated at once by flushing with copious quantites of clean, luke-warm water for at least 10 minutes while holding the eyelids apart. Medical attention should be sought as soon as possible. Much the same applies in relation to contact lens wearers: if paint splashes into the eye, the lens should be removed at once and the eye flushed in identical fashion. Medical attention should again be sought as soon as possible.

Inhalation

In conditions of poor ventilation, high concentrations of flammable vapour may accumulate, to which prolonged exposure may eventually cause dizziness and loss of consciousness. Where such conditions are known, it may be possible in the short term to wear a mask, or for longer working to use a respirator of approved design (see *Health Protection in the Spray Booth* below).

The real answer, however, is to ensure that there is good general ventilation and, where appropriate, local extraction ventilation, particularly to avoid the inhalation of fumes, vapours, dust or spray during the application of paint in a workroom. Such ventilation also prevents the accumulation of potentially flammable solid paint residues or solvent vapours.

The type of ventilation system should also reflect the nature of the paint in use within the booth or workroom. Because of the potential inflammability of the solid residues of cellulose paint, and because of the possible spontaneous heating up of solid residues from oil-based paint, for example, it is inadvisable to spray cellulose or oil-based paint in a workroom in which the ventilation system features dry extraction. Under these circumstances a water-washed extraction system should be used.

Ingestion

Eating, drinking and smoking cigarettes or cigars should not be permitted in any working area because of the risk of accidental ingestion. Food should not be brought into, stored, prepared or consumed in the workroom or in any place where paints and thinners are stored or handled. Depending on the chemical structure of the paint or thinner, accidental ingestion may even in minute quantities cause abdominal pain, vomiting, loss of consciousness and serious longterm complications.

If paint is ingested, medical attention should be sought at once.

Paints containing the heavy metal lead are by English law specifically labelled 'Containing Lead' and are subject to the **Control of Lead at Work Regulations, 1980** – under which eating, drinking and smoking are prohibited in areas where such products are used.

Medical Emergencies: Summary

Paint on Skin Remove promptly, while wet, if necessary with a proprietary petroleum-based product. (Do **not** use a solvent or thinner.) Wash thoroughly with soap and water.

 If skin irritation persists or a rash develops, seek medical attention.

Paint in Eye Seek medical attention at once. Flush out with continuous stream of clean, luke-warm water, holding the eyelids apart, for at least 10 minutes. (Any contact lens should first be removed.)

Paint Inhaled Seek medical attention at once. Move to fresh air and keep warm. Do not eat or drink. Do not smoke.

Paint Swallowed Seek medical attention at once. Drink as much water as possible. Do not induce vomiting (in case caustic material travels from the alimentary canal into the lungs).

Health protection in the spray booth

● Spray booth design. Booths and similar enclosures should be designed, installed and maintained to prevent vapour or spray from entering the operative's breathing zone and escaping into the general atmosphere of the workplace. Spray mist must be conducted by the exhaust ventilation away to a safe place at a safe distance.

 Wherever an operative is required to work within the booth, an efficient alarm system should be fitted (and maintained) to warn the operative when the air pressure within the booth has fallen to the minimum safe working level.

● Spraying with preparatory materials.
When using preparatory materials containing phosphoric acid or methylene chloride, eye protection, PVC gloves, boots and an apron should be worn, and a protective cream applied on the hands.

● Normal spray refinishing.
When any refinish product is being sprayed, a cartridge respirator conforming to British Standard 2091:1969 must be worn, and should be fitted with a vapour-particulate cartridge designed for paint spray and light fume protection. Sometimes a higher degree of protection using airline breathing apparatus is advisable (see paragraph on two-pack polyurethane products below), and in that case it will be stated in the manufacturer's technical literature and marked on the containers.

For dry sanding operations a cartridge respirator conforming to BS 2091:1969 and fitted with a particulate cartridge is recommended, although the vapour-particulate cartridge used when spraying will suffice.

Filters must be changed regularly, and face-pieces should be washed equally regularly in a sterilizing solution (such as a diluted disinfectant).
● Spraying two-pack polyurethane products activated with isocyanate hardener.
In two-pack paint systems, one part consists of an isocyanate adduct containing a small percentage of free isocyanate – a substance that is a respiratory sensitizer. A sensitized person experiences chest tightness or wheezing, watery eyes and a dry throat (later there may be a headache), and may eventually react to very low concentrations of isocyanate. Although on every occasion recovery is rapid when exposure to the isocyanate ceases, the following guidelines (together with good standards of industrial hygiene) should enable paint products containing isocyanates to be used without risk to health.

Wherever possible, operators applying two-pack products activated with an isocyanate hardener should work inside the spray booth, and should wear compressed airline breathing apparatus conforming to British Standard 4667 Part 3:1974. Particular care should be taken to ensure that the supply of air to the compressor is drawn from an uncontaminated source, and that an efficient oil-water and fume filter is fitted. Filters should be changed as often as necessary.

Anyone who enters a spray booth or enclosure for a short period (less than 15 minutes) while spraying is under way must be protected from inhaling the spray-mist by wearing a respirator conforming to British Standard 2091:1969 with a type CC canister.

Despite the above safety procedures, no one with a history of asthma or other long-term respiratory ailment should take any part in a process that involves isocyanates. Companies involved in spraying such products are advised to ask their operatives to undergo a full medical examination before requiring them to perform this work.
● Spraying with low-solubility lead-containing products. According to the Health and Safety Code of Practice, in support of the **Control of Lead at Work Regulations, 1980**, spraying with low-solubility paints is unlikely to result in significant exposure to lead. Nonetheless, it is essential to maintain high standards of hygiene in such matters as washing facilities and non-contamination of foodstuffs. Where there is a genuine possibility of significant exposure to lead, adequate protective clothing, suitable clothing storage and changing facilities are to be provided.

Toxic Chemicals: Poisoning

Many of the substances used in the paint industry are toxic to one degree or another. Some can be absorbed into the body through breathing or swallowing, or simply by skin contact. The effects may be local or general (systemic) and vary from a slight deterioration of overall condition to a seriously life-threatening state.

If the effects are evident within a short time – minutes, perhaps, or a number of hours – the poisoning is described as acute. But it frequently happens with the chemicals most in use in paints and solvents that poisoning is instead chronic, that the effects are not apparent for a considerably longer time, sometimes as a cumulative result of years of exposure in small quantities.

Both acute and chronic poisoning virtually always respond to treatment, although a complete cure of chronic poisoning depends on whether organic damage or pathological change has also occurred within the body during the much longer exposure to the toxic substance. For many such substances, however, the effect of a high concentration in the body for a short time is identical to the effect of a low concentration in the body for a long time.

Other effects of chemicals may be acute allergy, when the body suddenly registers high sensitivity to a substance that it may or may not have encountered before, or the loss of sensitivity, by which the body gradually registers less and less effect of the substance and may even come to feel the lack of the substance when absent – addiction. In fact, addiction is more common than allergy in the UK.

Symptoms of Solvent Poisoning: Summary

Acute Poisoning Solvents have an effect on organs of the body that contain fats (lipids) or fat-like substances (lipoids): organs affected include fat-storage tissues (such as bone marrow), nervous tissues (such as the brain) and the liver.

Symptoms are:
- apparent intoxication
- yawning and tiredness
- dizziness and vertigo
- nausea, followed by vomiting
- possible difficulty in breathing
- possible unconsciousness
- rarely, paralysis of the respiratory system (and without treatment, death)

Solvents dissolve skin fats, drying the skin, making it susceptible to infection or allergic reaction.

Chronic Poisoning Effects vary more in cases of chronic solvent poisoning. However, the most common symptoms are:
- irritability
- marked, continual tiredness
- bouts of dizziness and vertigo
- frequent sharp headaches

In most cases, symptoms fade and cease after a few weeks' absence of the solvent involved. Rarely, symptoms persist.

To avoid solvent poisoning
Guidelines for the avoidance of solvent poisoning are:
1 An operative must never mix solvents without knowing precisely what they are, and any potential hazards involved.
2 Solvents and similar liquids must not be stored in neutral containers and so possibly be confused with fluids that may be consumed by mouth.
3 Personal hygiene must be scrupulously observed before, during, and after handling paints or solvents. Solvents (such as turpentine, xylene or white spirit) may eventually sensitize skin and should not be used to clean hands. Instead, it is advised that mild, petroleum-based hand cleansers be used. But if it is essential that a stronger solvent is used, the hands should be washed thoroughly with soap and water afterwards and a fatty skin cream applied.
4 No one should be allowed to get away with claims of 'unusual tolerance' to the breathing of solvent fumes. An effective breathing aid must always be worn when painting in confined or badly ventilated spaces. In addition, suitable and approved protective clothing should be worn whenever appropriate.
5 The working area should be organized from the first in such a way as to eliminate all possible risks.
6 Ventilation should be adequate and approved. There should be an evenly distributed airstream across the entire suction opening, in which the flow of air should not be less than 50 cm per second (20 inches per second). Extra ventilation should be arranged when operatives are welding or are burning off paint.

Various considerations arise from these guidelines, notably in relation to the actual substances that are most commonly the cause of industrial poisoning in the field of paints and solvents, and in relation to the metabolic damage that results.

Solvents that cause weak chronic poisoning
Ethanol, acetone, esters, ether, aldehydes, and petrol hydrocarbons tend to give rise only to acute symptoms of intoxication (although they are inflammable). Ethyl acetate and butyl acetate provoke tears and coughing in someone unused to either, but cause no problems to those familiar with them.

Cellosolve [trade name] has a slightly stronger poisoning effect, but one that can reportedly end in damage to the kidneys.

Trichloroethylene and perchloroethylene (or tetrachloroethylene) – hydrogen chlorides that are important to industry as degreasing agents – give rise to symptoms of psychological disturbance. Once contact with either chloride ceases, however, a sufferer generally returns to normal very quickly.

Solvents that cause strong chronic poisoning
Benzene, methanol, carbon tetrachloride, tetrachloroethane and carbon disulphide belong in this group. Benzene features in the poison regulations of many countries because of the deleterious effect it has on the composition of blood. (A useful replacement for benzene is toluene or xylene, neither of which causes the same damage.) Methanol is today seldom used as a solvent: vapour poisoning is therefore rare. But the substance, also called methyl alcohol, is nonetheless frequently ingested as a liquid either voluntarily (as methylated spirits) or by accident. The symptoms of chronic (and occasionally acute) poisoning are well known: damage to the optic nerves, possibly leading to total blindness. The effects of carbon tetrachloride, tetrachloroethane, pentachloroethane and chloroform (used as an industrial solvent) are on the liver and kidneys and may cause serious problems, of which the first signs are jaundice and discoloration of the urine. Carbon disulphide poisoning results in general nervous symptoms and psychological disturbance. Damage is

mainly to the peripheral nervous system and may provoke allergic reaction, and may ultimately lead to paralysis.

When heated, halogenic hydrocarbons decompose to form halogenic hydrogen and phosgene. Halogenic hydrogen is a strong irritant, and its presence serves as a warning that phosgene – which can cause severe lung damage fairly rapidly, and has been used as an offensive weapon in war – is also present. Cases of phosgene poisoning occasionally occur when an operative spraying with a paint aerosol that utilizes the gas freon as propellant is too close to an electric heater or an open flame.

Rarely, tricresyl phosphate (a plasticizer in some plastics) causes systemic poisoning, resulting in gastric problems and possible loss of sensation at the extremities; recovery may be slow.

Poisonous pigments

Paints that contain poisonous elements are not common, and are generally carefully labelled as poisonous by the manufacturer. The manufacturer's instructions on use should be scrupulously observed. Such paints mostly contain the metallic elements lead or chromium.

Lead is a considerable health hazard: any contact with the skin means some degree of absorption. However, the borderline between tolerable lead absorption (almost everybody comes into contact with lead in one fashion or another a few times a week) and lead poisoning is difficult to draw and may depend on the individual anyway. It is estimated that the average person is physically able to excrete a maximum of about $0 \cdot 7$ milligrams of lead per day via the usual excretory channels. Obviously, if more than that is taken up by the bloodstream, lead poisoning will result. The symptoms are fairly clear. Poisoning initially shows up as constipation (lead colic, or 'painter's colic'). As lead in the circulation increases, the so-called lead line becomes evident as a darkish line where the teeth meet the gums. It is caused by the chemical conversion of the lead in the bloodstream at that point to lead sulphide. The lead line is more marked in people who neglect dental hygiene. Advanced lead poisoning results in loss of sensation and then paralysis in the extremities, a condition that gradually creeps farther up the limbs. Without treatment, the fingers and toes may go gangrenous.

Acute lead poisoning is a rare condition, but can arise in a person who has already absorbed a high degree of lead in the skeleton (which is one place in the body where lead can be stored relatively safely). If then some metabolic change takes place – perhaps caused by an infection or even a change of diet – that makes the blood more acid, what is known as a lead crisis may occur as the lead precipitates out and causes massive poisoning.

The element chromium is a carcinogen: contact causes cancer. But in paints it is the hexavalent chromium compounds (as opposed to trivalent chromium compounds) that present the most danger. They cause the skin condition eczema and painless sores on the skin that are extremely slow to heal.

Many elements included in paints involve risk in connection with welding and burning off paint. The most common, and the most problematical, are compounds of lead, cadmium and zinc. Welding or oxyacetylene cutting of sheet metal coated with a lead paint gives off a lead-laden smoke with a concentration of lead far in excess of what is hygienically permissible. Ventilation must allow for the fumes, and a respirator and other protective clothing are vital. Similar precautions must be taken when welding galvanized or otherwise zinc-rich sheet metal.

The hardeners in polyurethane and two-component epoxy paints

The isocyanates in some polyurethane paints and the aliphatic polyamine hardener in epoxy paints may both cause irritation to the respiratory passages that may in time turn into asthma and other allergic conditions, such as eczema. Precautions should be taken to avoid such irritation, but if it occurs, all contact with the type of paint involved will have to cease.

Health and safety: legal requirements

The **Health and Safety at Work Act, 1974**, places a duty on manufacturers and suppliers of any substances for use at work in England and Wales to ensure – so far as is reasonably practicable – that each substance is safe and without risk to short- or long-term health when properly used.

The Act equally places a duty upon employers to ensure – so far as is reasonably practicable – safe working conditions and the absence of risks to short- or long-term health in connection with the use, handling, storage and transport of all articles and substances. All plant, equipment and working conditions must comply with statutory requirements, such as those detailed in the **Factories Act, 1961**.

Acts similar, if not identical, to the Health and Safety at Work Act, 1974, are in force in most other countries.

The EC Council Directive on the classification, packaging and labelling of materials used by the paint industry insists on the following standard labelling on substances supplied by manufacturers:
● designation (name and nature) of the substance;
● full name and address of the manufacturer;
● general description of risk involved in transport, storage or handling (if any), including symbols relating to any such risk;
● statutory phrase detailing any specific risk;
● statutory phrase detailing specific safety measures required.

In general, it can be said that paints for vehicle refinishing are safe in use provided that:
● good standards of working practice and industrial hygiene are maintained;
● people handling paints (and other materials) have been fully and properly trained; and
● appropriate protective equipment and clothing is supplied, properly maintained, and utilized.

Storage

In England and Wales the storage of paints with a flashpoint below 22°C is governed by the **Petroleum (Consolidation) Act, 1928**, and **Statutory Rules and Orders No. 993 (1929)** and **No. 1443 (1947)**.

Under the Act, paints, thinners, and other products specified by the Act must be labelled either 'Petroleum mixture giving off an inflammable heavy vapour' or with a flame symbol and the words 'Highly inflammable', indicating a flashpoint below 22°C. The Act also lays down that the storeroom must be licensed and be constructed to approved standards. Most other countries have similar legal restrictions.

In England and Wales the storage of paints with a flashpoint between 22°C and 32°C is governed by the **Highly Flammable Liquids and Liquefied Petroleum Gases Regulation, 1972**.

Under the Regulation, paints in this group must

be labelled either 'Flashpoint in the range 22°–32°C' or with the risk-word 'Flammable', which in EC official terminology indicates a product that has a flashpoint of between 22°C and 55°C. More precise flashpoint details may be obtained from the data sheet relating to the relevant product.

Most other countries have similar legal restrictions.

Although materials with a flashpoint between 32°C and 55°C do not technically fall within the Regulation, good industrial practice conforms to it, ensuring that the label 'Flammable' is visible on such products.

Safe storage

Essential guidelines for the safe storage of inflammable materials (particularly paints or the solvents that go into paint), once the products have been satisfactorily labelled, include:

1 Storage of inflammable paints and solvents should be in a place or container constructed of fire-resistant materials and located at an adequate distance from all other buildings.

2 There must be no possibility whatever that inflammable liquids might leak on or into the surrounding area, or into any drainage system within or beneath the storage place.

3 Storage tanks may be constructed below ground level, partly below ground level, or completely above ground level. In the last case, containing walls should be specially strong to prevent leaks but also to limit the risk of fire.

4 Gauge-glasses in or on tanks containing inflammable liquids should be avoided; if there is a circumstance in which a gauge-glass has to be used, it should be fitted with a valve that closes automatically if the glass breaks.

5 Pipes to and from storage tanks should, if possible, be kept wholly above ground, in order to facilitate inspection; they should also be located where there is no danger of mechanical damage.

6 As a precaution against the dangers of static electricity, all pipes, ducts or containers for inflammable liquids should be bonded and earthed (grounded), and should be connected to supply tanks in such a way as to exclude the possibility of static sparking.

7 Storage tanks must be adequately vented; vents should be fitted with wire screens to act as flame arresters in an emergency.

8 Some authorities consider the safest method of

storing inflammable liquids is in small containers, such as drums or barrels, left out in the open air. If direct exposure of such containers to the sun is avoided, and provided the terms of guideline 1 above are followed, there is much to recommend this method.

Various considerations arise from these guidelines, and are of themselves almost as important to safe storage.

The workroom
The maximum amount of paint or other inflammable material kept in a workroom should be restricted to the requirements of one working day only, and should not exceed 50 litres (11 UK gallons/13·2 US gallons). All containers of paint and thinners should be kept securely closed, except during use. Empty containers – which present a greater fire or explosion hazard than full containers – should be disposed of on a daily basis.

Electrical installations
All electric light fittings and electric motors should be of the flameproof type. (Information about the specifications of flameproof electrical machinery and apparatus is available in the UK in the periodical supplements published on the subject by the British Standards Institute.) Wiring, and particularly all switches and fuse-boxes, should be external as far as possible – any necessary internal wiring should be in heavy-gauge, screwed, solid-drawn conduits. Mains-connected portable electric lamps should never be used.

Ventilation
It is essential that inflammable vapour is ducted safely and rapidly away, so that there is no possibility of a build-up that might lead to fire or explosion. If ventilation is mechanical, via an exhaust or a pressure system, care must be taken to allow no risk of ignition in the exhausted air. Ventilation is essential also in the interests of health.

Chemical incompatibility
Some specific inflammable products, for chemical reasons, must not be stored in proximity with certain others. Peroxide catalysts used in the manufacture of polyester products, for example, are strong oxidizing agents and should not be stored anywhere near a number of other substances, especially nitrocellulose sanding dust or any organic material.

General tidiness
Spillages must be cleaned up immediately. Deposits that are potentially inflammable on or in containers should be removed at the first opportunity; removal should not involve the use of iron or steel implements. Plant should be kept clean externally as well as internally. Oily rags and other contaminated materials should not be allowed to accumulate.

Handling and Mixing

There are many requirements also listed within the Highly Flammable Liquids and Liquefied Petroleum Gases Regulation, 1972 in relation to the handling and mixing of paints (and solvents that go into paint). As might be expected, some of the provisions echo the safety precautions for storage outlined above.

Under the Regulation:

1 All decanting and mixing should be carried out in an area that is well ventilated and at some distance from storage or application buildings.
2 Adequate ventilation must from the beginning be carefully designed and provided as far as possible to prevent dangerous concentrations of inflammable vapours.
3 The installation and use of electrical apparatus must from the beginning be carefully specified and rigorously controlled to limit the risk of fire or explosion, especially in areas where vapours are inevitably likely to accumulate.
4 All potential sources of ignition should be strictly controlled: possible sources of sparks from static electricity must be eliminated.
5 Smoking of cigarettes and cigars should be prohibited; matches should not be carried.
6 Products that are potentially hazardous must be kept separate, even when not chemically interactive. Anyone engaged in handling and mixing such products should wear protective clothing to avoid skin or eye contamination.
7 Accumulation of potentially flammable solid paint residues must be avoided as far as is possible. All places where dry paint deposits can accumulate should be cleaned frequently and regularly. (Nitrocellulose residues should be removed using non-ferrous scrapers.)
8 All spillages must be cleaned up as and when they occur, and materials absorbed on to sand, earth or other inert matter. It is imperative that no flammable material be allowed to enter the drainage system.

9 Any rags or other combustible material must after use be deposited in a metal container with a suitable (metal) cover, or be removed without delay to a safe place outside the building in which handling and mixing takes place.

10 Waste materials collected must be treated as a fire hazard, and be disposed of in accordance with the Control of Pollution (Special Waste) Regulations, 1980.

Fire Prevention and Fire-fighting Equipment

Adequate fire prevention and fire-fighting equipment, as approved by local fire authorities, should be provided and maintained in all areas where paint is stored, handled or mixed. Every factory should have a trained fire-fighting team; every person on the premises should be familiar with the fire alarm systems, the location of alarm points, fire escapes and emergency exits. Guidelines on facilities that should be provided in order to minimize the hazards associated with fire are as follows:

1 The structure of the buildings in which such operations occur should be of fire-resistant material.

2 There must be a fire escape, some means of flight from the scene of a fire, wherever it breaks out. This may or may not correspond with access for rescue from a fire – but if it does *not* correspond, there should be some additional means of access for rescue. Well defined passages to emergency exits should be maintained at all times. No outer door should be locked while there is any person on the premises, and all doors should preferably be provided with fastenings that enable the doors to open outwards under pressure.

3 Stored in an accessible but separate position, there should be supplies of fire-fighting foam, dry powder,

A guide to which portable extinguisher to use.

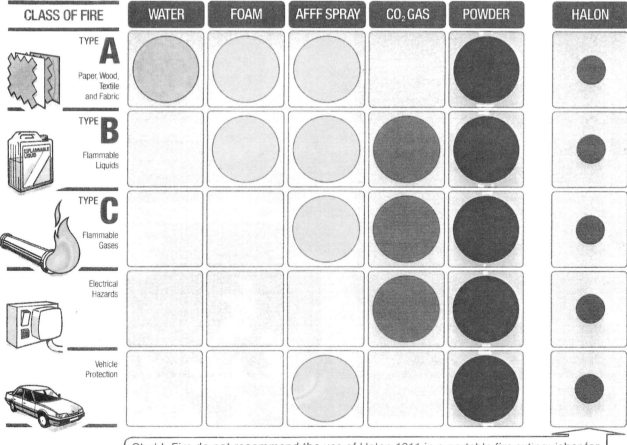

CLASS OF FIRE	WATER	FOAM	AFFF SPRAY	CO₂ GAS	POWDER	HALON
TYPE **A** Paper, Wood, Textile and Fabric	●	●	●		●	●
TYPE **B** Flammable Liquids		●	●	●	●	●
TYPE **C** Flammable Gases			●	●	●	●
Electrical Hazards				●	●	●
Vehicle Protection			●		●	●

Chubb Fire do not recommend the use of Halon 1211 in a portable fire extinguisher for those risks when a viable alternative exists.

carbon dioxide or Halon, and protective fire-resistant clothing, including respirators of an approved design, that have been maintained so as always to be ready for use. Filled sand buckets should be well distributed throughout the working area.

4 The building or buildings must be designed, sited and accoutred in such a way that the blast and effect of an explosion is minimized. Flame failure devices must be appropriately installed and maintained.

5 Ventilation must be adequate and appropriate, both overall and locally: extraction and exhaust ventilation must be sufficient, properly positioned, and correspond to sufficient, properly sited air intakes. Flow of air in and out must be recordably monitored. There must be the means of channelling air in and out mechanically as required.

6 All potential sources of accidental ignition through friction or static electricity should be eliminated.

7 All personnel must be familiar with emergency procedures in the case of fire or explosion. Specific duties in the event must have been allocated, and any special training undertaken, with refresher courses as necessary.

The various extinguishers must be regularly checked and must, of course, be located logically and conveniently.

8 During ordinary working procedures, restrictions on operating temperatures must be in force.

9 During ordinary working procedures, restrictions on drying/curing times must be in force.

One or two considerations arise from these guidelines.

● Fires in paint workrooms have two principal causes: a) solvents, and the fumes from them, are spread over a large area and are ignited all at once; b) gas and other fumes in otherwise empty containers are ignited and cause an explosion.

To avoid such fires:

a eliminate the possibility of the accumulation of fumes by cleaning up spillages of solvents immediately and by not using solvents to clean container walls and floors (proprietary cleaners are as efficient and safer);

b ensure ventilation is sufficiently local and effective;

c close all caps and covers when not in use;

d frequently check the state of the electrical

connections and earth (ground) – static sparks cannot occur between containers that are connected electrically;

   e never splash any flammable liquid when pouring;

   f never use plastic containers for solvents;

   g receptacles for rags and other materials contaminated by oils or paints that might oxidize rapidly and spontaneously combust must be numerous and convenient, and have self-sealing lids or covers; and

   h there should be a routine daily inspection of spray booths, filters and fans.

● Because spray dust from different types of surface coating may interact and possibly spontaneously combust, spray booths and equipment within must be cleaned thoroughly and at frequent, regular intervals. Respirator masks and goggles must be worn for this operation.

● Among the mechanical equipment and heating apparatus of larger works, overheated bearings can occasionally cause ignition. The installation of the self-oiling variety of bearings is recommended. In addition, steam pipes should be avoided altogether if possible. Where there have to be steam pipes, they should not be in contact with wood fittings, they should be brushed down daily, and all flammable materials must be kept away from them.

● Research or experimental work should be carried out in buildings different and separate from those in which manufacturing operations take place.

● Drying ovens. Before the oven is built, the refinisher must – in consultation with the local fire officer and the Factory Inspector – ensure that its site is such as to minimize the risk of fire while at the same time allowing the easy access and withdrawal of vehicles. Ventilation is at a premium with drying ovens: particular attention must be paid to extraction ventilation in order to avoid fire and explosion hazards. For more information on this specific subject, see Guidance Note PM25 issued (in the UK) by the Health and Safety Executive.

● Because of the fire risk, peroxide catalysts must be disposed of with special and extreme care.

● For the same reason, spray booth residues must not be stored or mixed with other products. Isocyanate residues should be adsorbed on to sand, earth or other inert material, and placed in a sealed container to be disposed of in accordance with the Control of Pollution (Special Waste) Regulations, 1980.

● Consideration should be given to the installation of

fixed, automatic sprinkler systems to provide fire protection in all areas where paint is stored, handled or mixed.

Fire-fighting Chemicals: Summary

Water Still one of the most useful fire-fighting elements, and especially when pressurized and directed from a fire extinguisher. Particularly useful in fires amid wood, paper or textiles.

Foam Foam sprays (Spray lances) provide a fast and powerful means of tackling both the wood and fabric type of fire and the petroleum, paint and gas type. Most also pass the electrical conductivity test of British Standard 5423:1987.

Dry Powder Dry powder is the most versatile of all fire-fighting mediums, useful for virtually every type of fire, including combinations (as occur in vehicle fires).

Carbon Dioxide and Halon These gases are used mostly in fire situations involving flammable liquids and electrical hazards, especially where delicate equipment and materials are at risk, for either gas itself causes no damage. Halon, however, is not ozone-friendly and its use in fire extinguishers is being phased out.

TOOLS: THE PAINTBRUSH

The classic tool for use with paint is the paintbrush, examples of which may be found in virtually every household in Europe and North America. Many professional house painters and decorators set great store by their selection of brushes, and indeed the restoration of many a car (and even carriage) may be perfectly finished with the help of the humble brush. But industry rarely uses the paintbrush, relying instead on applicators that can coat a larger or more detailed surface with smoother and more constant lamination.

   This section nonetheless features the nature and manufacture of the paintbrush, and merely gives reference to information about spray booths, the spray gun (and the various processes in which it is used) and electrodeposition that may be found in more relevant chapters elsewhere in this book. The earliest form of brush, invented probably only after humans had long used their hands to spread paint and create images, was a splayed twig. Today, a proper paintbrush has three major components: the bristle, the metal ferrule, and the handle.

The handle

Most paintbrush manufacturers grow their own timber for the handles. Seeds are collected from beech, sycamore, ash or alder trees that are particularly fine specimens in forests or parks, and are planted in spring in seedbeds. There they are carefully nurtured until the following winter when, as plants about 30 cm (1 ft) high, they are transplanted into close rows in what is known as the lining-out nursery. The plants stay in the rows for another two years, developing strong, fibrous root systems and being well cared for, before they are finally transplanted again, during the third winter after their planting as seeds, out in the woods.

The replanting is carefully controlled, so that the trees are perhaps closer to each other than they might have been in nature, in 1·5-metre (5-foot) squares, at 1,900 trees to the acre (roughly 4,700 to the hectare). This proximity causes the lower branches to die off in the early stages of each tree's growth, and so reduces the number of knots in the timber.

The rate of growth of hardwood trees in England varies according to the species of tree and the nature of the soil. Of the usual four, the alder is the fastest grower, in good conditions and not far from water averaging some 60–90 cm (2–3 ft) per year. Sycamore and ash grow about 37–45 cm (15–18 in) a year, and beech – the slowest of the four – generally makes about 30 cm (12 in) in any year.

After between 12 and 15 years, the trees are inspected and thinned out: bent, deformed or badly suppressed trees are removed. A further thinning out operation takes place after 18–20 years. Some of the poles taken as thinnings at this time may go to make smaller paintbrush handles.

Most trees are allowed to continue growing until they are around 23–25 cm (9–10 in) in diameter, by which time they are about 40–50 years old. Felled, they are cross-cut into planks 221 cm (7 ft 3 in) long, a size calculated as the optimum for the variety of shapes that are to be made from the timber. The vertical gang-frame saw used to cut the logs converts them into planks of exactly the required dimensions in no time at all, with its twelve 1·5-metre (5-foot) blades in a frame through which the logs are

Bevelled finish to bristles.

Rubber setting **BELOW FERRULE** ensures maximum pliability. (Left) Note the way the bristles are formed into an "arch". This preserves the fine flagged ends.

Finest hog bristles with forked (flagged) ends.

propelled by hydraulic power.

Stacked on pallets, the planks are taken to the kiln for drying. This is very necessary, for immediately after felling a tree trunk may hold up to half its own weight in residual water, a moisture content that has to be reduced in the kiln to about 10–12 per cent. (If wood is made any drier, it swells badly on renewed contact with the water in ordinary air.) Drying takes between 10 and 14 days, and is controlled and monitored electronically to achieve precisely the desired results.

The dried planks are then passed through a multiple-edging saw, which has three, four, or six circular blades, and which cuts each plank into strips of a desired width. The strips are then cross-cut into 'blanks' of the required length. Most blanks then go through an automatic spindle moulding, which shapes each handle on two sides and two faces, before passing through a battery of sanding machines that smooth off the edges; blanks with knots or areas of ugly discoloration, however, are rejected. For sealing and polishing, the handles are first placed in a rotating barrel containing a sealant, and then, on a specially designed board, are dipped in cellulose lacquer, a process that is repeated to ensure the best possible finish and polish to each handle.

The metal ferrule

The ferrule is the metal binding that joins the bristle (the actual brush) to the handle. Invented in 1905, it may today also have the manufacturer's name and logo embossed upon it. Most are fashioned from a nickel-plated steel strip. A single machine completes all the necessary operations automatically – the binding, sealing and folding, and even the embossing.

The bristle

Despite the use of the word 'bristle' in this context as a technical term, not all paintbrushes actually have brushes made of pigs' (or boars') hairs, which is the original meaning of the word: there are quite a few synthetic substitutes and one or two natural ones.

The bristle of the best quality for paintbrushes comes from Chongqing (formerly spelled Chungking) in China, derives from the Chinese wild pig, and is black. Artists and many other professional painters prefer **pure bristle** of this type, which has its own firm yet springy properties.

Medium bristle – a form of bristle intermediate between pure bristle and soft bristle – generally comes from the Qingdao (formerly spelled Tsingtao) district of China.

Soft bristles derive mostly from the Tianjin (formerly spelled Tientsin) district of China.

Extra stiff bristle, on the other hand, come from the wild boar of India. It is used only in the large distemper brushes.

Horse-hair brushes contain hair from the manes or tails of horses and are for the most part exported from South America. The material is held to be vastly inferior to bristles in elasticity and springiness.

Most **synthetic bristles** are made of nylon. They wear much longer than natural bristle, but do not have the capacity to hold paint as well as natural bristle does thanks to the fiscules that grow up the side of each hair, and the fine, flagged tips at the top.

The process by which bristle is fitted to the metal ferrule and then to the paintbrush handle is surprisingly long and complicated. The first operation is washing and straightening, effected by tying the bristle flat along aluminium tubes, and giving them a

The Chinese wild pig from which the bristles are taken.

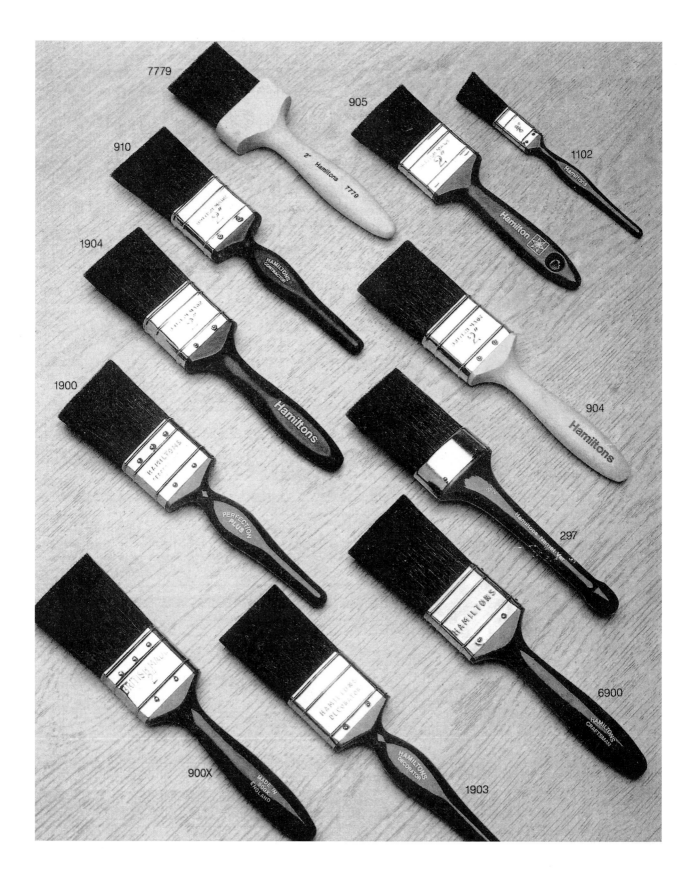

prolonged boiling. The bristles are then sorted and turned – sorted to remove any hairs too short for a paintbrush, and turned so that the fine tips (the flagged ends comprising two or three unltrafine strands to each hair) of the bristles are all together on one side and the coarse roots all together on the other. They are then sorted for length and put through a number of further processes, including another straightening, combing, mixing, and packing into bundles.

When the bristles are ready to be made into a brush head, they are given a final straightening by being boiled inside a metal cone for about five hours. (Bristles are hollow: as the boiling water penetrates each bristle it swells tight against others and against the straight side of the metal cone. The emphasis on straightness follows from the fact that straight bristle helps to paint smoothly.) Drying comes next, for some 30–40 hours in a carefully controlled drying oven. Bundles of bristles are then shaped to the width and thickness required; a bevelled (two-sided slanting) edge is then given to the top of the brush head, to assist both in the smooth release of paint from the flagged ends, and to make the brush last as long as possible.

The brush has then to be fixed within the ferrule. To hold the bristles there, they are set to a specific depth either within epoxy resin or, increasingly rarely, in rubber. Epoxy resin has the advantage of requiring a much shorter curing (setting) time than rubber – four hours as opposed to four days – and does not require the additional seven- to eight-hour high-temperature process of vulcanization that rubber does to acquire imperviousness to any known solvent.

Finally, the bristle is washed in strong disinfectant that not only cleans them but is designed to deter attack by moths which might otherwise find the organic material much to their taste. A hydro-extractor then dries the brush heads completely. They are lightly trimmed in a rotary trimmer to ensure that all the ends of the bristles are quite even. The handle is rammed in tightly, and centred. Riveting machines then pin the bristles to the ferrule, and the ferrule to the handle, and the ferrules are polished up.

A selection of good quality paint brushes from Hamilton, the British manufacturer.

Other tools

For information on the structure and use in painting of the spray gun, see Section 3: Methods of Application, page 86.

For information on applying a surface coating by means of electrodeposition, see Section 3: Methods of Application, page 113.

For detailed information on the structure and use of spray booths, see Section 4: The Spray Booth, page 182.

CALCULATION OF PAINT PER UNIT AREA

The amount of paint required for any given area depends upon certain variable factors:
- the intended thickness of the final film coating;
- the porosity of the receiving surface (substrate);
- the viscosity of the paint;
- the method of application; and
- the likely area of overspray (which may in turn depend upon the efficiency of the ventilation in the workroom, or upon the skill – or lack of skill – of the operative).

One method, with a pigmented finish, is to use the **Sheen Hiding-Power Test Chart**. First weigh the Chart. Then apply the intended coating material over the Chart until the black and white squares are just obliterated. Reweigh the Chart. Calculate the amount of paint required for the area you have in mind using the mathematical factors shown at the foot of the Chart.

Area in relation to paint type

In general, however, a rough and ready guide to the covering capacity of various types of finishing materials (the measure of viscosity timed using a standard viscosity BSB4 flow cup) is as follows:

	m^2 per litre	seconds
acrylic lacquer	8	16–19
cellulose lacquer	8	19–23
metallic lacquer	8	19–23

	m² per litre	seconds
base-coat/clear-coat finishes	8	19–23
sealant	8	19–23
etching primer		
mixed 1:1	8	with activator thinned to 20–25
primer	8	19–22
primer surfacer	8	19–22
primer filler	8	19–22
coach enamel	12	35–45
Permobel/Val–		
Flash 4:1	12	23–27
undercoat	12	35–45
synthetic primer	12	30–35
glaze-coat 6:1	12	35–45
varnish	12	25–30
Application by brush:		
enamel	13–15	138–167
undercoat	18–20	138–167
flat oil paint	16–17	138–167

Area in relation to substrate

The Paint and Painting Industries' Liaison Committee regularly publish an alternative listing of approximate coverage areas of various types of paint in square metres per litre, but with reference to the type of surface that has to be covered. The Committee is careful to point out that all figures quoted are intended to be thoroughly practical, representing averages achieved for brush application on large-scale painting work, and thus taking into account wastage and losses. For this reason, the figures quoted for certain types of paint may be somewhat smaller than figures suggested by the manufacturers.

A 14/60 Lagonda belonging to John Brown awaits restoration. John Brown's body will be treated with the care it deserves. The first 14/60 was produced in 1926. (Photo: Richard Bird).

surface	wood primer (oil-based)	water-thinned primer/undercoat as primer	as u-coat	aluminium sealer spirit-based	oil-based
finishing plaster		13–15			
wood floated rendering					
smooth concrete/cement					
fair-faced brickwork					
blockwork					
roughcast/pebbledash					
hardboard		10–12			
soft fibre insulating board		7–10	10–12		
fire retardant ins. board					
smooth paper-faced board		8–11	10–12		
hard asbestos sheet		7–10			
structural steelwork					
metal sheeting					9–13
joinery	8–11	10–14	12–15	7–9	9–13
smooth primed surface			12–15		

all figures square metres per litre.
Aluminium sealer is normally used over 'bitumen' painted surfaces.
On some roughcast/pebbledash surfaces, appreciably lower coverage may be obtained.

surface	metal primer conventional	metal primer specialized	plaster primer (including building board)	alkali-resistant primer
finishing plaster		o	9–11	7–11
wood floated rendering		b t a	8–12	6–8
smooth concrete/cement		i n	9–11	7–11
fair-faced brickwork		f	7–9	6–8
blockwork		i g	5–7	4–6
roughcast/pebbledash		u r	2–4	2–4
hardboard		e s	8–10	
soft fibre insulating board		f		7–9
fire retardant ins. board		r o	8–10	
smooth paper-faced board		m	10–12	
hard asbestos sheet		m a	10–12	8–10
structural steelwork	7–10	n u		
metal sheeting	10–13	f a		
joinery		c t		
smooth primed surface		u r		
smooth undercoated surface		e r		

All figures square metres per litre.
Convention metal primers are lead, chromate and calcium types.

surface	external wall primer/ sealer	under- coat	gloss finish	oil-based thixo- tropic finish	eggshell/ semi-gloss finish (oil-based)
finishing plaster	6–8	11–14	11–14	obtain figures from manufacturer	11–14
wood floated rendering	6–7	7–9	8–10		9–11
smooth concrete/cement	6–8	7–9	8–10		11–14
fair-faced brickwork	5–7	6–8	7–9		8–10
blockwork	4–6	6–8	6–8		7–9
roughcast/pebbledash	2–4	3–4			
hardboard		11–14	11–14		10–13
soft fibre insulating board		10–12	10–12		10–12
fire retardant ins. board		10–12	10–12		10–12
smooth paper-faced board		11–14	11–14		11–14
hard asbestos sheet	6–8	10–12	10–12		10–12
structural steelwork		10–12	10–12		10–12
metal sheeting		10–12	10–12		10–12
joinery		10–12	10–12		10–12
smooth primed surface		11–14	11–14		11–14
smooth undercoated surface			11–14		11–14

All figures square metres per litre.

surface	emulsion paint standard	contract	glossy emulsion	heavy textured coating
finishing plaster	12–15	10–12	o b t a i n	2–4
wood floated rendering	8–12	7–11		2–4
smooth concrete/cement	11–14	10–12		2–4
fair-faced brickwork	8–12	7–10		2–4
blockwork	6–10	5–9	f i g u r e s	2–4
roughcast/pebbledash	2–4	2–4		
hardboard	12–15	10–12		2–4
soft fibre insulating board	8–10	7–9		2–4
fire retardant ins. board	8–10		f r o m	2–4
smooth paper-faced board	12–15	10–12		2–4
hard asbestos sheet	10–12	8–10		2–4
structural steelwork			m a n u f a c t u r e r	2–4
metal sheeting				2–4
joinery	10–12	10–12		2–4
smooth primed surface	12–15	10–12		2–4
smooth undercoated surface	12–15	10–12		2–4

All figures square metres per litre.
Heavy textured coating is of interior and exterior types.

surface	masonry paint	oil-bound water paint	cement-based paint
finishing plaster	5–7	7–9	
wood floated rendering	4–6	6–8	4–6
smooth concrete/cement	5–7	7–9	6–7
fair-faced brickwork	4–6	6–8	3–6
blockwork	3–5	5–7	3–6
roughcast/pebbledash	2–4		2–3
hardboard soft fibre insulating board fire retardant ins. board smooth paper-faced board hard asbestos sheet	5–7	7–9	4–6
structural steelwork metal sheeting joinery smooth primed surface	6–8		
smooth undercoated surface	6–8		

All figures except for oil-bound water paint in square metres per litre.
For oil-bound water paint the unit is 4·536 kg (10 lb).

2 · PAINTS AND PIGMENTS

THE COMPOSITION OF A PAINT

Paint in general consists of
- the pigment,
- a binder,
- an extender,
- a solvent, and
- any of various additives.

Pigment, the colorant agent, consists of white or coloured particles usually of 0·2–5 microns in size; they can be of organic or inorganic origin. The pigment gives a paint its colour (its shade and intensity) and its covering or hiding capacity. To a lesser degree, the pigment may also be responsible for the paint's weathering properties, its texture (which affects the method of application), its resistance to chemical agents, and its gloss.

The **binder** creates a permanent, continuous film and is responsible for the paint's adhesion to the surface, its resistance to weathering and to chemical agents, and for several other qualities. In relation to the finish, the binder must be regarded as the most important ingredient of a paint.

Extenders or **fillers** are technically non-hiding pigments between 0·2 and 30 microns in size; they can take any of various crystalline forms. Their purpose in a paint is to lend body, to improve brush-out characteristics, to add resistance to weather and chemical agents, and to lower the cost. Although such fillers do not themselves possess any hiding power, they help to extend the hiding power of the paint's pigment to an optimum level by retaining the pigment particles at a specific distance from each other sufficient to cover effectively.

The **solvent** in a paint is usually an organic substance, a liquid that has a certain miscible capacity and in which the binder is soluble. What the solvent is responsible for is the quality of deformation and flow, wetting the surface while at the same time not increasing the drying time. In dispersions, the solvent is replaced by the dispersion agent, water. The term 'solvent' in the context of paint is not always or entirely accurate, for a 'solvent' that does not affect a binder is instead a diluent or thinner, and not a solvent as such at all. At the same time, the quantity of thinner that can be added to a solution of binder in solvent is limited: if more is added than the 'thinning limit', the binder will 'fall out'. A solvent's capacity for solubility is restricted to specific binder groups: a universal solvent has not yet been formulated.

Additives comprise a large and extremely diffuse group of products that are used to accentuate the best qualities of a paint. They may thus enhance a paint's thickening, wetting, drying, stabilizing, or any other properties. Of these products perhaps the most important today are the plasticizers, which are used to make the basic resin film more elastic and extensible.

These factors in paints are for the most part examined in greater detail later in this chapter, although one or two feature in more detail within other chapters in this book. While we are investigating the composition of paint in general terms, however, it is convenient here to look at what is perhaps the greatest difference between paint types. The above factors are all individual constituents, but it is in the way they combine to form paint that the difference is manifest.

Solutions and dispersions

In physical terms, then, a paint can be described as a mixture of fluids and solids – a mixture that represents either a **solution** or a **dispersion**.

A solution is a practically homogeneous mixture of two or more substances at the molecular level, although the molecular structure of each constituent is different. It occurs because there is a strong binding tendency between those particular molecular constituents. At the same time, solutions in which one constituent has unduly large molecules are known as colloidal solutions: the solvent in a colloidal solution may confusingly be described as the dispersion medium and the dissolved substance the disperse phase.

A dispersion in the context of paints, however, is a mixture in which there is no solubility between components. It can take the form of a **suspension** (a solid-fluid mixture in which solid particles are dispersed in the fluid dispersion agent) or an **emulsion** (a fluid-fluid mixture representing a combination of an oil and water).

An emulsion can be either of two types:
● an oil-water emulsion, in which the water is the surrounding medium and determines the deformation and flow characteristics (an example is milk);
● a water-oil emulsion, in which the oil is the surrounding medium (an example is skin cream).

Whereas oil-water emulsions can be thinned with water to an unlimited degree, water-oil emulsions can be thinned with water only with some difficulty.

Water is the dispersion agent in almost all dispersions. And because a dispersed substance cannot (in the context of paints) be soluble in the dispersing medium, the paint film obtained from a dispersion paint once dried is usually water-resistant. On the other hand the dispersing agent is generally water-soluble, and if too much is added, can reduce the water-resistance by quite a margin, which can be a serious limiting factor.

Composition of Paint Types: Summary

Unpigmented paints solution: a binder in a solvent
emulsion: a fluid non-water-soluble binder in water
suspension: a non-water-soluble solid in water

Pigmented paints suspension: a non-soluble pigment in water or solvent
dispersion: an emulsion, or a fluid pigment suspension

There are some characteristic differences between paints that are solutions and paints that are dispersions.
● Viscosity. The viscosity of a solution very much depends on the size of the molecules in the binder, on the capacity of the solvent to dissolve the solute, and the proportion of the contents that is inactive. The greater the molecular size and the higher the inactive proportion, the more viscous the paint.

The viscosity of a dispersion is basically determined by the viscosity of the dispersion medium. It is more or less independent of molecular size, and increases under the effect of the inactive proportion of its contents only when that proportion is itself of some magnitude.

Viscosity (and consistency) can of course be adjusted very simply through the addition of water or water-soluble thickeners such as casein or polyvinyl alcohol. But the range of properties available in a dispersion by regulation of its viscosity – taking into account the type and concentration of the binder and its molecular size, the degree of polymerization, and the solubility characteristics – is greater than that of a suspension if the technical conditions of application are identical in both cases.
● Adhesion.
In general, adhesion is better in solutions than in dispersions because of the better penetration, wetting and achorage in the receiving surface. Dispersions should not be expected to perform as well in view of the relatively poor wetting capacity and penetration, and in view of the high degree of polymerization. The film formed by a dispersion paint can almost always 'breathe' – that is, is not impervious to water vapour.

On the other hand, dispersions can be applied on a damp, or even wet, surface. Once dry, however, the paint film tends to be more sensitive because of the additives it contains (the dispersion agent or thickener).
● Drying and film formation.
In general, solutions take a longer time to dry than dispersions. But the binder in a solution may hold the solvent in the paint film, which leads to a reduction in overall quality.

In a solution, the formation of a film takes place through the evaporation of the solvent or solvents, or through the oxidation or hardening of the binder (see page 131, HOW PAINTS DRY. The binder can thus be described as in a way 'melting' together to form a continuous, homogeneous and relatively dense film.

In a dispersion, the way a film forms is still not completely understood. It is probable, however, that after excess water has evaporated, the remaining water withdraws from the capillary-like spaces between the binder particles and the pigment particles, so drawing the binder particles closer together. This theory assumes that there is an adhesive tendency between the particles without which a continuous film could not be formed, a tendency present in relation to the thermoplasticity of the binder. This in turn means that there is a critical minimum temperature for a dispersion paint under which film formation cannot take place. Such a critical minimum temperature is indeed measurable, and in most dispersion paints is approximately 5°C (41°F), although if necessary for specific conditions of application the limit can be effectively lowered by the addition of small amounts of solvent.

● Flammability and toxicity. Paints in solution (notably with organic solvents) are in many cases highly flammable and may also give rise to hazards of toxic poisoning. Flammability and toxicity are unknown with dispersions.

PIGMENTS

The number and variety of pigments used in modern paints is colossal. Paint manufacturers themselves employ experts in coloration whose job it is solely to experiment with pigments in order to find the shades and tones of colours, and the finishing properties, required by industry and the general public. No industrial sector is more involved in this demand than the car manufacture and assembly business, a sector that is also involved in other high-quality industrial colorant applications.

By definition, a pigment is a substance not soluble in water, in other solvents or in a binder. In principle, then, virtually anything that is insoluble in water may be used as a pigment. But there is then the consideration of the requirement of colour, and the characteristics that follow from whether the pigment has any tendency towards fine dispersion.

Knowledge of basic pigments has been current

among human artists for millennia. All the famous old masters of painting made their own binders in which the pigments were contained, and did so with skill and careful selection according to the precise effects they required. Such information was among the most valuable that an artist could pass on to his school or pupil.

From the time of the Renaissance, pigments were divided into the so-called earth pigments and certain other animal and vegetable products. By earth pigments they meant colorant elements that were found in the earth: the metallic salts such as the oxides, sulphates and sulphides.

This division between the two types of pigment is retained today, although the nomenclature is slightly more scientific and the sections are more stringently defined. The earth pigments are better known today as inorganic pigments – although earth pigments remains a group within the inorganic pigments – and the animal and vegetable products (which invariably contain carbon and hydrogen) are organic pigments. Moreover, it is now of much more importance that organic pigments are temperature-sensitive and relatively combustible, whereas inorganic pigments are generally not heat-sensitive and may be thought of as incombustible.

It was from the 1850s that chemical foundations began to research more thoroughly into pigments in the quest for new dyestuffs. The burgeoning chemical industry was largely bound up with the flourishing textile trade, and investigation was to a great extent concentrated on ways of colouring fabrics. The basic constituent of all research into the subject at this time was coal tar. Coal tar contains a wide variety of organic compounds, including benzol, toluene, xylene, naphthalene, phenol, cresol and anthracene, all of which may be isolated by means of fractional distillation. Only at the beginning of the 20th century was the scope of such research extended to include pigments – particularly organic pigments – for the paint industry, and the programme naturally enough also started off from the basis of coal tar. Among the first results of the programme was the discovery of aniline pigments.

Organic and Inorganic Pigments: Summary

Inorganic Pigments
● Earth pigments
● Synthetic earth pigments

- Metal powders
Organic Pigments
- Natural animal/vegetable products
- Synthetic products

Inorganic pigments

Earth pigments
Earth pigments are naturally occurring minerals and rocks that are mined, quarried or extracted, purified by sedimentation, dried, and then ground into a form usable as pigment.
- White earth pigments.
White earth pigments include:
Barite (natural barium sulphate) – heavy, and resistant to acids and alkalis; now used as a filler;
Terra alba (natural calcium sulphate), also called mineral white or gypsum – used exclusively as a filler;
Chalk (natural calcium carbonate), **talc** and **kaolin** (china clay) – all three used primarily as fillers.
No white earth pigment features in the manufacture of automobile paint, however.
- Coloured earth pigments.
Notable among the coloured earth pigments are **ochre**, **English red**, and **umber**. Ochre contains iron oxide; English red actually is red iron oxide; umber contains iron, manganese and other oxides.

Synthetic earth pigments
These fall into two groups, one representing naturally-occurring pigments that are synthesized, the other representing synthetic products that do not occur naturally. Synthesis involves a chemical process in which a chemist selects and combines different constituents, and the final product results from precipitation or smelting. The process gives products of high purity and brilliance, good covering power, and suitable particle size.
(acircular), of which the acircular is reckoned to give the better outdoor permanence; but although zinc white is used both indoors and outdoors with most types of binders except the most acidic or alkaline, it has a comparatively poor covering capacity.
- White synthetic pigments.
White synthetic pigments include:
Lead white (basic lead carbonate) – used from ancient times, it is not as white as zinc white, has larger particles, and may be used only for outdoor paints; it may however be combined with zinc white and other white pigments in linseed oil paint, or in

paint used to cover anti-rust-treated steel.
Lithopone (a mixture of zinc sulphide and barium sulphate) – available in grades that differ according to the proportions of the mixture; it is primarily used for house paints and is unsuitable for use on vehicles owing to its sensitivity to atmospheric pollution.
Blanc fixe (synthetic barium sulphate prepared from purified sodium sulphate and barium chloride solutions).
Titanium dioxide – available in two grades, titanium dioxide anatase and titanium dioxide rutile, distinguished by different crystalline form; titanium dioxide rutile is the more stable form and is used principally for outdoor paints owing to its higher resistance to atmospheric deterioration and lesser tendency to chalkiness.
Zinc white (zinc oxide) – available in different degrees of whiteness, purity and particle size, the colour of the seal on the container signifying the quality (white, green or red: white seal is the top quality); it also occurs in two different crystalline forms: round (nodular) and needle-shaped.
Titanium white (titanium dioxide rutile cut with blanc fixe or zinc oxide).
- Black pigments.
Black pigments are today based exclusively on soot (**smoke black**, **carbon black**) obtained by the combustion of organic compounds, principally by the partial combustion of gases. They are included here as inorganic because they are made up of finely dispersed carbon in elemental form (although many people regard black pigments by definition as organic).
- Coloured synthetic pigments.
Coloured synthetic pigments are abundant. They are divided into groups according to the constituent metal that gives rise to the colour, and include:

Iron pigments
Yellow iron oxide – obtained by the flocculation of an iron salt solution with alkali, followed by oxidation; it has very good properties (it is light- and chalk-resistant, fine-grained, and has good covering ability) and can be used in nearly all paint types.
Red iron oxide (more or less pure iron oxide) – available under different names at different concentrations of oxide: **oxide red**, **iron oxide red**, etc., at high oxide concentration, **English red**, **Venetian red**, etc., at low oxide concentration; it has good light resistance, good colour intensity, and good covering ability, is resistant also to calcium and chemicals, and

41

is usable in most binding agents indoors and outdoors.

Ferric ferrocyanide is blue, and is known as **Prussian blue** or **Paris blue**.

Lead pigments

Red lead (oxygen-rich lead oxide) – the most important lead pigment, generally prepared by the oxidation of molten lead, available in various grades: low-grade 26–32·5%, high-grade 32·5–33·5%, and fine-dispersed over 33·5%; it is used mostly with linseed oil to make anti-rust paint: a basic pigment, it reacts with acid binders by thickening, and with drying oils it forms what are called lead soaps, which are waterproof and elastic, and which of course make for a certain amount of rust protection; red lead also makes an iron surface passive and has high adhesive qualities, also preventing creeping rust; on the disadvantageous side, however, it has low light permanence and should be painted over with a covering paint after it has dried fully (usually over a month); it also easily forms a sediment layer and is poisonous.

Cadmium pigments

Cadmium sulphide is sold as **cadmium yellow** and **cadmium orange**, and cadmium selenide as **cadmium red** – these pigments are of great importance to high-grade automobile enamels and are characterized by very good resistance to light and to solvents, and high covering ability; the only disadvantage is the high price, which fluctuates according to the current cost of the cadmium, sulphur or selenium.

Chromium pigments

Chrome yellow (neutral lead chromate, or less commonly zinc chromate or barium chromate), **chrome orange** and **chrome red** (both basic lead chromate) – the most important pigments of this group, they are potentially of interest for automobile enamels, although if chromium pigments are cut with white inorganic pigments the paint tends to darken when subjected to continuous light.

Chromium oxide green – another important pigment, made by the annealing of potassium bichromate and sulphur.

Chromium oxide hydrate green – another important pigment, made by the annealing of sodium bichromate and boric acid.

Chrome green is a mixture of chrome yellow and Paris blue, and also exists in cut form.

Zinc pigments

Zinc yellow (zinc chromate) and **zinc green** (a mixture of zinc yellow and Paris blue) – the most important pigments of this group; zinc green also exists in cut form.

Mercury pigments

Vermilion (red mercuric sulphide) – most important of the mercury pigments, but it is extremely poisonous and quite useless for automobile enamels in that it darkens after only brief exposure to light.

Manganese pigments

Manganese blue (barium manganate) and **manganese violet** (manganese phosphate) – the most important pigments of this group.

Silicon pigments

Ultramarine blue, **ultramarine violet** and **ultramarine green**, all made by the smelting of aluminium silicate, sulphur, sodium carbonate and sodium sulphate – the best known pigments of this group; ultramarine blue is the most important and has high light stability, but has some sensitivity to industrial pollution of the atmosphere.

Cobalt pigments

Cobalt blue (a mixture of cobalt and aluminium oxides) – the only important pigment in this group; it is characterized by such high heat resistance as to be useful in the ceramic industry.

Molybdenum pigments

Molybdenum red (a double salt of lead chromate and lead molybdate) – the most important of this group.

Metal powders

The fine dispersion of bright metals such as aluminium, copper or brass yields what are known as metal powder pigments. Most of these have very high standards of permanence.

Metal powders based on copper that have afterwards been dyed using the so-called basic aniline dyes, however, are characterized by low light permanence: brief exposure to light removes the dye altogether so that the true colour of the pigment returns. This class of product is of absolutely no interest to the automobile enamel industry.

On the other hand, aluminium powders have recently gained favour in automobile enamels, especially applied in polychromatic finishes in which, generally, the aluminium powder is combined with a transparent organic pigment. Polychromatic enamel demands very good light permanence of the coloured pigment, which is highly stressed. Only organic pigments with extremely good light permanence can thus be considered for such finishes.

Organic pigments

Natural animal/vegetable products

Few of these substances – extraction products or juices of plants, fluids from animals – are in use today. When they were more common, the production method was to treat the liquids with metal salts and so create non-soluble pigments.

Indigo, for example, was extracted from the leaves of the indigo tree, a plant that was formerly cultivated on a huge scale in eastern India.

Indian yellow was the evaporated urine of Indian cows fed with mango leaves.

Synthetic products

Synthetic organic pigments – aniline dyes – are today produced in enormous quantity and constitute a major proportion of the pigments used industrially. Initially, as we have seen, such dyes were extracted from coal tar. Cracking products from the petrochemical industry are now also used as the basic raw material.

The colouring power of a synthetic organic pigment is much better than that of inorganic pigments, and they generally also have greater brilliance. Organic particles are softer than inorganic particles, with the exception of phthalocyanine colour, which approaches the inorganic in hardness and also in covering ability. In temperature resistance, inorganic pigments are superior, although for most types of binders the resistance of organic pigments is sufficient. But the temperature resistance and the light and weather permanence of an organic pigment does depend on the binder used, and considerable testing has often to be carried out in order to find the best and most appropriate. Inorganic pigments may also give a certain protection against corrosion, and act as stabilizers of the binders used: organic pigments lack these properties. But organic pigments are not poisonous, as some of the inorganic pigments are.

The principal pigments in this group include:

Phthalocyanines

Blue and green pigments formerly made of phthalic acid obtained by the distillation of coal tar – characterized by uniformly high standards of permanence and, for organic pigments, a fair covering ability.

Azo and diazo pigments

This group is produced through a process known as coupling: typical examples are **toluidine red** and **Hanse yellow**; the pigments are of varying permanence; moreover, they are not always entirely insoluble in solvents, and for this reason only a few of them are safe for painting over; nonetheless, these pigments are of interest to automobile enamel producers because they have very high light permanence, cut or uncut.

Anthrachinone colours

These products are obtained from anthracene, itself produced from heavy coal tar oil; they include synthetic **indigo** and a number of vat dyes; the enamel industry has in recent years become much more interested in vat dyes, which include a range of yellow, orange, red, blue and violet pigments, and which are characterized by excellent permanence and better temperature resistance than most azo and diazo pigments; together with phthalocyanine pigments, anthrachinone colours are of considerable importance to automobile enamel makers: several products from different makers are presently available.

Chinacridone pigments

These pigments are the latest addition to the organic pigments group; at the moment they comprise red and violet pigments only, but like the phthalocyanines and the vat dyes they are characterized by extreme permanence.

Alizarin pigment

Alizarin is the colorant in madder root, and was also formerly obtained from the anthracene of coal tar; it has now been virtually overtaken by the newer red organic pigments in the vat dye and chinacridone groups.

Luminescent pigments

Some organic and inorganic compounds have an ability to absorb radiation from outside the visible spectrum – such as ultraviolet light – and to emit it as additional visible light. The result is an extra brightness, the glow of luminescence.

The effect is either *fluorescent*, if visible light is emitted only when exposed to the activating radiation, or *phosphorescent*, if visible light is emitted for some time after the activating radiation has ceased or been removed.

Some specialized paints intended to give such an effect – such as the Day-Glo range – fade very quickly if left exposed to light. Because they are extremely transparent, they should be applied over a solid white ground. Approved methods of application are spraying, dipping, or using a silk screen: such paints tend to streakiness if brushed.

Pigments for waterborne coatings

These can be divided into two distinct types.
● Universal stainers. For the purposes of trade sales (decorative paint), a universal stainer is defined as a mixture of water, glycol, a non-ionic surfactant and a suspending agent (such as mica).

Pigmentation is either by stirring in an aqueous, fully dispersed, high-solids pigment dispersion paste, or by dispersing a press-cake or pigment powder. All these methods are equally suitable. In general, there are no problems with pigment dispersion or compatibility.

For the purposes of industrial sales (involving strong solvents), where the universal stainer may contain more glycol, less water, or less or different surfactants, pigment selection may become a little more restricted. This could be considered a situation half-way between decorative universal stainers and what are termed waterborne coatings.
● Waterborne coatings. It just so happened that as interest arose in waterborne coatings, new grades of pigments with better particle-size distribution control and rheology (flow characteristics) were introduced. This coincidence in timing served to give waterborne coatings a mystique that perhaps they hardly deserve. In particular, the myth developed that pigments require special conditions – that clean surfaces are essential, that for non-polar surfaces (such as phthaocyanine blue) flocculation resistance

treatment is required, in both cases to ensure that the medium can 'associate' with the pigment. But in fact, in general, pigments tend to be equally suited to waterborne coatings or the comparatively opposite approach: high-solids coatings.

Waterborne coatings nonetheless remain surrounded by technical and commercial secrecy, reinforcing the mystique accredited to them. Defined in simple terms, the coatings may become more familiar.

As solutions they comprise either amonnia- or amine-solubilized acrylic resins or micelles (colloidal particles) with coalescing solvents or co-solvents.

Dispersion of the pigment is usually in water or in a resin mixture, occasionally in a coalescing solvent or co-solvent.

Pigments used in the vehicle manufacture industry

The challenge to the makers of paints for the automotive industry is to produce the widest possible colour range of durable, solid, metallic and pearlescent finishes in high-solids and waterborne coating systems. Pigments with excellent technical properties are required. In particular, a high level of heat- and solvent-fastness is demanded, as are adequate dispersion behaviour and rheology (flow characteristics), with equivalently outstanding resistance to weather and atmospheric pollution. Very strict control of the quality of the pigment is mandatory in order to enable reproducible paint to be manufactured.

To obtain a diverse colour range a surprisingly small number of coloured pigments are used. For solid finishes iron oxides, mixed metal oxides and selected polycyclic organic pigments are the norm. For metallic and pearlescent finishes transparent iron oxides and selected polycyclic organic pigments are used. All finishes may contain carbon black.

The following review of pigments by colour is presented in order of increasing complexity of preparation and application, as experienced by paint makers to the automotive industry. The order is green, blue, violet, red, orange and yellow, and the review is then followed by a section on colour styling.

Green pigments
Green is the relatively problem-free area in the field. Phthalocyanine green pigments are of excellent

durability at all depths of shade in all finishes. Two types are available:

C.I. Pigment green 7: **Polychloro**
This ranges in hue from mid- to bluish green –
ICI C&FC products Monastral Green GBX   (bluer)
               Monastral Green GLX
               Monastral Green GNX   (yellower)
– and improved qualities with superior brightness and strength are now available. Such improvement has been achieved through a particle size that is slightly smaller (hence increased strength) and slightly narrower in distribution (hence increased brightness). Because the change in particle size is minimal, other properties – such as durability – remain unaltered.

C.I. Pigment green 36: **Polychromobromo**
A yellowish green that is ideal for green or yellow shades in order to eliminate – or at least minimize – the use of the deficient organic yellow pigments.

Blue pigments
A number of blue pigments can be considered for automotive paints, although some have better properties than others.

C.I. Pigment blue 15:1: **Tetrachloro-copper phthalocyanine**
A standard colour intermediate in hue between its own alpha and beta forms, its main use is in automotive metallic paints because it shows a dramatic green 'flip-flop' effect. In pale metallic shades, however, it can show colour instability after storage.

C.I. Pigment blue 15:2
There is a range of properties for this pigment.
ICI C&FC products Monastral Blue FBR
               Monastral Blue FBN   (light surface treatment)
               Monastral Blue RFN   (heavy surface treatment)
Monastral Blue FBR is bright and strong, with excellent flocculation resistance and rheology. But its major use is in decorative paints because in reduced shade in strong solvents it is unstable in storage, and recrystallizes to the beta form. Yet in metallic and pearlescent finishes it is stable in storage and is of

sufficient durability for the automotive industry, although it could be considered to give very bright and rather red shades. These finishes would have to be kept well apart from any solid finish.

Monastral Blue FBN is the standard quality for automotive paint. Unfortunately, light surface treatment tends to lend greenness, dullness and weakness.

Monastral Blue RFN under heavy surface treatment tends to be even duller and weaker, but it has the best flocculation resistance. It is used principally in refinishing mixing schemes.

C.I. Pigment blue 15:4
Pigment of standard quality for automotive paint.
ICI C&FC products Monastral Blue FGX
Monastral Blue FGX has competitive qualities and durability, but has a rheology (flow characteristics) superior to most.

C.I. Pigment blue 16: **metal-free copper phthalocyanine**
This pigment is used on a small scale for metallic automotive finishes. It is generally far more economical instead to use a mixture of high-quality C.I. Pigment blue 15:4 and C.I. Pigment green 7 (= Monastral Blue FGX and Monastral Green GBX), although this gives a slightly duller result.

C.I. Pigment blue 60: **identical blue**
This is the only other blue pigment in widespread use. A rather reddish blue pigment, with durability similar to that of the best phthalocyanine blue pigments, it features mostly in pearlescent finishes because it represents the organic pigment that gives the best opacity while retaining the desired polychromatic effect.

Other blue pigments of occasional use include C.I. Pigment blue 15:6 (for economy more often substituted by a mixture of C.I. Pigment blue 15:2 and C.I. Pigment blue 60, or of C.I. Pigment blue 15:2 and C.I. Pigment violet 23) and **indanthrone blue** (ICI C&FC products Monolite Blue 3R).

Violet pigments
There is little demand for bright violet as a colour in the automotive industry (and quite right too). Technical and commercial problems are relatively minor in connection with blue and green colorants, and the very restricted demand simply means that

such problems in connection with violet pigments can perhaps likewise be adequately met.

C.I. Pigments violet 23 and 37: **dioxazine violet**
    This pigment is widely used, although it suffers from poor durability in medium and pale shades, especially in metallic finishes.
ICI C&FC products Monolite Violet RN

C.I. Pigment violet 19, beta phase: **quinacridone violet**
This pigment has in the past been used chiefly for lending scarlet chrome pigments a bluer hue. In comparison with dioxazine violet its durability is even poorer.
ICI C&FC products Monolite Violet 4R

Red pigments
● Inorganic red pigments include:

C.I. Pigment red 101: **red iron oxide**
This is widely used as a dulling component in both the conventional form for solid colours and the transparent form for metallic and pearlescent finishes.

C.I. Pigment red 104: **scarlet chrome**
Like lead chrome yellow pigments, scarlet chrome shades are obsolescent and being phased out. Two are available:

ICI C&FC products Polymon Scarlet HF4 (yellow shade)
Polymon Scarlet HF5 (mid-shade)

● Organic red pigments are numerous, and include a range from yellower reds through mid-shade reds to bluer reds:

C.I. Pigment	common name	
red 168	dibromoanthanthrone	(yellower)
red 260	isoindolinone red	
red 216, 226	pyranthrone red	
red 209	dichloro-quinacridone	
red 254	DPP red	
red 178, 224	perylene red	
violet 19 (gamma ph.)	quinacridone red	
red 177	anthraquinone red	
red 179	perylene maroon	
red 122, 202	dimethyl-/dichloro-quinacridone	(bluer)

Of the yellowish-red pigments, dibromoanthanthrone (ICI C&FC products Monolite Red 2Y) has the best durability, although it is expensive. It can be used

with complete confidence at any depth of shade in solid, metallic and pearlescent finishes. All the same, its principal use is to make yellower the mid-shade reds such as quinacridone red, perylene red or DPP red.

    Of the mid-shade red pigments, DPP red is brighter and has better rheology than quinacridone red, but poorer durability in paler shades. Because of its excellent rheology, perylene red is widely used in strong solid colours, although it has poorer durability than either DPP red or quinacridone red. Anthraquinone red is not particularly good in either rheology or durability. Quinacridone red is available in two forms: an opaque yellowish shade, and a transparent bluish shade. In the past, the yellow shade has tended to be dull and weak, with poor gloss and rheology. A more recent product (ICI C&FC products Monolite Red 2BX) combines yellowness and opacity with excellent brightness, strength, gloss and rheology.

    The best pigments for bright, very bluish red hues with good durability are dimethyl-quinacridone (ICI C&FC products Monolite Rubine 3B) and dichloro-quinacridone. Perylene maroon, although dull, finds its principal use in strong metallic and especially pearlescent colours, in which its durability is adequate.

● Azo pigments of high molecular weight are used in full or very strong solid shades for lead-free transport finishes, where the criteria for durability may be more relaxed. They include C.I. Pigment red 188 (a monoazo), a yellowish red, and C.I. Pigment red 170 (also monoazo), a bluish red. Opaque qualities are available, although such qualities make them dull and weak.

    The condensed azo pigments are more expensive alternatives with better durability in strong solid shades. They include C.I. Pigment red 242 (ICI C&FC products Vynamon Scarlet 3Y FW), a yellowish red, and C.I. Pigment red 214 (ICI C&FC products Vynamon Red 3BN FW), a bluish red.

    All azo pigments are unsuitable for metallic and pearlescent finishes because of their poor durability.

Orange pigments
As with violet pigments, the scarcity of orange pigments available is to a great degree compensated for by the minimal demand.

C.I. Pigment orange 43: **anthraquinone orange**
    This is suitable only for pale shades because in

strong shades it is subject to darkening; it is also very expensive. Finally it may well be in the process of being phased out altogether.

C.I. Pigment orange 51: **pyranthrone orange**
    This pigment has poor durability in pale shades.

Yellow pigments
● Inorganic yellow pigments include:

C.I. Pigment yellow 34: **lead chrome yellow**
Lead chrome pigments are suitable for full and strong shade solid colours. It is possible to improve their resistance to darkening by coating them with layers of silicon, aluminium, tin, antimony or cerium oxides. Two have been readily available –
ICI C&FC products Polymon Yellow HF2   (lemon chrome)
                   Polymon Yellow HF3   (middle chrome)
– but these are now in the process of being phased out of use in automotive paints. Although there is nowhere any specific legislation prohibiting their use, and although they can be safely handled and transported with good industrial hygiene, the pigments do cause effluent and paint disposal problems.

C.I. Pigment yellow 42: **yellow iron oxide**
This is widely used as a dulling component, in the conventional opaque form for solid colours and in the transparent form of much smaller particle size for metallic and pearlescent colours.
Other inorganic yellow pigments of occasional use include C.I. Pigment yellow 53: nickel titanate and C.I. Pigment brown 24: chromium titanate. Both are weak in colorant power and are utilized mainly to improve gloss and opacity in appropriate solid colours. C.I. Pigment yellow 184: bismuth vanadate is more intense than nickel titanate but may show poor paint storage stability and acid fastness.
● Organic yellow pigments most in use are the *isoindolinones*. Tetrachloro-isoindolinones (C.I. Pigments yellow 109 and 110) are dull and weak; in strong shades they darken on exposure, and in pale shades they fade. The less chlorinated version (C.I. Pigment yellow 173) is brighter and has better durability in solid finishes. But all have relatively poor durability in metallic finishes.
Metal complexes of isoindolinones (C.I. Pigments yellow 177 and 179) and other polycyclic colorants

(C.I. Pigments yellow 117 and 129) offer some improvement in transparency and durability in metallic finishes.
Other organic pigments in occasional use include C.I. Pigment yellow 108: *anthrapyrimidine yellow*, which is dull and weak, and C.I. Pigments orange 48 and 49: *quinacridine gold*, which is also dull and has poor dispersion and rheological properties. (C.I. Pigment yellow 24: *flavanthrone* is no longer manufactured because of its high cost and its low redox – oxidation-reduction – potential which tended to cause loss of colour in metallic finishes after storage.)
● As for azo pigments of high molecular weight, they find limited use in full or very strong solid shades principally for vehicular finishes. The two classes (azo and condensed azo) are perhaps best represented by C.I. Pigment yellow 154: *benzimidazolone yellow* (azo) and C.I. Pigment yellow 155 *condensed azo yellow*. Because of poor durability, however, both are unsuitable for metallic or pearlescent finishes.
At the present time there is no yellow pigment thoroughly suited to all requirements of the automotive industry.

Colour styling

Trends are always changing, and trends in the the automotive paint industry are no different. Colours achieve a popularity, and different shades of those colours then vie for dominance. But even within that competition there are discernible patterns, a distinct growth in popularity in relation to some colours, some shades, some finishes, and a measurable reduction of interest in others. And in general these patterns are identical all over the world.
    The main technical difficulty for the paint manufacturer – who has little or no influence over the popularity or unpopularity of what is produced – in these circumstances is that it takes between three and four years for a particular colour shade to be devised and fully formulated, to go through the various stages of testing, and then to be selected and used by a vehicle manufacturer. Nonetheless, the present situation in terms of trends towards and away from the popular may be represented by the chart overleaf. It must be stressed that the chart is relevant at the time of writing. The ecology factor, for example, has seen green Mondeos and even Porsches in recent months. But will it last?

colour	shift	commercial interest
yellow/gold	towards green	a little
	towards red	a little
orange	towards red/rust	a little
purple	to brighter shades	a little
grey	towards red/brighter	moderate
red	towards yellow (brighter)	great, but for solid finishes only
	towards blue (but also brighter)	great, but for pearlescent finishes only
brown	towards violet (and/ or brighter)	great, but for metallic finishes only
blue	towards red	great
	towards green	great

There is an overall trend towards cleaner and warmer colours. Pale colours are becoming of less importance.

The demand is steady for black or white as colours. Green is also missing from this chart – no shift in popularity between different hues is discernible – but as a general colour it has managed to attract increasing interest in relation to pearlescent finishes. At the same time, the growth in pearlescent colours is markedly faster in North America and Japan than in Western Europe.

To match a particular shade, organic pigments of a similar hue are generally chosen, although complementary colour mixing of organic pigments is not favoured because of the risk of hue change on exposure. Nonetheless, mixtures of organic pigments can often show superior durability in comparison with the individual pigments at the same depth of shade. (Obviously it is advantageous in such a mixture if one pigment darkens by the amount another fades on exposure.) Durability is therefore evaluated in relation to the specific pigment formulation.

Pigments: the state of the art

Automotive resins are changing rapidly from single-coat to solvent- or waterborne base-coat/clear-coat systems to improve initial appearance and gloss retention. Such base-coat systems make new demands. The pigments must have good paint rheology, for example, to permit the high pigment loadings needed to afford opacity in thin films.

Most of the organic pigments described above are – or can be made – suitable.

Ultraviolet absorbers are often added to the clear coat in order to reduce the resin film breakdown. They have little effect on pigment durability.

In regard to organic red pigments, careful control of the particle size distribution of the individual crystals improved rheology, opacity and gloss without undue sacrifice of brightness and strength. The newer types of phthalocyanine blue pigments, now becoming increasingly available, should give fewer rheological problems. (The phthalocyanine green pigments remain trouble-free.)

In order to obtain adequate opacity, especially with pearlescent finishes, a base coat may be applied over a coloured sealer/surfacer coat. A complementary approach now is to use what are known as hyperdispersants. Some of the hyperdispersants now available are suitable for use in the automotive industry (the Solsperse agents, for instance). They improve the rheology and gloss of the paint, and get the best colorant properties from the pigments.

Automotive colour stylists are always seeking new effects. Perhaps the next noteworthy innovation – following the dramatic success of pearlescent finishes – will be micronised titanium dioxide. Micronised (more accurately described as 'ultra-fine') titanium dioxide comes in particle sizes of only tens of nanometres. The pigment is thus too small to be opaque and appears translucent. Commercial interest in it is for its use in resin film protection: it is a powerful absorber of ultraviolet light. For this purpose, care should be taken to use a stabilized grade. But ultra-fine titanium dioxide also possesses subtle optical effects in the visible spectrum. Incorporated into a metallic or pearlescent finish, it gives apparent colour changes depending on the angle from which it is viewed.

BINDERS

Binders are included in all paints, and are therefore the component of identification – the most important constituent – in most paint classification systems. As with pigments, the number and variety of binders is huge, their properties highly diverse, and the properties they impart to their paint types remarkable in their scope and the chemical science required to match them for appropriate use.

Above all, as a group binders relate specifically to the way paints dry. And for this reason, the classification of binders with their paint types and spraying characteristics is presented not here in this chapter on the general composition of paints, but in HOW PAINTS DRY, page 131.

EXTENDERS AND FILLERS

Extenders and fillers are for the most part pigments of very low covering ability. They are principally natural or modified mineral products ground into powder form, having little or no opacity in oil, and are added to paint

- to improve brushing properties;
- to prevent the settling of heavy pigments;
- to provide a reasonably keyed surface for subsequent coats;
- in combination with other pigments to aid the hardening of the paint;
- as a flatting agent (to give a matt finish); and
- to bulk out the paint and so reduce cost.

The standard extenders are quite few in number. They comprise:

- Barite (natural barium sulphate). A mineral that is alkali-, acid- and weather-resistant, used primarily in undercoats; it is especially effective in hardening the film and providing a keyed surface.
- Blanc fixe (synthetic barium sulphate). Has the same properties of resistance as natural barite, and is also used primarily in undercoats.
- Calcite (whiting, chalk: calcium carbonate). A soft, crystalline mineral that is not acid-resistant but is excellent at bulking out a coating; it is used mainly in filling compositions – putty and cement, for example.
- Kaolin (china clay: aluminium silicate). A soft, inert mineral formed by the disintegration of feldspar; it too is used in filling compositions, but can be used also for dulling, in undercoats, and as a base for dyes.
- Talc (asbestine: magnesium silicate). Used mostly in combination with calcite, talc is a light mineral unaffected by moisture; it is employed mainly as a suspending and flatting agent.
- Diatomite (kieselguhr). A siliceous mineral constituted by the fossilized skeletal remains of tiny plants; it is used for dulling, as a suspending agent (especially in white-line paints); in other industries it is used additionally as an abrasive.

- Dolomite (magnesian limestone). A chalky mineral used in filling compositions but also in dispersion paints.
- Witherite (barium carbonate). A mineral often found in combination with barite and with some of the same properties; it is used mainly to check the chalkiness of titanium in paints.

SOLVENTS, DILUENTS AND THINNERS

Solvents and thinners are used to adjust the viscosity of the binder or the paint until it is suitable for the intended method of application (brushing, spraying, dipping, or whatever). It is rare indeed for a paint to consist only of pigment and binder – although not unknown, for oil paints comprise nothing more than pigment and linseed oil.

When a coating of paint has been applied, the solvent in most cases evaporates completely so that only the pigment and binder – which together make up the film – remain. To the layperson this may give the impression that the solvent thus has no effect on the final result, the finish. But that is certainly not the case. In more detail the functions of a solvent are:

- to dissolve the binding agent, and by so doing,
- to give the paint the required application properties;
- to promote wetting of the surface to be painted; and
- to facilitate faultless film production.

Turning this information on its head, if a solvent remains unevaporated in the paint coat it tends to give an impression of

- reduced hardness;
- a higher degree of gloss;
- less brittleness;
- greater elasticity.

– and premature practical use of the painted surface in this situation leads to

- lower resistance to chemical attack;
- decreased protection against rust; and
- reduced mechanical strength.

Chemistry is of great importance. Each type of binder requires a specific solvent or type of solvent. Oils and fatty alkyds, for example, are best dissolved by mineral turpentine, whereas most other binders demand more active solvents such as aromatics (toluene or xylene), acetates or ketones. Accordingly, solvents may be classified either according to their origin, as **volatile vegetable oils**, **mineral oils** obtained by refining (aliphatic solvents), **tar oils** obtained by distillation of coal tar (aromatic solvents or benzol hydrocarbons), **synthetic solvents**, or **water**; or alternatively according to their chemical composition, as **esters**, **ketones**, **ethers**, **alcohols**, **aromatic hydrocarbons** and **aliphatic hydrocarbons**.

As an example of how much care must be taken in the chemical formulation of a paint involving a solvent, the special need for expert selection of solvent for a urethane lacquer might be instanced. No solvent should be used that contains anything that might react with ioscyanates – no alcohols, nor solvents that include a relatively high proportion of water; no white spirit, and no aliphatic hydrocarbons. Solvents more often pressed into service for this type of coating are ketones and esters (such as methyl isobutyl ketone, cyclohexanone, butyl and amyl acetates, and similar), both of which are strong solvent types fully capable of dealing with the polyester resins and polyisocyanates. But hydrocarbons can be used, if desired. In the main, hydrocarbons are not actually solvents as much as diluents: they are used really to make the solvent less expensive in relation to its quantity. Hydrocarbons most used for this purpose include toluene, xylene and naphtha, and some proprietary brands of the aromatics.

If the solvent's major function is to evaporate, then the rate at which it evaporates is clearly also of dominant significance. The **rate of evaporation** inevitably affects the application properties, the film formation, overall fluidity, and a few other factors. Measurement of the evaporation rate is on a scale on which the evaporation rate of ether is given the value 1. Thanks to the laws of physics, the evaporation rate is also related to the boiling point: the lower the boiling point, the higher the evaporation rate.

The circumstances of evaporation are also influential. Considerable amounts of solvent may evaporate as the paint travels from the spray gun to the surface to be painted, for example. Sufficient solvent of slow evaporation rate must remain in the sprayed paint coat to provide for good flow out – although not so much slow solvent that the surface drying is affected detrimentally, with the possible result of running and sagging. At the same time, a solvent must not have too fast an evaporation rate or too much would evaporate between the gun and the surface, resulting in 'dry' spraying, insufficient fluidity (causing a surface effect like orange peel), over-fast surface drying and poor through-drying.

Another property of a solvent that is as critical to its performance as it is to its permitted use is its **flashpoint** – the temperature at which it produces a vapour that is combustible. Naturally, the flashpoint is very specifically relevant to the potential fire hazard. Most insurance companies, fire control authorities and similar interested bodies issue precise regulations governing the permissible level of flashpoints for paint application without special measures. The permissible flashpoint levels differ from country to country, but as a general rule it can be said that solvents with a flashpoint below 21–25°C (70–77°F) are considered Highly Inflammable (and should be labelled clearly to that effect – see SAFETY: Storage, p.25).

Solvent Types, Examples and Properties: Summary

	boiling point °C	evaporation rate (ether = 1)	flashpoint °C
Volatile oils			
turpentine	150–175	34	35
dipentene	175–198	slow	54
Mineral oils			
white spirit	150–200	slow	35
Tar oils			
benzene	80–82	3	–15
xylene	135–145	13	23
Synthetic solvents: alcohols			
ethanol	78–79	8	14
butanol	114–120	33	34
Synthetic solvents: esters			
ethyl glycol	125–135	42	40
ethyl acetate	74–77	3	–2
butyl acetate	110–130	12	24
Synthetic solvents: ketones			
acetone	55–56	2	–17
methyl isobutyl ketone	75–85	6	–14

Other Useful Flashpoints

solvent	flashpoint °C
amyl acetate	32
cyclohexanone	44
diacetone alcohol	46
ethyl lactate	47
glycol mono-ethyl ether	43
glycol mono-ethyl ether acetate	52
isopropyl alcohol	12
methanol	0
methyl acetate	−13
methyl ethyl ketone	−7
n-butyl acetate	39
n-butyl alcohol	47
toluene	4

Volatile Oils

● Turpentine is the most important volatile oil in relation to the paint industry. A clear liquid that is between transparent and straw-coloured, it is obtained from the resin of coniferous trees, particularly pine trees, and its principal constituent is accordingly pinene. There are two main types of turpentine: one is made of resinous wood and black liquor and is generally known as wood turpentine or sulphate turpentine; the other is balsam turpentine. Balsam turpentine is made by distilling balsam (an oily, sticky resin generally containing benzoic acid) with steam. The result is turpentine and water, which are separated by means of their differing densities; colophony resin (also called rosin) is left in the distillation chamber. Turpentine produced in this way is of high quality, and for the market may be labelled by the country of its origin – French turpentine, American turpentine, Venetian turpentine, and so on. (Venetian turpentine is made from larch tree balsam.)

Balsam turpentine most often has a mild aromatic smell. Sulphate turpentine tends to have a slightly sulphurous tang.

Because turpentine is unsaturated (it has the molecular property of being able to take on additional atoms or radicals without losing its original ones) it can be oxidized by the air. This is the reason that turpentine both thickens after long storage (especially in vessels that are not airtight) and, to a certain extent, promotes drying. It provides an excellent solvent for oil, oil paint, oil-lacquer alkyd paint and the like.

● Dipentene, related to turpentine, evaporates more slowly and is stronger as a solvent than turpentine. It improves brushability, fluidity and through-drying while at the same time reduces the risk of film disturbance (wrinkling). But it is very strong and should be used in small amounts only. In fact it is so strong that if excess is used on a pre-painted surface, there is the risk of dissolving the previous coat of paint – which is why dipentene is a constituent in some paint removers.

Mineral Oils (Aliphatic Solvents)

Fractional distillation during the refining of crude oil yields a number of different hydrocarbons, each with an individual boiling point. Of these, white spirit has come into widespread use as a solvent and thinner.

● White spirit – called different things in different countries (*Testbenzin* in Germany, *essence minérale* in France, for example) – consists principally of saturated aliphatic hydrocarbons. In contrast with turpentine, it does not oxidize and is rather weaker as a solvent, although still strong enough to be a good solvent for oil, oil paint, oil lacquer and so forth. It is also generally cheaper than turpentine.

An odourless form of white spirit exists, but is a weaker solvent than the ordinary version.

● Paraffin – again called different things in different countries (kerosene in the United States, *Leuchtpetroleum* in Germany, *pétrole lampante* in France, for example) – is rarely used as a solvent in paint, but may be applied for its slow evaporation, which prevents quick setting of the paint.

Tar Oils (Aromatic Solvents or Benzol Hydrocarbons)

● Xylene, or xylol, and toluene, or toluol, are strong solvents used in many synthetic resin enamels (notably alkyd enamels and chlorinated rubber enamels) and as a diluent in cellulose enamels. Their rapid evaporation makes them unsuitable for brush enamels, and their strong dissolving power may often entail some risk of the dissolution of a previous coat of paint on the surface they are applied to.

● Benzene, or benzol – not to be confused with words for 'petrol' in European languages – has now been virtually phased out of its former use in paint owing to its high toxicity. However, it remains a valued diluent in quick-drying nitrocellulose lacquers.

Some solvents comprising a mixture of aromatic and aliphatic solvents are also commercially available.

Synthetic Solvents

This group includes alcohols, esters (of both glycol and acetate types) and ketones.
● Ethanol, alcohol, is used as a solvent for certain resins, such as shellac, Manila copal and colophony (rosin). It may also be used in cellulose enamels as a 'latent solvent' to increase the dissolving activity and strength of another solvent.
● Butanol, another alcohol, is also used as a solvent for specific resins, such as urea resin, and similarly used as a latent solvent in cellulose enamels.

The alcohols are additionally used as the dehydrating and damping agents in industrial nitrocellulose.
● The esters methyl glycol and ethyl glycol are used as a solvent for several resins and in cellulose enamels.
● The esters ethyl acetate and butyl acetate are strong solvents with high dissolving power, used (for example) in cellulose enamels. Because of its lower cost and greater solvent power, butyl acetate largely displaced amyl acetate from its former popularity, although amyl acetate evaporates more slowly and gives rather higher gloss and better flow properties.

Butyl acetate was the first ester that could be used in the formulation of 'high-flash' lacquers – lacquers that have a flashpoint above 23°C. In many types of spraying lacquers, however, butyl acetate benefits from the addition of latent solvents.
● But acetones and other ketones remain among the best solvents for use in cellulose enamels. Acetone is the most rapidly evaporating solvent normally used, and is also the most powerful solvent judged on the basis of the viscosity of its solutions.
● Less important synthetic solvents include hydrogenated hydrocarbons (such as decalin and tetralin) and chlorinated hydrocarbons (such as carbon tetrachloride and trichloroethylene). Major properties of these are that they dissolve fat and are non-combustible.

Acetates such as ethyl acetate and butyl acetate, and ketones such as methyl ethyl ketone, methyl isobutyl ketone and acetone, are examples of active solvents – solvents that dissolve the binder without any need for the presence or assistance of other substances (see latent solvents under Ethanol above).

In general a ketone is a stronger solvent than an acetate, so that if the same quantity of ketone and acetate thinner is added to a specific quantity of paint (in two different containers), the ketone-thinned paint is thinner than the acetate-thinned paint. One corollary of this is that at any given viscosity, ketone thinning produces a higher solid content – which gives the finished coat better properties and must also result in cutting down the working time.

It is also possible to dilute ketones more than the acetates.

Common diluents (used primarily to make paints and thinners less expensive) other than toluene and xylene are hydrocarbons such as industrial petrol.

ADDITIVES

The most important types of additive are:
● Anti-skin additives, most often special phenolic and amino compounds which prevent the formation of a skin but may at the same time delay surface drying.
● Fungicides to stop the onset of mould or other forms of mycosis.
● Thickeners.
● Plasticizers. Plasticizers by increasing the overall elasticity of the paint prevent a finished coat from being too hard and brittle, although the proportion added naturally also affects tensile strength, gloss, adhesion, thermoplasticity, the evaporation of volatile solvents and the paint's susceptibility to defects in the finish. Like most paint constituents, moreover, specific plasticizers are suited to specific types of paint and unsuited to others. They can be divided into two groups: natural and synthetic. The natural group includes fatty oils such as linseed oil and tung oil. The synthetic group includes phthalic acid esters such as dibutyl phthalate and dioctyl phthalate, and phosphoric acid esters such as tricresyl phosphate. Some types of alkyd resins can also serve as plasticizers.

Perhaps a more useful way of distinguishing between plasticizers, however, is in classifying them as gelatinizing or non-gelatinizing. The gelatinizing plasticizers do not sweat – do not exude moisture from the film under certain conditions – and may also have a swelling and dissolving effect on some binders. The phthalates and tricresyl phosphate are gelatinizing in relation to nitrocellulose. Castor oil, in contrast, is a non-gelatinizing plasticizer.

Non-saponifying chlorinated plasticizers are especially important for alkali-resistant paints.

● Drying agents or siccatives – substances that accelerate the drying of part or all of the constituents of the paint. One example (to which the general term 'siccative' is frequently applied as a technical term) is the type that acts as a catalyst to promote the drying of a binder that dries by oxidation. For this purpose one or more of the metals lead, cobalt, manganese and certain others may be utilized.

● Drying stabilizers – substances added to a paint that contains one or more pigments which, over time, would otherwise completely absorb the drying agents and thus prevent proper drying. The stabilizers are there to be preferentially absorbed by the pigments, leaving the drying agents free to fulfil their task.

HOW PAINT IS MANUFACTURED

A paint factory can be likened to a large chemical assembly-plant, in which finished raw materials – delivered by the makers or refiners, tested for their specific properties and for overall quality, and kept on site for use – are put together to create a reproducible product that is popular with the market.

A very few manufacturers actually have their own contracted specialists who produce the raw materials they require, to the specified quantity and quality.

Virtually all manufacturers have large and well-equipped laboratories for testing the raw materials and for testing the performance of products that are made, at various stages of production. In some cases, the customer – especially if the customer has individual requirements – might be invited to attend some tests or carry out his own.

In general, solvents and diluents after delivery from petrochemical corporations are stored in underground tanks. Binders are stored in tanks above ground. Pigments and extenders are for the most part kept in drums and sacks.

Pre-production

A new paint is formulated, made up in small batches,

Raw materials are dispersed by means of a 'dissolver'.

The dissolving station at work.

The paint will eventually be checked for viscosity, gloss, drying time, application properties and tinting.

The small-scale tinting unit which is used by the retailers.

and tested for the qualities desired, or to find out what qualities it has that might make it marketable. Tests include chemical and physical analysis, and scrutiny of such factors as ease of application, speed of drying, quality of film, and resistance to stress and weather.

Details of tests that a paint has to undergo, both in the manufacturer's laboratory and prior to delivery to the retail outlets, are outlined in the next sections within this chapter. Suffice to say here that no paint makes it through this methodical investigation unless it has something that gives it at least one desirable quality that no other paint made by the manufacturer has.

Mixing

When the product has been approved, it is put into production. The solvents and diluents are pumped in correct quantities through centrally controlled pipe systems into measuring and mixing vats. There, measured quantities of pigment are added, plus any extender required by the formulation.

The raw materials as mixed are stirred and dispersed by means of a 'dissolver', a cylindrical shaft within which there is a rotating saw-like disc. This unit is so effective at dispersion that dispersion paints and certain alkyd-based primers need no further treatment and can be pumped directly into the final vat for filling in delivery containers.

Other paints require further reduction in the size of the pigment particles. They are therefore conveyed to a mill (or perhaps more than one mill) for what is known as fine dispersion, or grinding.

Grinding

There are three common types of mill in which liquid paint is finely dispersed: the **pearl mill**, the **roller mill** and the **ball mill**.

● The pearl mill.

This method is both rapid and entirely adapted to modern continuous operation. Its use is therefore becoming increasingly common in paint manufacture. The paint is pumped under pressure into the sand-filled mill from below. Both sand and paint are forced to rotate by means of a number of discs. The resultant extremely strong currents mean that the paint is finely dispersed and ground in the very short time it takes to travel up through the mill. The paint is drawn off at the top.

Average capacity using a 120-litre (29 UK gallon) container is about 1000 litres (220 UK gallons) of finished paint per hour.

The pearl mill in which pigment is ground.

● The roller mill.

The roller mill consists of adjustable steel rollers rotating against each other (like a triple mangle) so that the paint is subjected to pressure and to shear forces which together reduce particle size. The paint is removed from the final roller in the row by a steel blade.

The usual number of rollers today is three. In former times it was two or even one. With one roller, the blade removing the paint was a 'pressure bar', a broad metal knife with a fairly large contact area. The pressure on the bar could be varied according to the paint type.

Three-roller mills are useful for several types of paint, but unfortunately have a relatively low capacity: at best 200–250 litres (44–55 UK gallons) per hour.

Rollers in this day and age are exclusively made of steel. In former times stone rollers might have been used.

● The ball mill. Possibly the most common method of fine dispersion in the paint industry at the moment, the ball mill consists in principle of no more than a rotating drum half filled with steel or porcelain balls of about 2–3 cm (1 in) diameter. The paint is introduced through a special hatch until all the balls are completely covered. The hatch is then closed and the drum set in motion. The pigment particles are ground down as they are crushed between the spinning balls. Average rotation speed of the drum is

LEFT *A roller mill. This unit consists of adjustable steel rollers.*

ABOVE *In contrast, a ball mill which consists of a rotating drum.*

ABOVE RIGHT *The paint is filled mechanically into delivery containers in different types of filling machines.*

RIGHT *The final mixing tank where tinting takes place with the aid of different tinting pastes.*

ABOVE FAR RIGHT *Spray test, one of the final checks.*

set at slightly under one revolution per second.

This method is, however, time-consuming. Although the desired pigment particle size naturally differs among the various types of paint, grinding time is a minimum of 14 hours, a maximum of around 30. Nonetheless, industrial units can contain up to several thousand litres of paint in one batch.

Final Batching

After the grinding the paint is pumped to the final batching. This is where more binding agent (and possibly solvent or thinner) is added while stirring, in order to obtain the desired viscosity. Non-white paints are tinted and adjusted for colour with the aid of one or more tinting pastes, introduced in exact proportions as established by the original formulation. Almost all of the tinting process is carried out by machine – and ideally, the goal of the manufacturer is to be able to mix all of the paint types produced at one factory with one type of binder base – but a few paints still require skilled manual tinting.

Checking and Filling

The paint is finally checked for viscosity, gloss, drying time, and its application properties, and the tinting matched for hue against a sample of the desired colour. The tests are described in the section below. Approved in all these details, the paint is passed on to the filling machines which put the paint into its containers for delivery to the customer.

The containers are properly packaged and labelled, and loaded on to the delivery vehicles.

PAINT TESTING

The process of producing a paint from first to last involves continual monitoring at every stage. However, there are two times when the paint undergoes the most stringent examination to find or check all the properties that it has or should have. These are 1) in the manufacturer's laboratory, on sample batches before the paint is put into actual commercial production, and 2) on each production batch immediately prior to delivery to the retail outlets.

BELOW *Painted panels undergoing various long-term tests. The panels are positioned to receive the maximum sunlight.*

Laboratory Tests

When investigating the fundamental properties of an industrial finish, the experienced professional looks first for three major factors:

- adhesion;
- drying time, and the ultimate hardness; and
- flexibility.

These are the factors that chiefly determine the practicability and durability of a protective coating to wear and tear. Only after these factors meet approval does the professional then go on to examine for solid content, heat resistance, humidity and chemical resistance, gloss, colour and colour changeability, and overall function fulfilment.

Tests for adhesion

The **Cross-Hatch** or **Grating Cut test** is widely used: its technical merits have been recognized by international standards authorities as a valid test method for the property of paint adhesion on a surface (which of course also takes into account contributory factors such as the flexibility of the coating, and the possible presence of secondary layers of coating between the test coat and the substrate). The method utilizes a cutting tool with either one or six cutting edges. The six-edged cross-hatch cutter, which has 1- or 2-millimetre gaps between blades,

has advantages over the single-edged tool for both safety and simplicity in use.

The six-edged cutting tool consists of a hardened steel cylinder ground to a high standard of precision so that its cutting edges are formed between outer edge guides. A lightweight, comfortable handle provides a firm handhold. The usual method is to make 10 parallel cuts at the 1-millimetre spacing across the surface of the paint, and then 10 more parallel cuts at right-angles across the first cuts, forming a square grid pattern. A piece of masking tape (or other tape) is applied to the grid and taken off again. The number of squares of paint removed by the tape is taken as a measurement of the adhesion.

The **Cupping Tester** is an instrument that tests the adhesive qualities of lacquers, paints and other protective coatings that have been applied to a metal substrate. A steel-faced ball punch of 20 mm (4/5 in) diameter is applied forcibly to the uncoated back of the test panel. As the panel is deformed under the blow of the punch, the coated surface is kept under observation. Any point at which cracking appears, or bits of the coating flake off, is carefully recorded.

The **Cylindrical Mandrel Bend Test** also tests the resistance of a coating of paint, varnish or similar product to cracking or detachment from a metal panel. This time, the test panel is simply bent around a cylindrical mandrel. The test can be applied as a

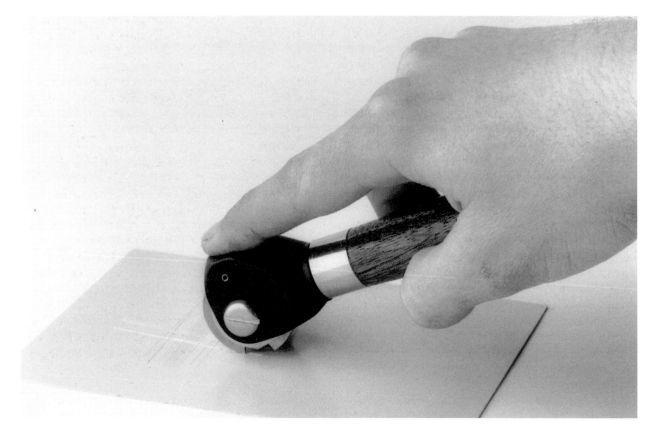

BELOW LEFT *The cross hatch cutter in operation.*

RIGHT *The cupping tester is an instrument that tests the adhesive qualities of lacquers and paints.*

simply pass/fail test at a known diameter of the mandrel, or as a point-of-failure test by using successively smaller mandrels until cracking or flaking is recorded.

Tests for hardness and wear resistance

There are many laboratory methods to test for hardness, a number of which involve simply damaging (or trying to damage) the paint coat in carefully specified ways – scratching, impacting or making and impression, for example. In addition, the tests for adhesion cited above may well also give indications of a paint's hardness and wear resistance.

One of the standard methods, however, is the **Pendulum Hardness Test**. The paint to be tested is applied to a steel or glass base. Once the surface has dried, two steel balls attached one each side of a free-swinging standard König-Albert pendulum are placed upon it. The pendulum is started swinging at a predetermined rate, causing the two balls to roll back and forth across the base. The rolling balls cause the paint to be depressed over a small area; the friction

nonetheless consumes energy and thus slows down the pendulum. The number of pendulum swings are recorded until a set minimum swing distance is attained. The softer the paint, the deeper the impressions, the lower the number of swings of the pendulum are recorded before the minimum swing distance is reached.

Wear resistance can be measured by a **Taber Abraser**, in which sample panels of measured weight are made to rotate against solid rubber wheels. The decrease in weight after a set number of revolutions of the wheels is measured, and corresponds to the amount of paint surface that has abraded off.

Tests for flexibility

The **Conical Mandrel Bend Test** is much like the Cylindrical Mandrel Bend Test used to determine the adhesion of a coated layer on a metal test panel (see above). This time the test panel is forcibly bent around a conical mandrel that tapers from a diameter of 37 mm (1½ in) to one of 3 mm (⅛ in). The panel is afterwards exanmined to find the minimum diameter

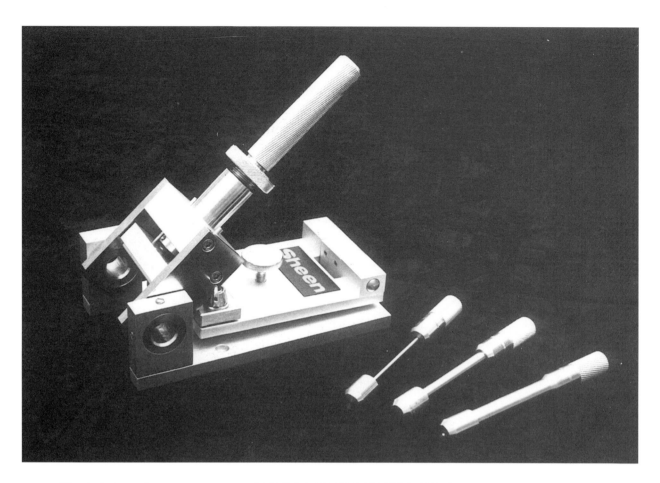

ABOVE *Physical Tests: the cylindrical mandrel band test.*

RIGHT *Physical Tests: mechanised scratch tester.*

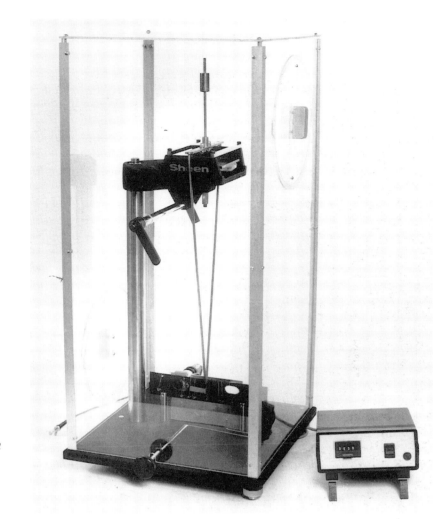

RIGHT *Physical Tests: the pendulum hardness test.*

BELOW *Physical Tests: the conical mandrel bend test unit.*

RIGHT *Physical Tests: the dry film thickness gauge.*

BELOW RIGHT *The positector coat thickness gauge.*

LEFT *The Wolf Wilbourn pencil tester.*

BELOW *The digital thickness gauge.*

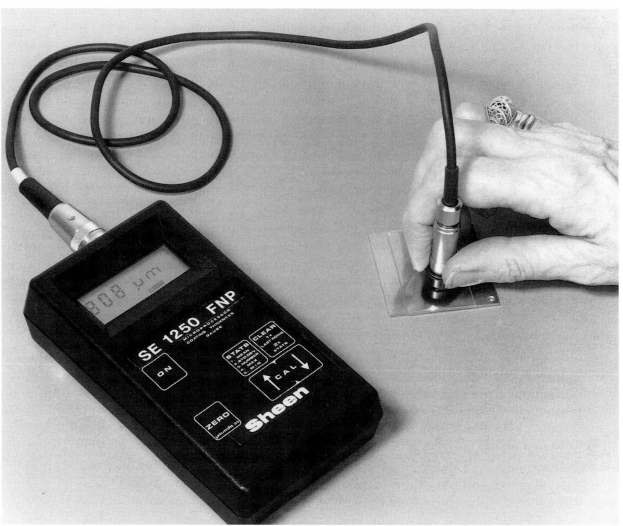

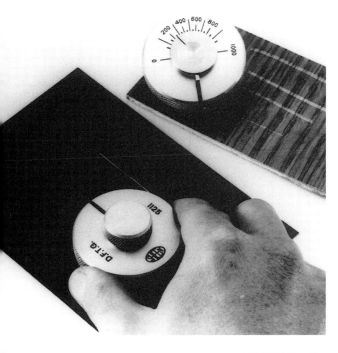

at which failure by elongation occurred.

The Cylindrical Mandrel Bend Test and the Cupping Tester (see Tests for adhesion, above) can also be used as tests for flexibility.

A version of the Cupping Tester is the **Erichsen Test**, by which a steel ball is thrust from below into a metal sheet, the top of which has been coated with the test paint. The size and location of the deformation in the sheet is taken as a measure of flexibility.

Tests for thickness of coat

● Dry coat tests. The thickness of a coat of lacquer, paint, varnish or any other kind of applied layer has much to do with its protective capacity, and for that reason both technical and economic considerations must be applied. Tests on coat thickness are a matter of daily routine in almost all paint laboratories.

There are a number of gauges and measuring devices commercially available for testing the thickness of a dry coating. Many operate by penetrating the coating with a point or blade.

One laboratory instrument of this type is the **Microcator**, which very simply determines the distance between the top and the bottom of the paint coating, and is calibrated in micrometres (microns).

A simpler device, for use in the field, is the **Rossman dial**, which has two fixed points and one moving point connected to the pointer on the dial by gearing. The two fixed points are placed on the coat surface, and the moving point penetrates to the substrate material.

If the substrate is of iron or steel that can be magnetised, the coat thickness can be measured non-destructively by electromagnetic conduction. One instrument in widespread use for this purpose is the **Permascope**. It consists of an amplifier, a probe and a gauge. The principle is that the magnetic flow across a gap in a magnetic circuit is proportionate to the size of the gap. The circuit can be set up so that the magnetic (iron or steel) base and the probe are separated by a gap that corresponds to the thickness of the coating, the resultant flow (dependent on the thickness) being recorded on the gauge, which is calibrated with two non-magnetic sheets of different thickness.

A similar, but perhaps handier, instrument is the **Elcometer**, which can be used by field personnel. The instrument also requires a magnetically conductive base but operates with permanent magnets. Calibration is similarly effected by means of non-

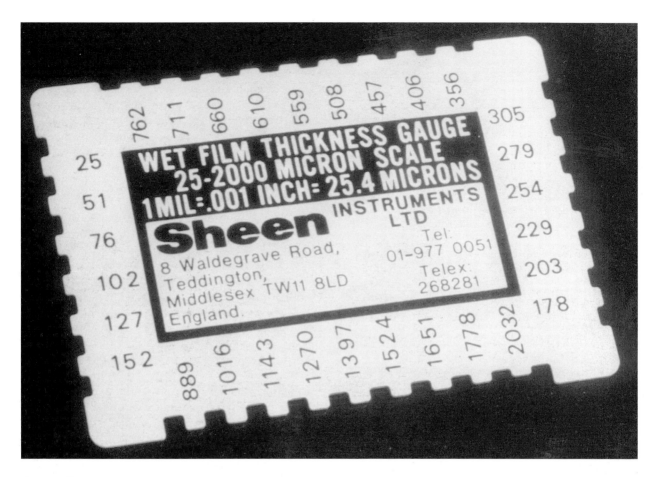

magnetic sheets of roughly the same thickness as the paint coat to be measured.

Other instruments are based on using the attractive force of a permanent magnet, which increases as the paint coat thickness decreases. This force can be measured by means of a spring that is tensioned until it finally overcomes the force of attraction. When it does, the coat thickness can be read directly from a calibrated scale. The **Microtest** is a well-known instrument of this type, which works with a balanced rocker. Another even simpler gauge is the **Test Pen**: roughly the same size as an ordinary ballpoint pen.

● Wet coat tests. Measuring the thickness of a wet coat is fairly straightforward: after all, at the very minimum all that is required is a calibrated card or sheet.

Of the more accurate instruments commercially available, however, the simplest type is probably the steel wet-coat gauge that resembles a **tapering comb**. The two end teeth, the equal longest teeth of the comb, represent the base line and are pressed

through the coat on to the base material. The last tooth to be wetted by the paint, as the teeth rise off the surface through the taper of the comb, indicates the thickness of the coat, for each tooth is stamped with a measurement (in microns and thous).

More accurate still is the **wheel gauge**, which has two coaxial side rims each side of a groove that gradually deepens. When the wheel is rolled through the paint, the groove picks up paint only to a certain depth, which can be read off on a gauge as the thickness of the paint.

Tests for covering ability

Various manufacturers produce **hiding-power charts** to determine or compare the covering ability of surface coatings. The best known are ultraviolet-cured and their lacquer is solvent-resistant; they are suitable for use with most organic water-based or solvent-borne coatings. The method is to apply the coating gradually and evenly over the black-and-white patterned chart. When the pattern is thoroughly obscured, the covering ability

ABOVE LEFT *The calling card wet film gauge.*

TOP *The test pen type dry film pull off gauge.*

ABOVE *The wet film comb gauges.*

RIGHT *The wet film thickness wheel.*

HIDING POWER TEST CHARTS **Sheen**

    Our hiding power charts meet the requirements of most popular tests used to determine or compare hiding power and contrast ratios of pigmented coating materials such as paint, emulsions and inks.
    Our charts are UV cured and their lacquer is solvent resistant. They are suitable for use with most organic, water based or solvent borne coatings.

301-A	**301-B**	**301-C**	**301-D**
		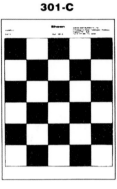	

SIZE OVERALL : 250 × 180mm

301-E	**301-F** **Glossy**	**301-G** **Uncoated**

SIZE OVERALL : 150 × 100mm

301-H	**301-J**	**301-K** **Glossy**

SIZE OVERALL : 420 × 300mm (A-3)

66

corresponds to the volume or weight of paint used per chart surface area unit.

Alternatively, the **Cryptometer** was developed to provide a simple and rapid subjective testing method for the measurement of opacity in terms of covering (hiding) and spreading properties. It continues to be extremely popular for production and quality control in preference to comprehensive practical testing or the complex measurement of reflectance values. (Practical tests and the measurement of reflectance values are nonetheless required methodology in some product specifications in relation to the testing of wet film rather than a dry coating.)

The Cryptometer itself consists of an optically flat glass plate, half black and half white, that is used as the base. Each half of the base has a scale engraved on it along one edge, starting from the division in the centre. Two glass discs, each with a couple of metal supports at one end, are placed on the base in the black and the white areas. The length of the two discs' metal supports are not the same, so that when placed on the base the discs rest at different angles in relation to the flat base. A 'wedge angle constant' (K) is recorded for each disc, ranging from the smallest angle $K = 0.002$ through $K = 0.0035$, $K = 0.004$ and $K = 0.007$ to the largest, $K = 0.008$. The most-used constants are the pair $K = 0.004$ and $K = 0.008$.

One of the discs is selected as appropriate to test the paint: usually $K = 0.008$ for light-coloured paints and $K = 0.004$ for dark-coloured paints. A blob of paint is put on the centre of the base, close to the black-white dividing line. The chosen disk – let's make this a test for light colours, using the disc $K = 0.008$ – is placed over the paint, its metal supports on the white area of the base. The disk is pressed down firmly so that the paint under it is spread out without air bubbles, forming a shallow wedge between discs on the base. This wedge moves with the disc, and the disc is then moved until the black-white dividing line is just obliterated. The scale reading is then recorded from the black scale where the edge of the disc makes contact with the base.

In testing a dark-coloured paint, the other disk is used and the scale reading is taken on the white area.

The thickness of the paint, in millimetres, over the black-white dividing line is calculated by

Hiding power test charts, a simple comparative method to gauge covering ability, as advertised by Sheen Instruments.

multiplying the scale reading by the wedge constant K of the disc used, and corresponds thus to the minimum film thickness necessary to properly cover an area. The coverage or spreading power for this thickness can be obtained for conversion charts compiled for every disc.

Tests for washability
The **Gardner apparatus for determining washability** works on the simple principle of moving a brush backwards and forwards across a painted surface that is kept constantly moist with a detergent (such as washing soda), and recording the results over time.

Delivery Tests

The tests carried out prior to delivery of a paint to the retail outlets are every bit as stringent as the tests carried out on the sample batches in the laboratory before the paint is put into production. In fact, they may be even more scrupulous. Certainly, many of the same tests are carried out, including a number described in this section and not specifically mentioned in the section immediately above.

In particular, tests at this stage concentrate on examining
- the viscosity;
- the particle size;
- the drying time;
- the gloss; and
- the shade. Tests on other less common properties may naturally also be carried out, some of them at the behest of customers with special requirements.

Tests to determine viscosity
Viscosity – fluidity or, more precisely, resistance to flow – is an important property of paint. The more viscous it is, the more slowly it flows. Whether the paint is to be applied with a brush or by other more advanced methods, it must have a viscosity that suits the method of application. For this reason, every batch of every paint manufactured, no matter how standard the product, is checked for its viscosity.

The simplest method of checking viscosity is to monitor the rate of flow of the paint through a **flow cup** over a measured time and at a measured temperature. A flow cup of the type ordinarily used in the paint industry is a cylindrical metal (often aluminium) container with a steeply tapering brass funnel leading to an exit hole at the bottom. There

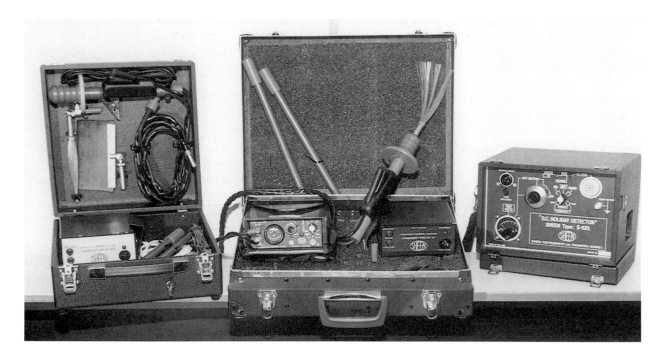

may be a wide rim or reservoir at the top of the cylinder, and the exit hole with its funnel surround generally screws on to the end of the cylindrical bore. There are many flow cups available for the purpose, most of them in standard sizes. The size most commonly used for paint viscosity measurement has an exit hole 4 mm (just under 1/6 of an inch) in diameter. A flow cup with an exit hole of 3 mm (just under 1/8 of an inch) in diameter is occasionally used for very lightweight, thin paints. Examples of the usual type, however, are **Ford Cup 4** and **BS/B4**. In other countries the standard flow cup of this size may be called other things but the name normally also ends with the figure 4 (as **DIN 4** in Germany).

Under ideal conditions, the rate of flow through the flow cup would be proportional to the kinematic viscosity (expressed in 'strokes' and 'centistrokes', calculated with reference to relevant flow formulae or to tables corresponding to the flow cup used, at a temperature of 25°C/ 77°F), which is dependent upon the specific gravity of the draining liquid. But conditions are seldom, if ever, ideal in relation to the ordinary use of a flow cup, and measurements can be regarded only as a reasonable basis for making flow comparisons under strictly comparable conditions.

Other important considerations to be kept in mind when using a flow cup are that
a the bore ratio (length of the cylinder divided by the inside diameter of the exit hole) should be as large as possible – preferably 10:1 or more – in order to provide a smoothly streaming laminar flow;
b the liquid sample should drain slowly (but not so slowly as to make time measurement outlandish) through the relatively long and narrow bore, placed in the true vertical, under the combined influences (only) of gravity and atmospheric pressure;
c the temperature of the draining liquid should be measured and controlled only in the efflux stream, after it has come through the bore; and
d special precautions should be taken if thixotropic or other non-Newtonian liquids are to be tested for viscosity, for there is no definite rate of shear generated in a flow cup.

As is evident from the foregoing, the use of a flow cup requires a few other items of equipment:
a thermometer accurate to within 0·5°C
a container to receive the paint from the flow cup
a stopwatch
To use a flow cup:
1 Place the flow cup on a stand in a draught-free place and in a temperature between 20°C (68°F) and 30°C (86°F).
2 Strain the sample into a clean container and ensure that it is at a similar or identical temperature.
3 Put your finger under the exit hole to block it while you fill the cup until the paint just begins to overflow into the reservoir (or 'gallery'). Fill the cup carefully in order to avoid the formation of bubbles.

4 Level the top of the paint in the cylinder by drawing a scraper across the rim of the flow cup.

5 Place the receiving container beneath the exit hole.

6 Remove your finger from the exit hole and, at the same instant, start the stopwatch.

7 Watch the flow of paint as it emerges from the exit hole. As soon as there are signs that the flow is breaking up into individual droplets, stop the watch and note down the elapsed time.

8 Record the result of the test in the form xx seconds, flow cup number x, at $xx°C$.

To be able to use a flow cup on a regular basis it is necessary to maintain it in good condition. An aluminium-brass type should last indefinitely (although some plastic flow cups are now available)

but requires attention after every occasion it is used. Clean the flow cup and receiving container in a suitable solvent after each test. If the exit hole becomes clogged or narrowed by dried deposits, soften the deposits with a suitable solvent and clean them off with a soft brush or rag – never with an abrasive material! Check the dimensions of the flow cup from time to time. If they have changed and are outside the specified tolerance, discard the flow cup. Alternatives to flow cups are **viscosimeters**. Rotation viscosimeters determining the force required to rotate an immersed body, recorded against time, are used to check the viscosity of thixotropic (or 'short') paints. Cone-and-plate viscosimeters are used to give a very rapid result on tiny samples: the values obtained are given in the units called *poise*.

LEFT *The holiday detectors. These can test for defects not only in paint, but also in p.v.c., rubber, glass and other anti-corrosive protective coatings. Pinholes or porosity are indicated by an audible and visual alarm indicator. The test voltage is set according to the Dielectric Strength of the material, which is the voltage at which the coating*

begins to break down. This must not be exceeded, naturally enough.

BELOW *An assortment of flow cups, as provided and described by Sheen Instruments.*

Flow Cups

These efflux cups provide a simple method of determining the consistency of paints, oils, resins, emulsions, printing inks, etc., they comply with the relevant national specifications (ASTM, BS, DIN, ISO) as detailed below: Zahn-type Flow cups have a stirrup style handle so that they may be dipped into the liquid under test to determine its consistency.

BS Flow Cups (BS. 3900 1971)	Ref. 401
Ford Flow Cups (old pattern)	Ref. 403
DIN Flow Cups (DIN 53 211)	Ref. 404
Zahn-type Flow Cups (ASTM D4212)	Ref. 405
Ford-Flow Cups (ASTM D1200)	Ref. 406
ISO 2431/BS 3900 (1983)/DIN 53224	Ref. 417
Flow cup stand including spirit level	Ref. 418
AFNOR Cup (French Specification)	Ref. 419
Frikmar Cup	Ref. 420

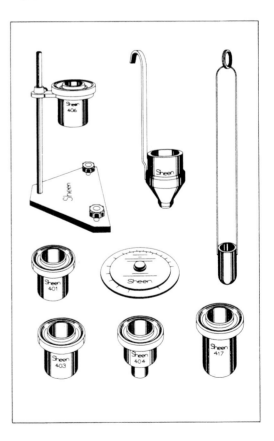

Comparative Viscosity Table

(in seconds)

Ford Cup 4	BS/B4	DIN 4
15	17	14
16	19	15
17	20	16
18	21	17
19	22	17
20	23	18
21	24	19
22	26	20
23	27	21
24	28	22
25	29	22
26	30	23
27	31	24
28	33	25
29	34	26
30	35	26
31	36	27
32	37	28
33	38	28
34	39	29
35	41	30
36	42	31
37	43	32
38	44	32
39	45	33
40	47	34
41	48	35
42	49	36
43	50	36
44	51	37
45	52	38
46	53	39
47	55	40
48	56	40
49	57	41
50	58	42
51	59	42
52	60	43
53	62	44
54	63	45
55	64	46
56	65	47
57	66	48
58	67	48
59	68	49
60	70	50

Ford Cup 4	BS/B4	DIN 4
61	71	50
62	72	51
63	73	52
64	74	53
65	75	54
66	77	55
67	78	56
68	79	56
69	80	57
70	81	58
71	82	58
72	84	59
73	85	60
74	86	61
75	87	62
76	88	63
77	89	64
78	91	64
79	92	65
80	93	66
81	94	66
82	95	67
83	96	68
84	98	69
85	99	70
86	100	71
87	101	72
88	102	72
89	103	73
90	104	74
91	106	74
92	107	75
93	108	76
94	109	77
95	110	78
96	112	79
97	113	80
98	114	80
99	115	81
100	116	82
101	117	82
102	118	83

Tests for particle size

The correct particle size ensures a sufficient degree of dispersion of the pigment or filler in the binder and solvent, in turn also avoiding the risk of such problems as inferior gloss, chalkiness, or leaving a deposit.

There are several established methods to measure particle size. One of the most used, and among the simplest, is the **Hegman Grind Meter**, which comprises a surface that has gradually deepening grooves engraved in it. The grooves are filled with paint, the top of which is levelled off with a special metal scraper. Direct optical observation can then ascertain where particles stick up proud of the grooves, and the particle size can be read off the scale at the side.

Tests for drying time

Many different devices have been produced in order to measure this important property. One of the simplest is the **Beck-Koller Time Meter**, a unit that draws a needle at a constant rate along a strip of the test paint. The speed of the needle is regulated so that the needle will not reach the end of the strip before the paint has had a chance to dry. The result is that the needle makes a groove or line as it is drawn through the wet paint, but from the point where the paint is dry no groove or line is visible.

Tests for gloss

It is important that different batches of what is supposed to be the same paint are identical in the gloss effect – a variation between batches could well be unacceptable to a customer.

One of several instruments for measuring gloss is the **Gardner Gloss Meter**. It has a photoelectric 'eye': a light beam is projected at the test paint surface and a photoelectric cell measures the intensity of the reflected beam. A dial on the instrument gives the reading.

Tests for shade

For years, shades have been checked and matched mostly by the naked eye – though by the eye of a well trained and experienced operative. Such operatives are now becoming sadly rare, however, for it has become quite uncommon for paint manufacturers to have their operatives trained to a sufficiently developed sense of colour awareness. And although such experts do still exist, particularly in the field of automobile painting where there remains a wealth of colours and shades, the efforts of manufacturers have generally been aimed at producing apparatus to control tinting with special basic tints in order both to produce consistent shades and to reduce the colour-checking element.

The basic, normal, and above all slow, method of testing a shade is to compare an original shade established as the desired standard on a piece of metal sheeting with a test sample applied in an identical way on to another piece of the same sheeting. This method, which generally involves forced drying of the test sample in an oven, may nonetheless take up to three days before an accurate comparison can be made. The comparison is then carried out in normal daylight – not direct sunlight – and at a distance of around 40–50 cm (16–20 in). In countries that experience long, dark winters it may be necessary to standardize shades using specified artificial lighting. It is important always to remember that one coat of

The gardner gloss meter.

The colour eye instrument.

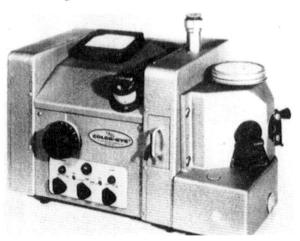

paint can look very different under different forms of lighting.

But for advanced measurement of shade, the machine most used is a **Colour Eye**, a spectro-photometer that in this sense is actually used as a colorimeter. Four filters are used for the purpose: one blue, two different red ones, and a green. The basic method is to compare light reflected from the test surface against light reflected from a plain white surface. In the machine a photoelectric cell is fed alternately with the light reflected from the sample and the light from the white surface. The difference generates an electric current of a corresponding output, registered on a dial.

The values given are recorded as X, Y and Z values, representing the proportion of light received through the filters, according to the standard for physical paint measurement established by the CIE (International Lighting Commission) as early as in 1931. Designated X (red), Y (green) and Z (blue), the values correspond to coordinates that not only allow colours to be defined and expressed in terms of mathematical precision, but allow the definitions also to be plotted graphically in what is called a CIE diagram.

For the measurement of production samples against an established colour, the white surface in the Colour Eye is replaced by a surface of the established colour.

The Colour Eye can be connected to a computer for direct evaluation in McAdam units (CODIC) or for paint composition formulation (COMIC).

The pin-hole detector. When the wetted sponge is applied to the surface and the return earth loop connected to the substrate, current can only flow where there is a flaw.

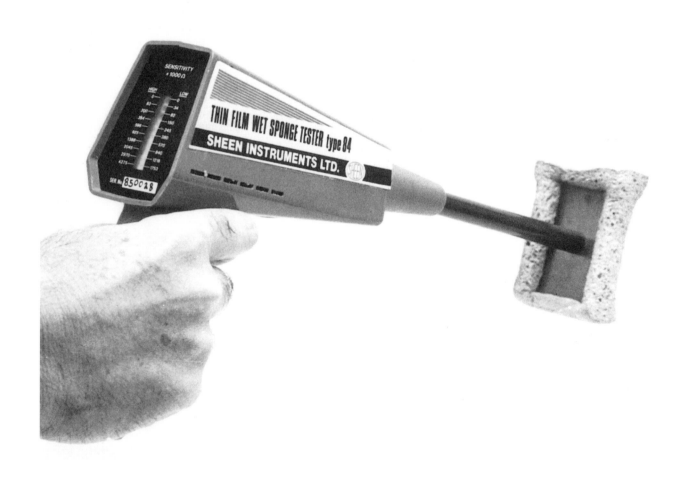

Another useful instrument for measuring the colour of a dry paint film is the **Microsheen Colorimeter**. This has six filters, readings from each of which are calibrated to give percentage values from 0 to 100, in which 0 represents matt black and 100 represents plain white (as the white surface supplied). Test results can be compared with readings of the established colour for reproduction.

DEFECTS THAT OCCUR IN PAINT UNDER STORAGE

There are three major defects that occasionally occur in paint that is stored for any length of time. For each defect there is a straightforward means of prevention.

Bodying
Bodying is the thickening of paint in its container. It is alternatively known as fattening, jellying or livering, depending on the visible effect.
● The causes are: loss of solvents, and oxidation or polymerisation.
● The way to prevent it is to keep the container tightly sealed, and to store the paint in a cool place.

(Thickened lacquer paints can often be made usable again by the addition of a thinner of good quality.)

Gassing
Gassing is the formation of gas in the container, which then causes pressure to build up within the container.
● The causes are: a chemical reaction between constituents, and/or the extreme age of the paint.
● The way to prevent it is never to keep a stock of paint that is too large for use within a planned period, to use the paint you have in the sequence in which you acquired it, and again to store the paint in a cool place.

Settling
Settling or caking is what happens when the pigment sinks to form a sedimentary layer at the bottom of the container.
● The way to prevent it is to invert the container at regular intervals, to use the paint you have in the sequence you acquired it (so that old stocks are used up first), not to store thinned paint at all (thinned paint settles much faster than unthinned paint due to its lower viscosity), and once more to store the paint in a cool place.

3 · THE APPLICATION OF PAINTS AND PIGMENTS

SURFACE PREPARATION

It is of vital importance that surfaces to be painted should first receive thorough preparation and pretreatment. However high the quality of the paint, if the adhesion of the primer to the substrate is not perfect the paint film is not properly supported, and breakdown is inevitable in the form of peeling, flaking, cracking or blistering. This means not only that refinishing will have to be undertaken much earlier than would otherwise be necessary, but that refinishing is the more difficult because of the necessity to strip the old paint process right back to the bare substrate again. To ignore or to skimp surface preparation is thus an entirely false economy.

Cleaning woodwork
Clean down wood to remove all dust, dirt, or other contaminants. Then sandpaper down the wood surface until it is quite smooth, and dust off. Apply primer as soon as possible thereafter.

Cleaning hardboard
Clean down to remove all dust, dirt, or other contaminants. Then apply to both faces and all edges a coating of a mixture made up of approximately equal parts of extra-pale varnish and white spirit. Allow this mixture to dry (overnight). Apply primer.

Cleaning metal
Metals invariably have to have surface impurities removed prior to any painting process. Such impurities in general do not adhere well to the metal surface anyway. Paint applied over them will in turn be unlikely to adhere to the surface. If paint is to serve its purpose of protection and decoration, it is imperative that a full adhesive bond developes between the metal and the paint film. The strength of this bond depends upon both surface cleanliness and surface roughness.

Impurities can be of a variety of types. Ferrous metals tend to rust while in store, and the surface may therefore have been deliberately covered in mineral oils, vegetable oils or fatty lotions. Other materials used as lubricating aids may have been applied to the metal in the rolling mill or in subsequent fabrication processes, including graphite, talc or wax. Residues particularly difficult to remove are fingermarks, polishing compounds, and the burned-on material that surrounds a weld. Black firmly-adherent mill scale and spots or pits of reddish-brown rust are often also present and must be removed prior to finishing.

On a non-commercial scale, the usual method of preparing a metal surface is:
- to remove all coatings down to the bare surface with a proprietary paint-remover;
- to remove all traces of paint-remover, and apply primer.

On a commercial and industrial scale, methods of cleaning metals may be divided into
- those to remove grease, oil, and loose solids – involving solvent methods, emulsion cleaning, or alkaline methods;
- those to remove mill scale and rust – involving weathering and wire-brushing, pickling, grit-blasting, and/or flame-cleaning.

Cleaning processes can evidently also be classified as relying on physical or chemical means. Physical methods include the use of solvents and emulsions, and produce a physically clean surface, whereas alkali cleaning (for example) is a chemical method and produces a chemically clean surface.

So important is the cleaning of metal surfaces before painting that it should be considered at the design stage of manufacture of an article. Closely folded lap joints and tack-welded sheet steel can result in the trapping of salts, causing later paint failure in moist conditions.

Removing Grease, Oil and Loose Solids

Solvent methods

● The solvent wipe. This was one of the original industrial methods of cleaning – simply wiping the surface with a rag soaked in white spirit. The process rarely leads to good results, tending not so much to remove grease as to spread whatever grease there is all over the surface. Moreover, fluff and dust from the rag may also be deposited, to appear later as blemishes in the paint film. For these reasons, and because the method is labour-intensive and not open to mechanization, the solvent wipe is no longer used in industrial workshops today.

● Sprayed solvents. Solvent spraying, using solvents such as paraffin (kerosene) sprayed on under pressure, is another method that has in the past been used to degrease metal surfaces. It is not popular today, however, possibly due to the high cost of paraffin and other such solvents, and the difficulty of recycling the solvents once contaminated with grease or oil.

● Trichloroethylene vapour. Trichloroethylene vapour degreasing is undoubtedly the most popular of today's degreasing methods for the small consumer (who may not be able to afford the more costly installations of alkali cleaners). The method makes use of trichloroethylene's special properties: a good solvent for mineral and vegetable oils, it has a heavy vapour such that when boiling in a deep tank the boiling liquid and its vapour can be maintained with very little loss. Other great advantages are that it readily boils at a temperature lower than the boiling-point of water, and it is non-inflammable.

The method involves suspending the cold metal article over the boiling trichloroethylene within the deep tank. The vapour condenses on the colder metal and drops back into the boiling liquid, carrying with it the oily surface impurities. After a time, and when condensation has ceased, the article is removed from the tank and appears degreased, dry and warm.

To prevent the vapour from escaping, a series of water-cooled copper coils are located inside the tank,

near the top. If the vapour ever reaches that height, it condenses and falls back down into the boiling liquid. Steam, hot water, electricity and gas are all suitable methods of heating the trichloroethylene, although safety devices must be incorporated into the system to ensure that heat is immediately cut off should the cooling coils fail or if, after long use, the quantity of grease and oil present causes the trichloroethylene to overheat.

A useful factor in the process is that because the grease or oil is non-volatile, it remains in the boiling liquid at the bottom of the tank and the metal article is continually being washed above with pure trichloroethylene.

Advantageous as the method is, however, there are also one or two disadvantages to it. It does not remove solid particles or fatty lotions (such as lanolin) as well as it removes grease or oil: a proportion inevitably remain on the metal surface. Two or more vapour baths may be necessary for metal articles of thin gauge which are particularly greasy. Under certain conditions – especially if water is present – heated trichloroethylene can hydrolyse to produce hydrochloric acid, which has disastrous effects on both the containing tank and on the metal article being cleaned. Mild alkaline or acid acceptor inhibitors are normally incorporated in supplies of trichloroethylene to be used in vapour degreasers in order to minimise this risk. Vapour escape from the tank is dangerous for several reasons: trichloroethylene is toxic if inhaled, and decomposes when exposed to a naked flame to produce even more toxic gases, notably phosgene. Precautions must be taken not only to keep the tank sealed as much as possible, but also to ensure that there is no flame (such as a lighted cigarette) in any areas where there is risk of vapour escape.

After a suitable period of use, sufficient grease and oil will have collected in the trichloroethylene liquid to have raised the boiling-point appreciably. The trichloroethylene should then be changed and distilled to purify it for reuse. In some of the more modern plants this distillation process is an integral part of the equipment.

The method may alternatively be carried out using perchloroethylene instead of trichloroethylene. Some parts of industry favour this substance because it has a rather higher boiling-point, which implies a longer condensation period on light-gauge work and consequently superior degreasing.

● Trichloroethylene liquid. Trichloroethylene liquid

and liquid-vapour degreasing plants were designed to improve on the vapour process. Although they are used for cleaning before paint finishing, they are more often used prior to electroplating, where a chemically clean surface is essential. Immersing a metal article in boiling liquid trichloroethylene produces a mechanical scouring effect that helps to remove solid particles on the surface. Thin-gauge metal sheets and sheets closely packed are degreased more efficiently than with trichloroethylene vapour.

Soluble oils and greases present on the sheets dissolve in the liquid and contaminate it. This problem is overcome in either of two ways. A single-unit plant can be run with its own distillation still, constantly purifying the solvent. Alternatively the plant may have several sections, so that an article is immersed in each boiling trichloroethylene vat in turn, starting with the vat containing the heavily contaminated solvent and ending with a vat of clean solvent. Condensed vapour is collected from the cooling coils and passed on to the final vat, causing this to overflow into the penultimate vat, and so on. The plant can operate in this way for a considerable time, changing the solvent only in the first vat from time to time.

A single-unit liquid plant may be used in conjunction with a vapour degreaser in a composite plant, for extra degreasing capacity. There are some integrated plants now on the market in which cleaning, phosphating, and paint dipping are all carried out in trichloroethylene solution.

● Trichloroethylene-soluble substances. For cleaning articles that contain constituents which are soluble in trichloroethylene – such as certain resins, plastics and adhesives – arklone (trichlorotrifluoroethane) may be used instead. It has a very low boiling-point, 47°C (117°F) and is a weaker solvent than trichloroethylene. It can alternatively be used as an aqueous emulsion.

● Ultrasound. Modern practice in liquid degreasers where a very high degree of cleaning is demanded is to use ultrasonic vibrations in order to improve the scouring action. The vibrations are produced by a generator that gives electrical pulses which a transducer converts into mechanical vibrations. The transducers can be either magneto-restrictive, using a metallic alloy rod, or electro-restrictive (piezo-electric), using a quartz or ceramic crystal. The rapid soundwaves beat against the surface to be cleaned, producing a 'cold boiling' effect in the solvent, the vibrating gas bubbles that occur through cavitation

stripping off solid particles. Typical of this method is the use of ultrasonic vibrations of 40 kHz from a 500-watt generator. Such a machine is used for high-precision plating work involving a liquid degreaser beforehand and a vapour degreaser afterwards.

To obtain an even greater degree of cleaning – as required for example in the electronics industry – it is possible to use these ultrasonic vibrations under considerably reduced pressure. This has the effect of removing any entrapped air on the surface of the article, allowing good contact for the solvent and consequently more efficient cleaning.

Emulsion cleaning

Emulsion cleaners, of the single-phase or di-phase varieties, comprise a useful addition to the methods of degreasing utilized by industry. The type available in the form of a **spray** is generally made up of a small percentage of paraffin (kerosene) or similar solvent emulsified with water plus wetting agents and, possibly, alkalis. The single-phase soak or **immersion** types consist of a solution of emulsifying agents in paraffin.

The article for cleaning is either immersed in a cold, single-phase concentrated cleaner, or is sprayed at high pressure with a warm, diluted di-phase type. Grease and oil on the surface of the article become emulsified and can be washed off with water (either by immersion or by spraying). This process is also fairly effective in removing solid particles if high enough pressure is used.

The resultant surface is ideally suitable for the formation of a fine crystalline phosphate coating, especially a manganese phosphate coating, which can be problematic after normal alkali cleaning. Alkali cleaning in addition tends to permit rusting more readily afterwards than emulsion cleaning. The single-phase immersion type of emulsion cleaner has another advantage in that it is not contaminated with grease or oil because the dipping and withdrawal of the article only adds a layer of cleaner to the article's surface. (The grease and oil are washed away with water elsewhere.) A tank of single-phase emulsion simply requires topping up from time to time, and not chemical renewal as is the case with alkali cleaners.

Alkaline methods

Alkali cleaning is by far the most popular method for large installation: it is comparatively economical in use and produces a well cleaned surface. The cleaner saponifies any vegetable oils present, emulsifies the mineral oils, and flocculates the solid surface particles. In fact the cleaner is designed to have a preferential wetting characteristic for the metal, so displacing the contaminant particles. Alkali cleaners require an adequate concentration of alkali together with sufficient surfaction agents to give the maximum lowering of surface tension.

As with emulsion cleaners, there are two main methods of applying an alkali cleaner: by **immersion** or by **spray**.

● Immersion cleaning. The simplest immersion type may consist only of two or three mild-steel heated tanks, the first for alkali, and the second and third (preferably there is a third) for subsequent washing with water. In general, the stronger the alkali, the higher the temperature, and the longer the article is immersed, the better is the cleaning action. A compromise has to be made, however, between several opposing factors including the large and unwieldy amount of foam that is produced and the consequent effect on the following phosphating process in which high temperature and the concentration of alkali produce a very coarse phosphate coating rather unsuitable as a basis for paint films.

The efficiency of the immersion type can be improved by vigorous agitation with compressed air. This simulates the mechanical scouring action that would be obtained by actually boiling. Alternatively, mechanical agitation in the immersion alkali may be used to produce a more thorough cleaning action.

The plant can be heated by gas or by superheated steam, and is controlled thermostatically so as to avoid overheating. Around and beneath the alkali tank there is ordinarily a well large enough to receive all the tank's contents in case a 'boil-over' should take place. Scum and flocculated contaminant particles rise to the surface and are removed over a weir by the introduction of fresh water. It is essential to control the concentration of alkali by taking regular volumetric checks and adding sufficient dry alkali cleaner to bring it back to working strength. To reduce heat loss, many small hollow glass or polypropylene spheres may be floated on the surface of the alkali solution.

In the washing stage, the greatest efficiency is attained by using high-velocity running water and the smallest size of wash tank practicable. Two tanks are normally used, the second to remove any alkali traces still remaining after the first. Any alkali left on the article if it then goes on to the phosphating process would neutralise the acids in that process and so retard the formation of an adequate phosphate film. Traces of alkali in the final wash water can be detected by means of conductivity measurements that can be taken automatically.

The final wash must be as hot as possible in order to reduce drying time, or rusting might occur on such a clean surface.

● Spray cleaning.

Modern industrial plants have now for the most part changed to spray degreasing, rather than immersion, for three main reasons. Firstly, the mechanical action of the spray produces more rapid results, particularly in relation to removing solid contaminant particles. Secondly, a spray system fits in well with a conveyor system, by which the article to be cleaned is conveyed from one part of the process to the next. And thirdly, it is possible not only to reduce the time during which article and alkali are in contact, but also to reduce the temperature and concentration, which also contributes to a subsequently finer phosphate coating. In this way, a 15-minute immersion cleaning might correspond to a 2-minute spray cleaning.

Positioning of the spray jets and the loading of the conveyor must be organized with great care, to ensure that every part of each article to be cleaned gets the required degree of cleaning. Such a plant has to be housed in a tunnel, and is followed by a succession of cold- and then hot-water sprays in sufficient number. The alkali concentration must be regularly controlled, and precautions taken to keep as minimal as possible any traces of alkali carried from one wash to the next. Filters in the alkali circuit should ensure that blockage of the spray jets does not occur. The design of the plant should from the first prevent rusting of the clean metal (which can take place in just a few minutes of an article's being allowed to remain moist and exposed to air).

To prepare these alkali cleaners, one or more of a number of different chemicals are used, including sodium metasilicate, sodium orthophosphate, tetra sodium pyrophosphate, sodium borate, and a large range of wetting agents. If high temperatures are required to remove very heavy greases, non-ionic wetting agents are useful to reduce foaming. For the cleaning of aluminium and zinc and their alloys, special alkali cleaners are necessary that do not attack the base metal, as would happen with the standard cleaners used for ferrous metals.

● Improved alkali cleaning. We have already noted (above) that an alkali cleaner affects a subsequent phosphate coating in a way that poses potential problems. What may happen is that a monolayer of absorbed alkali acts as a nucleus for crystal growth of the phosphate. It is possible to activate the alkali – with titanium phosphate, for example – to control this crystal growth.

The efficiency of alkali cleaning can be enhanced by making the article to be cleaned the cathode in an **electrolytic process** in which the rapid evolution of hydrogen produces an intensive scrubbing action. In cases where hydrogen embrittlement could constitute a serious disadvantage, the article can be made the anode in the system. Electroalkaline cleaning processes such as these are sometimes used to clean components prior to electropainting.

Steam cleaning

Steam has not enjoyed much success as a cleaning medium. Recently, however, a plant has been devised that is suitable for cleaning articles used in the machine-tool industry, such as heavy castings that cannot readily be lifted in and out of cleaning tanks.

A blend of steam and a superheated cleaning solution is manually sprayed on to the surface of the casting. With a control valve it is possible to vary the ratio of steam to cleaner. After cleaning, the casting can be washed and 'dried' with the high-pressure steam.

Removing Mill Scale and Rust

As its name implies, mill scale is formed during the rolling process. It consists of several layers of different oxides of iron, together making a hard, shiny black deposit on the surface of the metal that generally exhibits good adhesion. Because it is so adherent it is possible to paint over this scale if only a limited life is anticipated for the paint film anyway. But in the presence of an electrolyte (a salt), the mill scale and base metal will form an electrolytic cell, which will cause rapid electrochemical corrosion. For optimal results, then, it is necessary to remove mill scale so that the paint can develop its own full adhesive bond to the metal, and to avoid the possibility of flaking.

Rust, which can be considered a hydrated red oxide of iron, forms a loosely adherent film. It is quite futile to paint over it: failure of the paint film occurs rapidly due to loss of adhesion. Furthermore, the presence of rust under a paint film in moist conditions leads to a growth of the rust by extended attack on the metal.

A major difference between mill scale and rust is that rust is readily soluble in acid and mill scale is not. The removal of mill scale thus is ordinarily effected by 'pickling' in a strong acid that eats away underneath the scale, and so lifts it off the metal surface.

In all rust removal processes it is imperative that priming paint be applied immediately after cleaning: a very clean iron surface rusts very quickly even in ordinary atmospheres.

Weathering and wire-brushing

The traditional method of treating large-scale structural steel and girder-work is to allow it to weather and then to scrape the surface all over with a wire brush. The theory is that weathering loosens the bond of the mill scale even as the rust forms all round and beneath; on then wire-brushing, both mill scale and rust should be removed.

The method is rarely 100-per-cent effective. In fact, when it is regarded as a success it is often attributable to the efficacy of the red lead in the oil anticorrosive primer generally applied immediately after wire-brushing. Even if powered by electricity, wire-brushing seldom removes all the scale – it often just polishes it – and the wire bristles cannot penetrate to really deeply-pitted rust anyway. Moreover, the polished surface produced by wire-brushing and chipping frequently causes poor adhesion of the next paint coating. But it must be said that the use of a wire brush is more effective than that of steel wool, which leaves a surface contaminated with fine steel particles that can make for rapid galvanic (or electrolytic) corrosion.

Acid pickling

Any one of three acids is generally used for pickling: hydrochloric acid, sulphuric acid, or phosphoric acid. The first two remove both rust and scale; phosphoric acid removes only rust. Phosphoric acid is the most expensive, but has the advantages that it is less corrosive and that any residue in the pores of the metal create an insoluble iron phosphate coating that improves corrosion resistance. Conversely, any soluble iron chloride or iron sulphate residually remaining in the metal from either of the other two acids would lead to early breakdown of the paint film under moist conditions. To counteract such a possibility, a sulphuric or hydrochloric acid pickle is often followed by a very dilute hot phosphoric acid final wash.

Another disadvantage of hydrochloric or sulphuric acid pickling is the tendency towards pitting – a condition in which localized areas of the metal surface undergo deep acid attack due to galvanic causes. To reduce the amount of pitting, a pickling inhibitor may be added: this has the effect of slowing down the reaction with the metal but only slightly reducing the reaction with the oxide. A number of different combinations of substances are used as inhibitors, including many organic heterocyclic bases and sulphur compounds. The use of inhibitors also reduces the amount of hydrogen generated, and so lessens the hydrogen embrittlement of the steel caused when nascent hydrogen is absorbed at the metal grain boundaries, producing internal stresses.

In addition to pickling inhibitors, oxidizing-type accelerators and wetting agents are often incorporated in proprietary pickling solutions.

Phosphating after acid pickling produces a very coarse coating which, although not too appropriate for paint adhesion, is ideal for cold-forming.

The actual plant and methodology involved in the process of acid pickling strongly resembles those involved in immersion alkali cleaning. Wood- and lead-lined tanks were formerly used for hydrochloric and sulphuric acids respectively, but the modern trend is to use synthetic polymers to line the vessels. Hydrochloric acid can be used cold, but the other two acids require heat to work efficiently, and with either of them small polypropylene spheres are again floated on the surface to conserve heat and reduce acid spray from the hot pickling tanks. The acid strength must be carefully controlled for uniform results. One or more washing tanks are used – after a sulphuric or hydrochloric acid pickle, two efficient washes are essential, whereas phosphoric acid types need only a gentle wash in water, the water often containing 1 per cent or so of phosphoric acid. Following this part of the processing the clean, active surface must not be inadvertently allowed to rust again.

In sulphuric acid pickling, traces of iron produced in solution initially have an accelerating effect on the pickling rate, but as the iron concentration increases so the reaction becomes progressively slower. When the iron in solution reaches a level of around 10 per cent, the rate is too slow for (commercially) economic use: the pickle is normally discarded and replaced by fresh acid. Phosphoric acid pickles do not have to be changed so often: because iron phosphate is insoluble, the iron content of the pickle does not rise above a specific level.

If the work is contaminated with unduly large quantities of oil and grease, it may be necessary first to degrease using another method altogether prior to undertaking pickling, in order to avoid contaminating the pickling tank.

It is possible to use the spray technique with the acid pickling process. One such plant is used for the continuous pickling of steel strip from the rolling mills. Warm, dilute sulphuric acid containing a little hydrofluoric acid is sprayed on to the warm strip. After pickling, the acid is neutralized with alkali, and the strip is washed and dried. High strip speeds can be used, and it has been demonstrated that the incorporation of ultrasonic vibration mechanisms can speed the process up even further.

Other chemical methods
Rust – but not mill scale – can be removed by long immersion in strong alkali cleaners together with a chelating agent to combine with the oxide. The method is particularly useful in cases where it is necessary to preserve initial dimensions as far as possible, for there is no attack on the base metal.

A modern development in derusting processes is immersion in molten caustic soda containing a little sodium hydride produced by the passage of hydrogen through the back. The sodium hydride reduces the rust, and the surface is cleaned without any danger of attack on the base metal or of hydrogen embrittlement.

There are now several composite preparations on the market that are claimed to perform more than one operation concurrently. A blend of acid, organic solvent and non-ionic surfactant, for example, will degrease and derust at the same time.

Sand-, shot- and grit-blasting
The abrasive action of a fine, fast jet of particles of sand or grit is an extremely effective method for removing rust and scale. The resultant surface is clean and dry, and can vary considerably in texture according to the size and nature of the abrasive used. A fine texture is more suited to paint application, for a coarse structure requires more coats to even out the 'hills and valleys'.

The original process utilized sand propelled at speed by compressed air through a special head. But sand tends to break down on impact, yielding fine silica dust, with the consequent risk of silicosis to the operator of this system if the dust was inhaled. The next development was wet sand-blasting, by which water was used to damp down the hazardous silica dust.

Today, angular hardened steel or chilled-cast shot is the common choice for 'grit'-blasting. Because of its high price, however, surplus grit has to be collected up and the fines separated (often with a cyclone separater) in order to reuse as much as possible. Grit-blasting in this way can be carried out only on comparatively rigid metal surfaces – any thin-gauge parts would be deformed by the oncoming action of the 'grit'.

For the blasting an article is normally placed inside an enclosed booth. The operator works either from the outside, viewing through a porthole with hands in rubber gloves, or actually inside the booth, in which case fully protective clothing is essential. The operation is quite fast, similar to paint application by spraying, and special attention can be paid to welds or extra-rusty areas on the surface.

One especially useful model is available that has a head consisting of two concentric tubes, surrounded by a circular brush of crimped nylon. The grit is jetted through the central tube and out under pressure on to the surface, where its motion is deflected outwards, and it is then caught in a vacuum emanating from the outer tube, sucked back through and so recycled, after filtration and the removal of fines. The machine is portable, is much cleaner to use than most, gives ready penetration of complex shapes, and does not need such elaborate protective clothing. Presently it is most used in the ship-building industry and for cleaning finished structures such as bridges prior to repainting.

Whereas plant that uses compressed air as the motive force tends to employ angular abrasive materials and is more commonly utilized on finished structures, the high-speed impeller or airless type of blast-cleaning throws the abrasive medium off a large wheel, uses mostly round shot, and is ordinarily put to work cleaning flat sheets prior to fabrication.

Both compressed air and water may be used in combination with grit where only a very fine surface texture is required. Air and water pressures can be controlled to regulate the final texture. Naturally, however, in those processes that use only air pressure it is essential that the air and grit are totally dry, or the grit will clog and the surface begin to rust again immediately.

• Recent developments. A plant has been developed for the cleaning and descaling of rods, tubes and wire in which the stock is pulled through a vacuum chamber while grit is accelerated on to the metal. Because of the lack of air, the force of impact of grit on metal is much greater than in the normal process; cleaning is both rapid and efficient. The vacuum is additionally pressed into service to extract the used abrasive media, which is then cleaned, graded and reused.

Today, hardened glass beads (ballotini) are frequently used in place of any other type of 'grit'. There is no risk of silicosis with glass, and it does not contaminate the the surface of the metal as sand or metal 'grit' can.

Flame-cleaning

Flame-cleaning is one of the more modern methods of derusting and descaling and for generally preparing a surface for the application of paint. Like grit-blasting, it can be used only in connection with rigid surfaces.

The method is to allow an oxyacetylene flame to pass over the metal surface, which has the effect of cracking the mill scale layer, causing it to flake off, and of removing any rust, moisture or organic matter in a very short space of time. Loosely adhering residues of rust and scale can then be removed by light wire-brushing. But a priming coat of paint should then be applied immediately, while the surface is still hot. The heat has the effect of improving the adhesion bond between metal and primer.

This is one of the few methods applicable to derust a structure on site, and among other locations has been successfully undertaken on bridges prior to repainting.

METAL PRETREATMENT

The involved topic of metal pretreatment can best be considered in two sections:
• phosphating, as applied to ferrous metals; and
• pretreatment processes available for non-ferrous metals.

The information here presented is concerned almost entirely with preparation for paint finishing. Other purposes for which metal pretreatment may be performed – cold-forming, decoration and wear reduction, for instance – although mentioned in passing, are not considered in detail.

The Phosphating of Ferrous Metals

Phosphating has been a process used in industry in Britain from the beginning of the 20th century. Steel struts were given a rust-proofing treatment by being boiled for an hour or more in a solution of phosphoric acid containing iron filings. The same basic principle is still used today. Modern techniques are now able to speed up the process to just a few minutes' work (or in some cases to surprisingly short durations). The development was carried out mostly in the United States, where it was discovered that phosphating could be accelerated to commercially economic production times by the incorporation of metals such as copper and nickel, and of mild oxidizing agents.

In essence, phosphating comprises **the deposition on the metal surface of insoluble metal phosphates that are actually chemically bonded to the surface**. Not only does this give the deposit great adhesion but it can be either crystalline or amorphous in structure – with the result that the process creates a rust-resistant layer itself (even if scratched in use, the underlying metal surface does not corrode as rapidly as it would without the phosphate), and also provides an excellent 'key' to subsequent paint films.

Phosphating solutions are for the most part based on iron, zinc, or manganese acid phosphates dissolved in dilute phosphoric acid. Whereas these acid salts of phosphoric acid are readily soluble in dilute phosphoric acid, neutral (ternary) salts are soluble only if the phosphoric acid content is more than a certain critical level.

When an iron article is immersed in a phosphating mixture, the iron is attacked by the acid, lowering the acid's concentration at the metal surface to a level that is below the critical value at which ternary phosphate is soluble. After an appropriate duration the ternary phosphate consequently crystallizes out on the metal surface, first at the grain boundaries and then over the whole surface. Once a complete layer of phosphate salt has been deposited the reaction ceases and no further deposition occurs. The process is therefore balanced and self-regulating, but dependent upon the presence and correct concentrations of acid and acid salts.

Phosphating using this method, while yielding a satisfactory film, nonetheless requires considerable processing time at high temperatures – near boiling, in fact. Another potential disadvantage is that whatever acid salt is used initially (iron, zinc or manganese), the final film always contains some iron.

Accelerators

For commercial reasons it was evidently essential that some means be found to speed the rate of phosphate deposition. At first other metals were used as catalysts. Some of these (copper, for example) gave rise to problems with drying after painting.

The biggest advance came with the introduction of mild oxidizing agents which acted as depolarizing agents. The action of acid on metal causes the generation of hydrogen gas which, when formed on the surface of the metal, does not simply escape but remains as a gaseous film on the surface, thus dramatically slowing the reaction. The oxidizing-depolarizing agents had the effect of reacting with and removing this layer of hydrogen, enabling the metal-acid reaction to proceed more smoothly. They reduced the time of reaction from hours to minutes.

In general there are four types of oxidizing agents used: **nitrate**, **nitrite**, **peroxide** and **chlorate**.

The nitrate type was formerly most used with zinc phosphate solutions, either containing or not containing iron. Nitrate- or chlorate-accelerated zinc phosphate requires comparatively high temperatures of operation but needs no special replenishing technique, as is the case with the more reactive oxidizing agents (such as a nitrite or hydrogen peroxide) which require constant addition – often by drip-feed – to maintain the ideal concentration in the phosphating solution. On the other hand, the use of hydrogen peroxide or nitrite, with or without nitrate, enables lower temperatures to be used.

Zinc phosphate coatings generally respond better to acceleration than either iron or manganese phosphate coatings.

But the use of the accelerators demands the incorporation of a more efficient washing stage: any oxidizing agent left on the phosphate film represents a potential source of corrosion (although organic nitrites are not corrosive if left in seams).

Following the water-wash stage, a final rinse in a very dilute chromic acid, or a chromic-phosphoric acid mixture, further improves the corrosion-resistance of the coating. This should always be succeeded first by subjection of the coating to a strong jet of compressed air (or similar process) to ensure that any residual pockets of liquor are removed, and then by a final drying operation in a forced draught convection oven or an infra-red oven.

Coatings by weight

The film weight of the phosphate coating deposited is

81

commonly measured in milligrams per square metre (mg/m^2) of surface; $1,100\ mg/m^2$ corresponds to roughly 1 micron (0·001 mm) in thickness. For control purposes, the weight of a coating can be readily determined by weighing a specific size of specimen plate after coating, dissolving off the phosphate coating in a strong alkali, and reweighing.

Industrial coatings vary from $320\ mg/m^2$ to $22,000\ mg/m^2$, or even higher in certain cases. A British Standard covers the properties and uses of a wide range of thicknesses, but in general they can be divided into three types: **light**, **medium** and **heavy**.

● Lightweight coating. Light coatings, in the range 320–$4,300\ mg/m^2$, are essentially for use under a protective layer of paint. The extra-light weights give mainly improved paint adhesion, whereas the heavier weights possess in addition a certain amount of rust-inhibitive capacity. Accelerated zinc phosphate coating is the process most commonly used for light coatings, and is the form in service for the bulk of phosphating in industry carried out as a preliminary to painting.

● Medium-weight coating. Medium-weight coatings, $4,300$–$7,500\ mg/m^2$, are used prior to painting in circumstances where the maximum possible resistance to corrosion is demanded. If weights heavier than $7,500\ mg/m^2$ are used under paint, there is a danger that the resultant dried paint film may flake from the surface, particularly if that surface undergoes deformation, because these comparatively thick coats of phosphate tend to split on impact or on bending. Medium coatings are, on the other hand, more often used for finishing techniques other than normal painting. Metal parts can be finished with mineral oils, greases, wax, stains and lacquers, or lubricants, for example, yielding a usefully corrosion-resistant film. This type of finish is applied to some machined steel parts on which a heavy build of paint is undesirable. Phosphate plus oil is also used with medium coatings on products that have metal-to-metal moving contact – as, for instance, the moving parts of an internal combustion engine – considerably reducing the normal rate of wear due to friction.

● Heavyweight coating. Heavy phosphate coatings of between $7,500\ mg/m^2$ and $22,000\ mg/m^2$ can be used in their own right as a corrosion-resistant covering, without any further treatment. In fact they are used mainly as a preliminary to cold-forming and drawing operations. The nature of the crystalline deposit of ternary phosphates, particularly zinc, is to be able to undergo slip without becoming detached

from the metal. Moreover, the coating is very porous and is therefore capable of absorbing large quantities of lubricant. For cold-forming or drawing processes, then, the metal is first given a heavy phosphate coating that is then allowed to absorb a lubricant – a vegetable oil, maybe, or metallic soap: zinc stearate, for example – and is thus able to go on to cold-forming operations of a type that were formerly quite impossible or prohibitively expensive.

Phosphating plant

Early phosphating plant was of the immersion type, but this has been replaced in most commercial cases by the spray type, which has the advantages of being practical on a large scale, of greater speed in operation, and of being well suited to production on a conveyor system.

● Immersion systems. Tanks in immersion systems are normally constructed of heavy-gauge good-quality mild steel protected from further action by its own layer of phosphate deposit. Rubber- or synthetic rubber-lined tanks make for greater length of service provided that the heating arrangements in the tank are such that the rubber suffers no degradation. Heating can be effected via steam coils inside the tank, or by gas via immersion tubes, or by any of a variety of other arrangements – side heating, perhaps, or heating on both sides of a well which allows the insoluble sludge that always forms to accumulate without adverse effect on the efficiency of the heating method.

After the appropriate immersion time in the hot phosphating solution – from half an hour for heavy coatings to five minutes for the lightweight types – the article is washed in a hot-water tank and then given its final dilute chromic acid dip prior to drying. The drying oven must be efficient, maintained and monitored to avoid any subsequent formation of blisters in the final paint film.

● Spray processes. Conveyor systems in spray processes for metal pretreatment in the car industry include a sealed slot over the tunnel to isolate the conveyor track and chain from chemical spray. Each stage is separated by a suitable silhouette to prevent carry-over from one pretreatment solution to the next.

Application times in spray phosphating have largely been reduced to between 1 and 2 minutes, and the temperatures of the solutions have similarly been substantially lowered. Spray pressure is not obliged to be as high as for sprays used in alkali cleaning, but otherwise the plant and process are very similar. For phosphating, however, jets and pumps have to be constructed of stainless steel.

The work must not be allowed to dry off between the water wash and the chromate rinse, or rusting might occur. If the conveyor is stopped for any reason, there must be extra water sprays on hand to keep the work moist. Equal care must be taken in the drying-off stage after chromate rinsing to ensure that the liquid does not evaporate off the work and form runs or tears, or localized failure of the final paint film might occur. Today, final rinses are mostly of deminieralized water: in the past, many 'snail trail' corrosive defects have been attributable to the use of water containing too high a proportion of soluble salts.

Most spray-phosphating plants comprise a section of a composite conveyorized unit involving degreasing, phosphating, priming, and possibly stoving units all on the conveyor line.

Sludge disposal

An unfortunate but inevitable result of phosphating processes is the deposition of large quantities of insoluble sludge, consisting of ternary phosphates (mainly iron) formed by slow oxidation. On formation the sludge is fine and light. If allowed to remain in contact with heated surfaces, however, the soft sludge turns into a hard scale that eventually requires chemical descaling and physical chipping to get rid of it satisfactorily. On the other hand, if the sludge is permitted to remain in suspension in the bulk of the phosphating solution, it too is deposited with the normal phosphate coat and adversely affects the adhesion and corrosion resistance of the coating.

An early method of treating this sludge was to allow it to settle and then to decant it. Such a slow process is evidently unsuited to the requirements of today's commercial economies which are geared to high-speed production.

Various mechanical devices intended to run on a continuous basis have been brought in to try to control the sedimentation of the sludge. Examples are centrifuges, which require considerable maintenance, and cyclonic separators, which have proved fairly effective. But probably best of all are the mechanical band filters through which the sludge is continuously passed on a moving belt of filter paper near the bottom of the tank.

Fume dispersal

Chemically resistant exhaust ducts and fans must be provided to disperse the copious quantities of fumes generated by the phosphating process.

Monitoring of the phosphating process

Optimum results are dependent upon accurate control of concentrations, temperatures, duration of immersion, and the absolute cleanliness of the surface being treated. Much of the more mechnical operations – like keeping the phosphate tank topped up, and checking the conductivity of the final rinses – are now carried out automatically.

But from the first the design of the plant, jigging and workpieces should be carefully considered in order to reduce to a minimum the 'drag-out' of solution from one tank, and its carry-over to the next tank. In time any carry-over causes contamination. The arrangement of spray jets and workpieces must be such that all parts of the article receive the full treatment, that there are no shielded areas. Jets are most commonly either of two main types: the 'vee', which produces an almost straight stream or coarse spray and is directed on to the article's surface with great force, and the 'whirl-jet', which gives a fine spray. The choice of the correct type and positioning of the jets is critical for rapid phosphating, especially on articles of complex shape.

With immersion phosphating, care is needed in jigging to avoid possible airlocks.

Defects and their explanations

● Uneven and patchy phosphate films are often related to inadequate degreasing. In the case of alkali cleaning, the cleaner should be used at a higher temperature and with greater agitation in order to improve results. If an emulsion cleaning process has instead been used, it is probably the washing-off stage that has not been adequate. If on the other hand trichloroethylene degreasing has been applied to an article originally covered with solid contaminant particles, a wipe with a dry or solvent-laden lintless rag after degreasing should improve the phosphate coating by removing the particles.

● Coarse and patchy coatings can result from a surface that has been treated with an acid pickle or with a hot alkali cleaner that was too strong. The end product may be a coating that is not really appropriate to a paint film being applied over it, a condition thought to be caused by crystal growth starting from a nucleus of absorbed alkali or salt retained by the metal surface. The problem has been tackled in two ways:

a just prior to phosphating, the surface undergoes a process that has the effect of refining the grain size; examples are treatment with oxalic acid or with alkaline solutions with titanium salts (the latter of which may be incorporated in the alkali cleaner itself); and

b agents such as condensed phosphates or various organic compounds are added to the phosphating solution; the procedure is almost routine in continental Europe.

● Stains and run-marks on a phosphate film can be due to overlong periods between the various tanks (as might be the case, for instance, if the conveyor was halted for some reason). Most modern accelerated phosphate solutions are used in conjunction with lower temperatures anyway, and this defect has largely disappeared.

● Failure of the final paint coating by blistering on longterm water soaking may be the result either of contamination in the final rinses (check for the presence of mineral salts in the water) or of contamination falling from the flightbars, jigs or conveyor belt during the later stages of phosphating. In practice the latter snag is overcome by washing the conveyor with water jets at the relevant location.

Alkali phosphating pretreatment processes

Sodium dihydrogen phosphate and accelerators form the basis of very lightweight coatings sometimes called non-coating phosphates. They are 'non-coating' because the alkali metal stays in solution and does not form part of the coating. The resultant film can be up to $1,000 \text{ mg/m}^2$ in thickness and gives a bluish amorphous layer that is suitable for paint application.

If wetting agents are incorporated with the alkali phosphate solution, a light cleaning effect may be obtained in addition to phosphating, although there are obvious limits to the process. An improvement is the use of two such cleaning-phosphtaing stages, in which most of the cleaning and a little phosphating take place in the first stage, and the normal phosphate film is deposited in the second stage (after which the usual washing and chromic acid stages are required). The process has been developed mainly in Germany. Such lightweight coatings have proved a great success in applications for which the highest degree of corrosion protection is not urgent – on metal furniture, toys or lawnmowers, for instance.

They have also been used as an adhesion aid prior to the application of adhesives for PVC laminates or plastisols.

Alkali metal phosphates with accelerators and surfactants have additionally been used in a process in which they and steam are together sprayed on to large, heavy articles, and subsequently rinsed with steam by itself.

Typical Vehicular Pretreatment Schedule

	process	(minutes)
1	Partial immersion in alkali cleaner at 55°C while all the upper surfaces are sprayed with the same solution	3
2	Water rinse at 65°C	0·5
3	Water rinse at 60°C	0·5
4	Phosphating treatment at 55°C, part immersion part spray, as 1. above	1
5	Cold water rinse	0·5
6	Chromic acid conditioning at 60°C, part immersion part spray, as 1. above	0.5
7	Warm airjets play on the body	
8	Drying in an oven maintained at 135°C	3
9	Underbody dip or, more common now, electrodeposition of primer	
10	Application of normal surfacer coat (to be followed by colour coats)	

Other phosphating pretreatment methods

● Trichloroethylene. We have earlier seen trichloroethylene as an effective degreasing solvent, but it is possible to use trichloroethylene for cleaning, phosphating and even painting. The phosphating agents are dissolved in the solvent, and the whole process is non-aqueous.

● Electrolysis. Electrolytic phosphating to effect the rapid build-up of thick films, using plant similar to that used for electroplating, has been considered for certain specific applications.

● Simpler methods. Where the cost of full plant is prohibitive, or where large castings cannot readily be moved, it is possible to use phosphating solutions directly from a conventional spray gun or even to apply them by hand with a brush or wire wool.

● Self-etch priming. Perhaps half-way between a paint primer and phosphate pretreatment is the self-etch primer. These are made up of a polyvinyl butyral resin pigmented with zinc chromate, to which a phosphoric acid solution is added immediately prior to use. A thin, firmly adherent and corrosion-resistant film is produced which, because of its surface roughness, forms an ideal key for subsequent paint coatings. In addition to iron, it can be used on aluminium and other light metals.

Pretreatment for Non-Ferrous Metals
As with pretreatment on ferrous metals, one of the primary objectives in chemically pretreating the surface of a non-ferrous metal is to improve paint adhesion. Adhesion on non-ferrous metals is generally of a lower order in any case than adhesion on ferrous metals.

This part of the chapter is divided into sections relating to pretreatment on specific metals and their alloys, in the order:
- aluminium and alloys,
- zinc and alloys,
- magnesium and alloys, and
- other metals.

Aluminium and its alloys
Aluminium is the most commonly used non-ferrous metal. Although it is not subject to corrosion to the same extent as iron or steel, there are many conditions (such as marine exposure) under which it has to be protected by a paint film. The rate of corrosion of aluminium depends upon its purity: the pure metal – which has a low tensile strength – is reasonably resistant to corrosion. Magnesium and silicon alloys also enjoy good corrosion resistance, but it is the copper alloys – which have a high tensile strength – that are more readily corroded.

In contact with other metals, especially under marine conditions, aluminium is particularly prone to severe electrolytic corrosion, which can have adverse effects on the tensile strength. Apparently inert, aluminium is in fact a highly reactive material – its apparent inertness stems from a very thin surface layer of oxide which, if removed, rapidly reappears. It is partly for this reason that aluminium in sheet form has a somewhat greasy nature, and paint does not generally find good adhesion upon it.

Of the various chemical pretreatment materials for aluminium on the market, most are chromates, phosphates, fluorides, molybdates, or combinations of these four types. As with phosphating ferrous metals, it is possible to obtain two distinct kinds of coating structure: crystalline or amorphous.
- Chromate pretreatments.
Best known and most used of the aluminium pretreatments is the **alkaline-chromate treatment**, also called the Modified Bauer-Vogel (or MBV) treatment. Between around 3 and 15 minutes' treatment in a hot sodium carbonate-sodium chromate bath is sufficient to produce a greyish, iridescent, crystalline film of chromate-oxide of weight ranging from 500 mg/m^2 to 5,000 mg/m^2. Because the solutions used are alkaline, it is possible to incorporate a small degree of degreasing in the same tank, which renders the total process less complex. But washing must for the same reason be thorough. In fact, a final rinse in very dilute chromic acid is a good end treatment, followed by drying in the normal way.

The process is not suited to spray adaptation because of the high temperatures involved. Lower temperatures are possible, however, in a modified process that uses titanium or chromium carbonate as catalyst.

The **acid-chromate process** (in combination with fluoride or phosphate) forms a useful yellow-brown amorphous oxychromate film that is certainly suitable for subsequent paint finishing. Processing duration and temperatures are both generally less than with alkaline-chromate types, which means that this method is appropriate for spray application and for continuous strip plants. More care is required in prior degreasing, because of the acidic nature of the pretreatment, but the after-rinses are not so critical. At the same time, a final rinse in a dilute phosphoric acid solution often offsets the effect of any soluble salts introduced in water used during pretreatment.

The plant used, the working conditions, and the overall regulation and control of the chemical pretreatment on aluminium in many ways resemble those attached to ferrous-metal phosphating as previously described. An additional ion-exchange technique can be used, however, to maintain the strength of the solutions.
- Other aluminium pretreatments.
Zinc phosphate-fluoride or zinc chromate-fluoride with condensed phosphates form beneficial pretreatment solutions that can be used universally for iron, aluminium or zinc surfaces in rapid dip or spray processes that yield a crystalline deposit suitable for subsequent paint application.

Phosphate conversion coatings are available suitable for use on aluminium, steel and zinc surfaces. These coatings represent a convenient pretreatment method for plants that provide continuous strip coating, especially those in which a variety of metals may be coated in succession.

Anodizing is an electrolytic process by which a firmly adherent film of aluminium oxide may be deposited. Any of a variety of electrolytes may be employed, such as chromic acid, and the resultant film is so resistant that it may be left unpainted thereafter (although the surface is fine for a subsequent paint film). More expensive as a method than most other chemical pretreatments, it is nonetheless used in the aircraft industry.

Self-etch priming – as described a little earlier, on page 84 – is an ideal pretreatment for aluminium. It is a process complementary to other chemical pretreatment methods, suitable for hand application on both finished structures and on workpieces in the finishing-shop.

Zinc and its alloys

Zinc surfaces occur mostly as die-castings, or in the form of electrodeposited, galvanized or sprayed metal on an iron base. Under normal conditions zinc does not corrode – but if acid, alkali or electrolytes are present, corrosion can occur, and rapidly. Painting over zinc is problematical, for zinc is a reactive metal: it attacks the paint medium, forming zinc soaps that destroy the adhesion between paint and metal. The chemical pretreatment of zinc therefore interposes an inert layer between them.

Some pretreatments for zinc have already been described above, in information given about pretreating iron or aluminium.

Iron phosphate has been used to pretreat electrodeposited zinc (although electrodeposited zinc is in fact sometimes delivered from the mill in a chromated condition: see below). Low-temperature zinc phosphate is used for the treatment of hot-dip galvanized surfaces and die-castings, often followed – after rinsing – by a dilute chromic acid wash. In general, lightweight phosphate coatings are most suitable for subsequent paint application; heavy coatings give poor welding and forming properties.

A white deposit of hydrated zinc salts readily forms on zinc surfaces exposed to moisture. The basic carbonate that forms in this way is known as white rust, and represents a substance that even phosphating – the best pretreatment of zinc for painting – cannot prevent from occurring. It is to retard the formation of white rust that zinc may be chromated at the mill. The chromate must be removed before phosphating or applying a self-etch

primer, but can in fact present a good basis for some other primers.

Magnesium and its alloys

Because of its low specific gravity, magnesium and its alloys find many uses in the aircraft industry. A reactive metal, it may attack a paint medium resulting in the rapid formation of an oxide film (as does aluminium), but the oxide is more alkaline and non-adhesive than that of aluminium. To paint untreated magnesium is thus to invite the breakdown of the paint within a short time, both by saponification of the paint medium and by loss of adhesion. Moreover, because it is so reactive a metal, it is generally necessary to protect magnesium surfaces at all stages of fabrication with mineral oils or fatty lotions.

The most commonly used forms of magnesium pretreatment are therefore anodizing and chromating. Anodizing in a solution of ammonium bifluoride, with a little chromate, produces a firmly adherent film of mixed oxide and fluoride which, although not particularly resistant itself, forms a good basis for subsequent coatings. A number of different chromating solutions have been used, with varying degrees of acidity, and produce a firmly adherent yellow-brown chromate film that once again gives a satisfactory key for paint films.

Self-etch primer – see page 84 – is also often applied over anodized or chromated magnesium surfaces.

Other metals

Cadmium surfaces, as encountered on plated parts, are pretreated in much the same way as zinc surfaces for subsequent paint application.

Copper, brass, chromium plate and stainless steel have seldom to be finished with paint, although lacquers are sometimes applied. Some chemical pretreatment methods have been devised for these metals, but in general self-etch priming has been established as perhaps the most satisfactory process.

METHODS OF APPLICATION

Cold spraying

For many people, spray painting is what they associate with car manufacture: they have seen industrial films and advertisements in which robots lunge and twist, spraying coats of paint on car bodies in the paintshop of international vehicle factories. But the fact is, almost every manufactured article that is not its natural colour has been sprayed using a spray gun.

● The advantages of spraying. Other than dipping, spraying is undoubtedly the fastest method of applying a paint coating to any type of surface. One person with a spray gun can competently cover as large an area per hour as five people with brushes, and in many cases considerably more than five, with the equivalent saving in time. In addition, two sprayed coats are generally equal in thickness to three brushed coats: some two brushed-coat jobs can be perfectly as well carried out as a single-sprayed job. And the finish of a sprayed surface, moreover, is infinitely superior to a brushed one – there are no brushmarks on a sprayed job, especially if quick-drying paint has been used in the spray gun. Whereas brushmarks are fundamentally a series of ridges and furrows in the paint, a sprayed coat properly applied is quite even in texture and thickness throughout its whole area – and is in consequence longer lasting than a brushed coat of similar apparent thickness.

Finally, the surface on which paint is sprayed is not as critical as that on which paint is brushed. Whether it is steel or timber, brick or concrete, the spray gun covers it efficiently, speedily and economically.

● Special spray effects. Some types of paint used by building decorators and paint contractors can indeed only be applied effectively with a spray gun. These include stone paints and anti-condensation paints that must be sprayed on to give a really effective finish. Modern multicolour decorative paints – with which several colours can be applied in one application – can produce a pleasing mixed-colour spatter effect when sprayed that is quite impossible to obtain with a brush. Plastic texture paints, in particular, demand spraying on in order to ensure a uniformity of stipple; it also enables tinted plastic paint of one colour of stipple to be superimposed on another colour. Spatter, realistic marble and veiling effects with other types of paint are also exclusive to spray application, which can achieve blending, shading and the intermingling of colours much more easily than is practicable with brush or roller. And of course spray application of metallic finishes (such as bronzing) on plaques or statues and the like is far superior to any other method, producing an evenly

metallic appearance. Other special finishes available for spraying include dry cork granules to combat exceptional condensation, flock for textural effect, and dry glitter for spectacular decoration.

The decorator's, signwriter's, car-customiser's and artist's airbrush is a refined sort of spray gun that achieves a professional, almost printed, effect when used in combination with stencils or masking-tape.

● Surface preparation. It is vital to remember, however, that preparation of the surface to be painted is just as important with spraying as with any other method of application. Ignorance on this point has in some quarters earned paint spraying a quite unjustified reputation for producing a surface that does not key as well as a brushed surface, that is somehow not as durable. Every paint supplier readily provides advice on a complete painting cycle for any specific project, and that advice will begin with surface preparation as well as the types and quantities of primers, fillers and undercoats that are suitable. The unwitting use of such preliminary materials containing different resin bases, for example, can cause early breakdown of the final coating. Some paint manufacturers also recommend brush-painting the first coat of primer on a bare wood surface, rather than spraying, in order to fill the open grain without risk of trapped air pockets.

● Industrial spraying. In industry, paint finishing is almost always done in a spray booth of either the dry or water-wash type (for more information on spray booth types, see page 182, THE SPRAY BOOTH). Air from a compressor outside the booth, piped through an air filter and regulator (transformer) in the booth, connects the regulator with a pressure-feed paint tank in or near the booth. Air and paint hoses lead from the tank to a pressure-feed spray gun.

In some installations, alternatively, the atomization air hose connects the regulator directly with the spray gun, and there is only the single hose from the tank. The pressure-feed tank may additionally be replaced by a pump that pipes paint from some remote paint mixing and supply room.

Equipment for spraying is more costly than brushing equipment, but if it is properly cared for, spray equipment lasts for many years without incurring any further expense. Brushers and rollers, on the other hand, have a very limited lifespan, especially if used on rough surfaces. The cost of spray equipment is also offset by its speed of operation and economy in paint with no loss of quality.

● Spraying technique. Just as brushing requires a technique in order that the paint is applied most effectively with the least effort, so spraying requires a similar technique. It is not particularly difficult to pick up, and consists mainly not only of knowing how to use the spray gun but also of knowing in detail how the spray gun and its associated parts work.

Some spray gun manufacturers offer instruction on the use and maintenance of their equipment, and a refinisher would be well advised to take advantage of the offer, especially if he or she has never handled a spray gun before.

At the same time, spraying is one of the arts about which it can truly be said 'Practice makes perfect': experience is valuable, and even a short time's use of a spray gun can turn a rank amateur into a relative craftsman – although a certain amount of natural aptitude helps.

The spray gun

The spray gun is essentially a tool into which air and the paint (or other material) are introduced through separate passages, to be mixed at the air cap in a controlled pattern, and released as a jet.

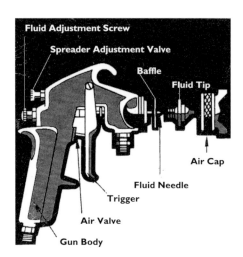

ABOVE *Diagram showing the principal parts of the spray gun.*

BELOW *The paint is atomized when air hits the paint stream.*

FACING PAGE *Parts of the spray gun needing lubrication.*

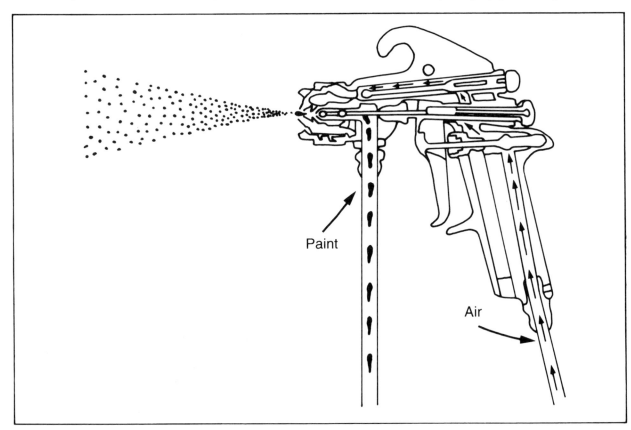

Paint

Air

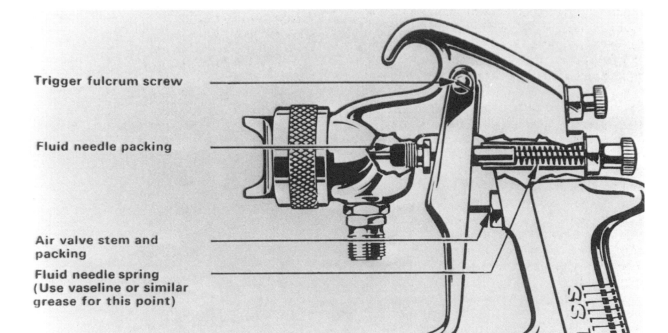

Trigger fulcrum screw

Fluid needle packing

Air valve stem and
packing

Fluid needle spring
(Use vaseline or similar
grease for this point)

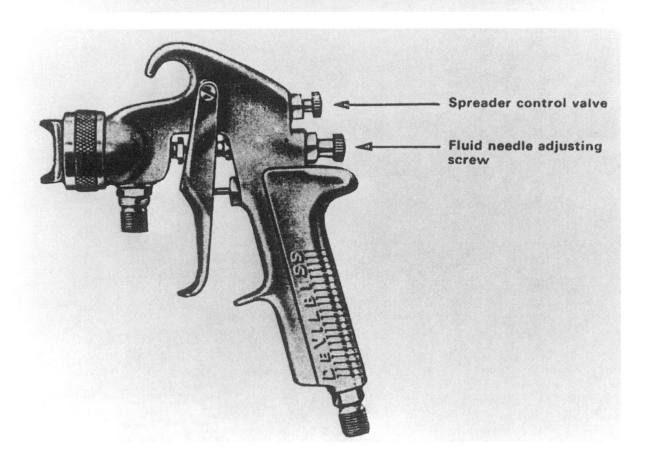

Spreader control valve

Fluid needle adjusting
screw

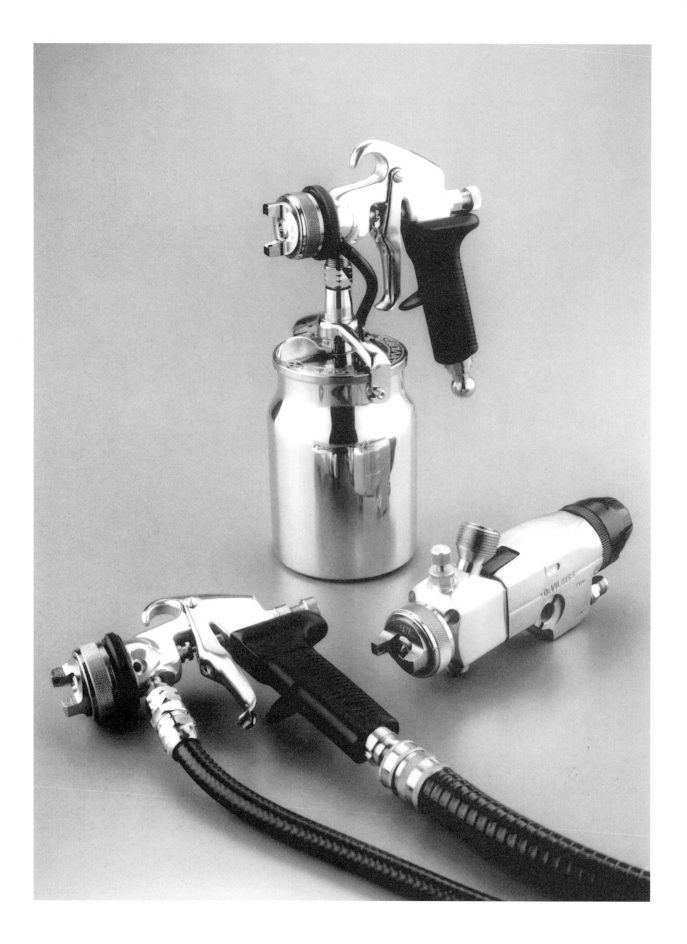

Spray guns can be classified in several different fashions. One method is by the location of the paint container: whether the gun has an attached container or cup, or whether the container is remote. Alternatively, another method of classification is by the system through which the paint is fed to the spray gun: whether the paint is kept in a container under pressure that forces the paint to the gun (a pressure-feed gun), or whether some means of suction is used to draw the paint to the gun (a suction-feed gun). Yet other classification schemes relate to whether the paint is mixed internally or externally, and whether the gun is of the bleeder or non-bleeder type.

● A pressure-feed gun. In this type, it is the pressure maintained on the paint in its container that forces the paint both into the gun and from the gun on to the surface to be painted. The system is used most often when large amounts of paint (or similar material) has to be sprayed, when the paint is itself too heavy to be siphoned from a container, or when particularly fast application is demanded. Typical use of a pressure-feed system is for spraying of a production line in a manufacturing plant.

● A suction-feed gun. In a suction-feed spray gun, a stream of compressed air creates a vacuum at the air cap, causing the paint in the container to be siphoned up to the air cap and out on to the surface. The vent holes in the cup lid must be open. This type of spray gun – easily identified by the fact that the fluid tip extends slightly beyond the face of the air cap – is usually limited to containers of the capacity of a quart

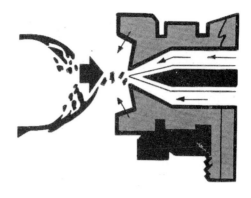

The external mix gun.

(1·14 litres, two pints) or less, and is accordingly most often used where many colour changes and smaller quantities of paint are required, such as in vehicle refinishing.

● An internal-mix gun. In an internal-mix spray gun, air and paint are mixed inside the air cap before being expelled. The system is used mainly where low air pressures and air volumes are employed, or when slow-drying paint is being sprayed – typically, for example, in spraying the outside walls of a house withn a one-quarter or one-third h.p. compressor.

● An external-mix gun. Air and paint in this type of gun are mixed and atomized outside the air cap. External-mix spray guns can be used with virtually all types of paints, and are especially practical for spraying fast-drying paints such as lacquers, or when a finish of high quality is desired.

● A bleeder gun. There is no air valve in a bleeder-type spray gun: air passes through the gun continuously, and the gun's trigger controls only the

LEFT The duo-tech guns – cup gun, pressure feed and automatic versions.

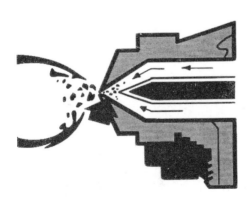

The internal mix gun.

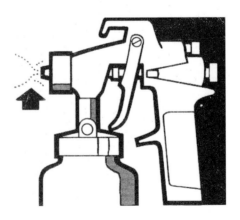

The bleeder type gun.

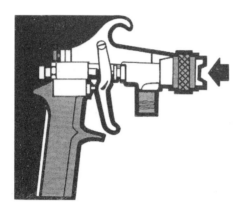

The non-bleeder type gun.

BELOW *The air cap, fluid tip, nozzle size and fluid needle.*

release of the paint. The system is normally used in combination with small compressors of limited capacity and pressure that have no pressure-controlling mechanism.

● A non-bleeder gun. The trigger of the non-bleeder type of spray gun regulates the flow of both air and paint, and there is an air valve to control the flow of air through the system in relation to the trigger. The system is normally used in combination with compressors that have some form of pressure-controlling mechanism.

● The automotive industry's choice. In the vehicle refinishing industry non-bleeder external-mix siphon-feed spray guns are almost universally used. Smaller jobs, such as panel repair, which generally demand only small quantities of paint, most commonly require a suction-feed spray gun with a one-quart cup (container). Larger jobs for which greater

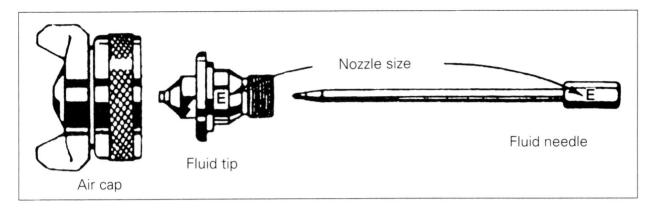

Air cap, fluid tip and fluid needle combinations. In this case, 'E' denotes a tip diameter size of 0.070 in.

amounts of paint are necessary might involve the use of a pressure-feed system with a separate two-quart or larger paint container.

The principal components of a spray gun are illustrated in the diagram. Some guns are equipped with a removable spray-head unit comprising the **air cap**, the **fluid tip** and the **fluid needle**. These three items are in practice regarded as a unit anyway, because they are directly responsible for the quality of the spray pattern and finish: together they are known as the **nozzle combination**.

As the trigger is pulled back, the mechanism first makes contact with the air valve stem, which turns on the air. It then retracts the fluid needle from from the fluid tip, allowing paint to flow. Releasing the trigger reverses the process. There is always air for atomization at the air cap for the air supply is first on and last off in relation to the trigger's movement.

● The air cap. There are various styles of air cap, producing different sizes and shapes of spray patterns appropriate for different forms of coverage. The greatest contrast in styles is between the internal-mix and the external-mix types.

Internal-mix caps (used with pressure-feed systems only) mix the air and paint inside the air cap before propelling them through a single slot or round hole.

External-mix caps (used with either suction- or pressure-feed systems) expel air through one or a number of holes to atomize the paint: they are thus classified as single-orifice or multiple-jet caps. Multiple-jet caps have several advantages over caps with a single orifice:

a better atomization of the more viscous types of paint, or of ordinary types of paint in low-pressure systems;

b higher atomization pressures can be used on the more viscous types of paint with less risk of a split spray pattern; and

c superior equalization of air volume and pressure from the cap gives better uniformity of spray pattern.

Selection of an air cap should therefore be on the basis of a combination of several different factors:

the type and volume of paint to be sprayed
the size and nature of the surface to be sprayed
the paint-supply system (suction- or pressure-feed)
the volume and pressure of air available
the size of the fluid tip to be used
The fluid tip.

The amount of paint that actually leaves the front of the spray gun depends on the size of the fluid tip opening when the fluid needle is retracted by the movement of the trigger. Fluid tips are available in a great variety of sizes in order to deal with paints of a range of types and viscosities, and to permit different volumes of paint to be sprayed at different speeds of application.

The standard fluid tip diameter sizes are (as decimalized fractions of an inch):

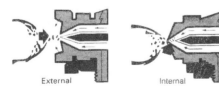

A cross section of external and internal mix air caps, side by side for comparison of flow.

AS	0·140
AC/CS	0·110
D	0·086
DE	0·078
E/EE/EX	0·070
FF	0·055
FZ	0·047
FX	0·0425
F	0·041
G	0·028
H	0·018

The sizes are stamped in the form of the relevant letter or letters on the fluid tip and fluid needle (both of which should show the same marks). Sizes in most general use are E, EX, FF and FX. The EX combination is used with suction-feed systems, whereas the other sizes are mostly for pressure-feed systems.

Fluid tips are ordinarily of hardened steel. Tips of stainless steel and some much harder alloys are available for use with corrosive or abrasive materials.

The rate of flow through the fluid tip is adjusted by the fluid needle adjuster, which controls how far the fluid needle travels when the trigger is pulled.

● The nozzle combination. Selection of a nozzle combination involves consideration of

the spray gun model
the type and viscosity of the paint
the size and nature of the surface to be sprayed
the volume and pressure of air available
the desired speed and/or quality of the finish

As a general rule, the largest possible spray pattern consistent with the size of the surface to be sprayed should be used: this reduces spraying time and the number of gun passes. Final finish coats should on the other hand probably be sprayed on with a nozzle combination featuring fine atomization and smaller pattern size in order to produce a finish of high quality.

The paint discharged in ounces per minute from a suction-feed spray gun is relatively stable, because it is largely determined by atmospheric pressure. Based on a standard-mix refinishing material with comparatively low viscosity, and at a flow rate equating to 50 pounds per square inch at the gun, a 0·070-inch fluid tip discharges around 12 ounces per minute, and a 0·086-inch fluid tip around 14 ounces per minute.

The paint discharged by a pressure-feed gun, however, depends more on the inside diameter (ID) of the fluid tip and the pressure on the paint in its

container – the larger the opening, the more paint is discharged. Based on a refinishing material with a viscosity of 25–30 seconds in a number 4 Ford flow cup, a 0·042-inch ID tip discharges between 10 and 30 ounces per minute, a 0·055-inch ID tip between 30 and 50 ounces per minute, and a 0·070 ID tip between 50 and 70 ounces per minute.

If the fluid tip ID is too small for the amount of material flowing through the gun, the discharge velocity will be too high, and the air coming from the air cap will not be able to atomize it properly, causing pattern distortion. If the fluid tip ID opening is conversely too large, control is lost over the material issuing from the spray gun, and there may not be enough air to atomize it correctly.

The nozzle combination's parts must be matched with each other and to the job in hand. Spray gun catalogues include charts to help a user do this.

A nozzle combination on a removable spray-head presents several advantages over one that is integral to the spray gun:
a it is easy to make a quick change from one type of paint or one colour to another – one spray gun with several heads may well answer the puprose of what might otherwise require several guns;
b easier cleaning and maintenance; and
c in the case of damage or during repairs to the spray-head, only a new spray-head is required, not a new gun.

Operating a spray gun in a suction-feed system
The typical components of a suction-feed system for paint spraying are:

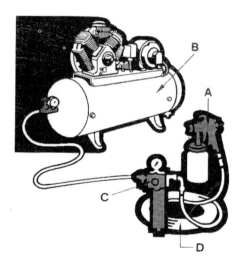

The suction feed system components.

This SIP Airmate Compressor is useful for spraying small areas, but a larger tank and more powerful motor is recommended for a full respray unless you are blessed with patience.

- a suction-feed spray gun with cup (A);
- an air compressor (B);
- an air regulation mechanism (C); and
- lengths of air hose (D).

   Setting up the system for operation involves:

1 Connecting the airline from the compressor outlet to the air regulation mechanism inlet.

2 Connecting the air hose leading from the air regulation mechanism outlet to the air inlet on the spray gun.

3 Reducing the paint to proper consistency, mixing, and straining it into the cup (container), and attaching the cup to the gun.

4 Opening the air outlet valve on the air regulator and adjusting the atomization air to approximately

50 pounds per square inch at the gun (if necessary by referring to a pressure-drop chart).

   For maximum pattern size, open wide the spreader adjustment valve on the gun: turn counter-clockwise until it stops.

   For maximum paint delivery, screw out the flow-adjustment screw to a wide-open position (reached when the first thread of the screw is visible).

   To check that all is working properly, spray a horizontal test pattern, holding the trigger open until the paint begins to run. Paint distribution should be even across the full width of the pattern. (If it is not, the problem is with either the air cap or the fluid tip – see *Spray problems and answers* below.) If distribution is even, rotate the air cap back to normal position, and begin spraying.

Operating a spray gun in a pressure-feed system

The typical components of a pressure-feed system for paint spraying are:

- a pressure-feed spray gun (A);
- a pressure-feed cup or tank (B);
- an air regulation mechanism (C);
- appropriate lengths of air and paint hose (D); and
- an air compressor (E).

   Setting up a system with a pressure-feed cup involves:

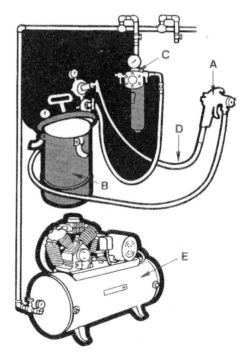

The pressure feed system components.

95

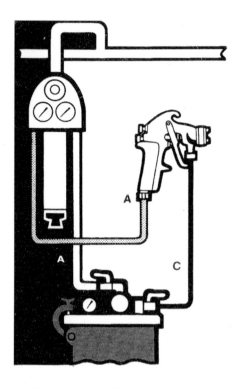

The pressure tank spraying hook-up.

1 Connecting the air hose (A) from the air regulation mechanism to the air regulator on the cup.
2 Connecting the air hose from the tank air regulator (B) to the air inlet on the spray gun.
3 Connecting the paint hose from the paint outlet on the cup (C) to the paint inlet on the gun.

Setting up a system with a pressure-feed tank involves:
1 Connecting the regulated air hose from the air regulation mechanism to the air inlet on the spray gun.
2 Connecting the mainline air hose from the air regulation mechanism to the air regulation inlet on the tank.
3 Connecting the paint hose from the paint outlet on the tank to the paint inlet on the gun.

For maximum pattern size, open wide the spreader adjustment valve on the gun: turn counter-clockwise until it stops.

For maximum paint delivery, screw out the flow-adjustment screw to a wide-open position (reached when the first thread of the screw is visible).

There is a standard routine to check that all is working properly, and that the gun is balanced for correct spraying. First shut off the atomization air to the gun. Set the paint flow rate by adjusting the air pressure in the air container – use about 6 pounds per square inch for a remote (non-attached) cup, and about 15 pounds per square inch for a two-gallon (9-litre) or larger container. The paint flow can be adjusted in either of two ways:
a) Remove the air cap, aim the gun into a clean container, and pull the trigger for 10 seconds. Measure the amount of paint that flowed during that time, and multiply by six (alternatively pull the trigger for 30 seconds and multiply by two) to find the paint flow rate in ounces per minute. Standard refinishing requires about 14–16 ounces per minute. If the flow rate is less than this, increase the air pressure in the container, and repeat. If it is more than this, reduce the pressure slightly. When the flow is correct, reinstall the air cap.
or **b)** Pull the trigger, and adjust the pressure in the paint container until the stream of paint discharging from the gun squirts a metre or more (3–4 feet) before it starts to drop. This indicates a paint flow of about 14–16 ounces per minute.

Then turn on the atomization air to about 50 pounds per square inch at the gun. Spray a fast test pattern on a clean sheet of paper, and check particle size in the painted surface. Increase or reduce air pressure until an even particle size is achieved. Now spray a horizontal test pattern, holding the trigger open until the paint begins to run. Paint distribution should be even across the full width of the pattern. (If it is not, the problem is with either the air cap or the fluid tip – see *Spray problems and answers* below.) If distribution is even, the system is ready for you to begin spraying.

The spraying technique
● Using the spray gun. The gun should be held so that the spray pattern is perpendicular to the surface at all times, and at a constant distance of approximately 20 cm (8 in) from the surface. Triggering should begin just before the edge of the surface to be sprayed is in line with the nozzle. The trigger should be held fully depressed, and the gun moved in one continuous motion until the other edge of the surface is reached. The trigger is then released, shutting off the paint flow, but the motion is continued for a short distance until it is reversed for the return stroke.
Each stroke should overlap the previous one by 50 per cent. Less than this proportion of overlap results in streaks on the finished surface – a 50-per-cent

overlap gives uniform coverage.

● Refinishing applications. Areas giving difficulty – such as corners or edges – should be sprayed first. Hold the gun 2 or 3 cm (an inch or so) closer than normal, orscrew the spreader adjustment control in a few turns. The result, either way, is a smaller spray pattern, although if the gun is merely held closer, the stroke has to be faster to compensate for the normal quantity of paint being applied otherwise to a smaller area of surface.

Try to retain the 50-per-cent overlap even on these difficult areas.

When spraying curved surfaces, try once more to keep the gun perpendicular to the surface at any given point. This may not always be possible, but it is an ideal to aim at.

Very narrow surfaces may require a different gun or spray-head that provides a smaller spray pattern. Alternatively, a full-size gun may be used with the air pressure and paint flow reduced, and with careful triggering.

● Cleaning and maintenance. A suction-feed spray gun and cup should be cleaned using a standard sequence of actions. First loosen the cup cover, and while the paint tube is still in the cup, unscrew the air cap about two or three turns. Hold a cloth over the air cap and pull the trigger. Air diverted into the paint passages forces paint back into the container. Empty the cup of paint in this way, and replace it with a small quantity of solvent. Spray solvent through the gun in order to flush out residues in the paint passages. The remove the air cap, immerse it in clean solvent, and dry it by blowing with compressed air. Unclog any blocked holes in the air cap preferably by soaking in solvent but if necessary by reaming out the blockage with a straw, match stick, or other fairly soft probe. Replace the air cap on the gun. Wipe off the gun with a solvent-soaked rag, or brush the air cap and gun with a fibre brush and thinner.

A pressure-feed spray gun also has a standard cleaning sequence. Hold a cloth over the air cap and pull the trigger, to force paint back into the open container. Clean the container and add solvent. Turn off the atomization air, pressurize the system, and run the solvent until clean. Dry the hose by again loosening the cap and container lid, and forcing air back through the gun and hose. Clean the air cap (as above) and fluid tip. Clean out the tank, and reassemble for future use.

A device called a hose cleaner can be used to force a mixture of solvent and compressed air

through paint hose and paint passages. A manually operated valve then stops the flow of the solvent, allowing the air by itself to dry the equipment. The parts of a spray gun that require regular lubrication are:

the fluid needle packing
the air valve packing
the trigger bearing screw

A drop or two of oil should from time to time be put on the fluid needle packing to keep it soft. The fluid needle spring should be coated with petrolatum.

Spray problems and answers
● Air leaking from the front of the gun. Generally caused by any of the following possibilities:

foreign matter on valve or seat
worn or damaged valve or seat
broken air valve spring
sticking valve stem due to under-lubrication
bent valve stem
packing nut on too tight
gasket damaged or missing

● Paint leaking from the front of the gun. This sometimes occurs in pressure-feed systems when a fluid needle is not seating properly, and is generally caused by any of the following possibilities:

worn or damaged fluid tip or needle
lumps of dirt lodged in fluid tip
packing nut on too tight
broken fluid needle spring
needle or tip of incompatible size

● The gun will not spray at all. A frustrating state of affairs that occasionally happens in in both suction- and pressure-feed systems, the result perhaps of:

no air pressure through the gun
fluid tip not open enough

In pressure-feed systems there is an alternative possibility which is:

paint pressure too low with internal-mix cap

In suction-feed systems the fault may lie in:

the paint too heavy for the suction-feed
an internal-mix air cap being used

● Jerky or fluttering spray. In both suction- and pressure-feed systems, this might be due to:

insufficient paint in the container
container being tipped at an excessive angle
paint passage obstructed
loose or cracked paint tube in cup or tank
loose fluid tip or damaged tip seat

In suction-feed systems only, there are other possible explanations:

the paint is too heavy for the suction feed

air vent in cup lid clogged

loose, dirty or damaged coupling nut on cup lid

dry packing, or loose fluid needle packing nut

the paint tube is resting on the bottom of the cup

● Defective spray pattern. Where the pattern is particularly heavy on one side or at top or bottom, the fault most often lies in one of these possibilities:

partly blocked horn holes

partly obstructed or dirty fluid tip

dirt on air cap seat or fluid tip seat

– diagnosis of whether the obstruction is on the air cap or fluid tip can be effected by making a solid test spray pattern and then rotating the cap one half turn and repeating the test pattern: if the defect is inverted the second time, the obstruction is on the air cap; if not inverted, it is on the fluid tip.

Where the pattern is instead heavy at the centre of the pattern, this can be caused by:

too low a setting of the spreader adjustment valve

too low an atomizing pressure

paint too thick or too thin for the fluid tip

Where the spray pattern is instead split, or is spotty, uneven, and slow to build, the malfunction is most often due to:

air and paint not properly balanced

– this can be corrected by reducing the width of the spray pattern using the spreader adjustment valve, or by increasing paint pressure (and therefore speed of use).

Where the spray pattern is dry, the sprayed coat is short of liquid material, which is most often caused by:

too high air pressure

the gun held too far from the surface

the nozzle not adjusted for surface distance

the paint not reduced or thinned correctly (in a suction-feed system)

Refinishing spray coats

● The spray gun is mainly used to spray paint in any of three basic types of coats: a **tack coat**, a **full wet coat** or a **mist coat**. The tack coat allows the application of heavier wet coats without sagging or runs. It is a light covering coat sprayed on to the surface and allowed to dry until it is just tacky (which takes only a few minutes). The finish wet coats are then sprayed over the tack coat.

A full wet coat is a heavy, glossy coat applied in a thickness almost heavy enough to run. Skill and practice is required to spray on a coat like this.

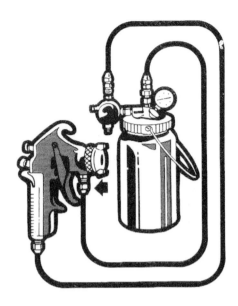

The pressure feed gun with remote 2qt. cup.

A mist coat is sometimes required for final metallic colour matching. It is applied in a fashion similar to a tack coat but the composition of the finish is usually very different. The paint manufacturer normally supplies instructions for mixing and applying a mist coat.

Spray paint containers

Containers of paint (or other materials) for spraying vary considerably in size according to the type of spraying system in use. There are nonetheless two common types: **cups**, which are attached to the spray gun itself, and **remote pressure cups** or **pressure tanks** located at some distance from the gun.

Cup containers typically have a capacity of one quart (1·14 litres, two pints) or less, and are used where comparatively small areas of paint are to be sprayed. They are attached to the gun with a lid assembly (or cup attachment) that either clips on or screws into the cup container. The lid assembly may or may not be independently detachable from the spray gun.

The appearance and function of a cup container differs according to whether it is to be used in a suction-feed system or a pressure-feed system.

● The suction-feed cup. The top of the suction-feed container cup has a vent hole which allows atmospheric pressure to play a part in the mechanics of the spray gun. When the gun's trigger is pulled so that compressed air exits from the air cap, a vacuum is created there. The pressure in the container is at once – thanks to the vent – higher than that at the tip end, and paint is forced up the delivery tube in the cup, through the spray gun paint passages, and out through the fluid tip, where the compressed air atomizes it in passing.

This type of container is particularly useful in spraying relatively thin (low-viscosity) material, such as lacquer, synthetic enamel or a stain.

● The pressure-feed cup. There is no vent in a pressure-feed container cup. The compressed air that atomizes the paint at the fluid tip also forces the paint from the container up to that point.

This type of container is particularly useful for spraying materials that are too thick for suction-feed equipment, such as some enamels, flat wall paints and wood fillers. It is often of a larger capacity than suction-feed cups, generally twice the size: two quarts (2·28 litres, four pints).

There are two types of pressure-feed cup: the **regulator type** and the **non-regulator type**.

The regulator type, as its name suggests, has a built-in regulator to control the pressure on the paint independently of the atomization air pressure, permitting better control of the spraying operation. Apart from the regulator control, there is generally also a gauge to indicate the paint pressure, a valve to release pressure from the cup, and a safety-valve to prevent excessive pressure build-up.

The non-regulator type has no such mechanisms and thus no means of additionally controlling paint pressure. Uncommon in professional finishing paintshops, it is mostly used with relatively small air-compressing systems.

The greater degree of control afforded by the regulator device means that the regulator pressure-feed cup can duplicate production finishing operations that would normally require a pressure-feed tank of a much larger capacity.

● The pressure-feed tank. The pressure-feed tank, examples of which range in capacity from 2 to 120 gallons (9·1 to 546 litres), is pressurized with compressed air, which forces paint out of the closed tank through a hose to the spray gun. The rate of paint flow is controlled by increasing or decreasing the air pressure in the tank.

Tanks are available with either top or bottom outlets, and with a range of possible accessories. Smaller, light-duty tanks are most often made of welded steel and are subject to inlet pressure restrictions. Larger tanks are ASME-coded and made of drawn steel. When abrasive or corrosive material is to be sprayed, the tank shell (the inside body of the

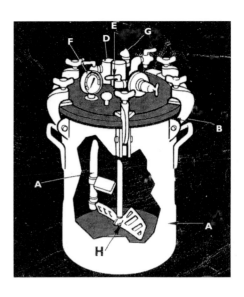

Pressure feed tank. (A) The Shell. (B) Clamp-on lid. (C) Fluid tube. (D) Header. (E) Regulator. (F) Gauge. (G) Safety valve. (H) Agitator.

tank) may be coated or lined with protective material, or an **insert container** – a pail-like vessel containing the special material – may be placed inside the tank so that the tank itself does not come in contact with the material.

The main advantage of a pressure-feed tank is its ability to feed a constant flow of paint to the gun over an extended time, and in a positive and uniform manner. Consequently, pressure-feed tanks are most commonly used where continuous production is required to be maintained. Agitators within the tank

Single regulator tank.

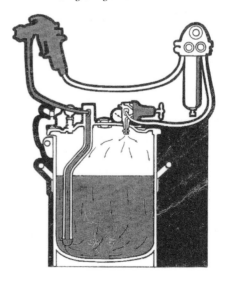

can ensure that the paint is consistently mixed in suspension.

Tanks are fitted with regulators that control pressure in either one or two ways: they are accordingly known as **single-regulator tanks** or **double-regulator tanks**. A single-regulator tank has a regulator that controls only the pressure on the paint within the tank. A double-regulator tank has one regulator that similarly controls the pressure on the material in the tank, and another that independently controls the pressure of air going into the spray gun for atomization at the fluid tip. With this type of tank, the paint pressure may be higher or lower than the atomization air pressure, depending on the height at which the gun is operated above the tank, the degree of atomization required, the size and length of communicating hose, the speed of operation, and the type of paint (or other material) being sprayed.

● Container maintenance. After every use, paint containers such as cups, tanks and insert containers should be completely cleaned, inside and out, with an appropriate solvent. The most efficient method is to clean while the paint is still wet.

Cleaning a suction-feed cup, remember to inspect the vent hole in the lid (as advised previously). Cleaning a pressure-feed container, inspect and clean the sealing surfaces, gaskets and clamps.

Hoses and connections

In spray painting there are two types of hose: air hose (usually red in colour) and fluid hose (usually black in colour).

● The air hose. In professional systems, the air hose is almost always coloured red, although in smaller low-pressure systems it may instead be covered with a black-and-orange braided fabric.

Single-braid rubber-covered hose comprises an inner tube, a braid layer, and an outside rubber cover, all vulcanized into a single unit. Double-braid hose, used for exceptionally high working pressure, consists of an inner tube, a braid, a separator or friction layer, another layer of braid, and an outer rubber cover, all vulcanized into a single unit.

The hose from the regulator to a gun or tank should have a minimum inside diameter (ID) of 5/16 inch (8 mm). Tools requiring more air may demand hose of ID 3/8 inch (9·5 mm) or more.

If the air hose is too small for the system, the spray gun is starved of air, with the resultant characteristic defects in operation.

● The fluid (paint) hose. Fluid hose is normally

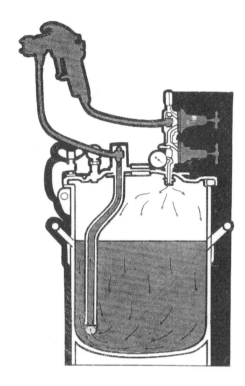

The double regulator pressure feed paint tank.

The threaded connection.

constructed in much the same fashion as air hose but with an outer covering that is black, or occasionally brown, in colour. Moreover, the inner tube is lined with special material that is impervious – or at the least, highly resistant – to solvents.

Hose with an ID of 3/8 inch (9·5 mm) is suitable for production guns in normal finishing. Guns used in maintenance finishing work may require hose of ID

1/2 inch (12·7 mm). Working with materials of high viscosity could demand hose of ID as much as 3/4 inch (19 mm) to 1 inch (25·4 mm).

● Pressure drop. Pressure drop is the loss of pressure due to friction in the hose or pipe between the source of air and the point of release. Obviously, the longer the hose, the greater the pressure drop – without any further complications such as corners or kinks.

At low pressure and in short lengths of hose, pressure drop is negligible. As the hose is lengthened, however, the pressure must be increased accordingly, and on a curving scale. All too often it is the innocent spray gun to which the air supply is starved through using hose of inadequate ID that is blamed as being defective.

● Hose maintenance. A hose that ruptures in the middle of a job can ruin – or at the very least, delay – the work. Always take care when leading a hose across the floor: it should not be pulled around sharp objects, run over by vehicles, kinked, or subjected to extreme heat. When not in use, hoses should be stored hanging in coils within an equable temperature.

The outside of both air and fluid hoses should be wiped down with solvent at the end of every job.

To clean the inside of the fluid hose, a hose cleaner should be employed – a device that forces a mixture of solvent and air through both fluid hose and gun to rid paint passages of paint residue. The paint gone, the supply of solvent can be turned off, leaving the air to dry the paint passages.

Pressure Drop at the Spray Gun

air hose ID	pounds per square inch lost			
	over 5 ft (1·5 m)	over 15 ft (4·6 m)	over 25 ft (7·6 m)	over 50 ft (15·2 m)
¼ inch				
40 psi gauge	0·4	7·5	10·5	16·0
60 psi gauge	4·5	9·5	13·0	20·5
80 psi gauge	5·5	11·5	16·0	25·0
⁵⁄₁₆ inch				
40 psi gauge	0·5	1·5	2·5	4·0
60 psi gauge	1·0	3·0	4·0	6·0
80 psi gauge	1·5	3·0	4·0	8·0
⅜ inch				
40 psi gauge	1·0	1·0	2·0	3·5
60 psi gauge	1·5	2·0	3·0	5·0
80 psi gauge	2·5	3·0	4·0	6·0

psi = pounds per square inch

Pressure Arriving at the Spray Gun

pressure at regulator	air hose ID	pounds per square inch arriving			
		over 5 ft (1·5 m)	over 15 ft (4·6 m)	over 25 ft (7·6 m)	over 50 ft (15·2 m)
40 psi	¼ in	36·0	32·5	29·5	24·0
	⁵⁄₁₆ in	39·5	38·5	37·5	36·0
	⅜ in	39·0	39·0	38·0	36·5
60 psi	¼ in	55·5	50·5	47·0	39·5
	⁵⁄₁₆ in	59·0	57·0	56·0	54·0
	⅜ in	58·5	58·0	57·0	55·0
80 psi	¼ in	74·5	68·5	64·0	55·0
	⁵⁄₁₆ in	78·5	77·0	76·0	72·0
	⅜ in	77·5	77·0	76·0	74·0

psi = pounds per square inch

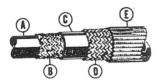

Braid covered hose.
(A) rubber tubing.
(B) woven braid.

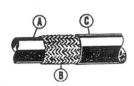

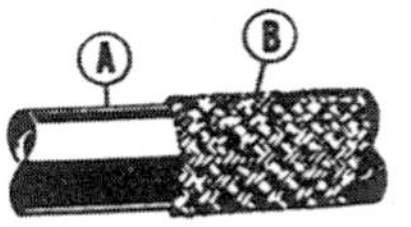

Single braid hose. (A)
Inner tube. (B) Braid.
(C) Outside cover, all
vulcanised into single unit.

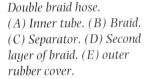

Double braid hose.
(A) Inner tube. (B) Braid.
(C) Separator. (D) Second
layer of braid. (E) outer
rubber cover.

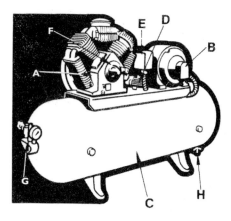

Stationary compressor outfit. (A) Pump. (B) Motor. (C) Air storage tank. (D) Check valve. (E) Pressure switch on larger models. (F) Oil filter. (G) Oil/water trap. (H) Drain tap.

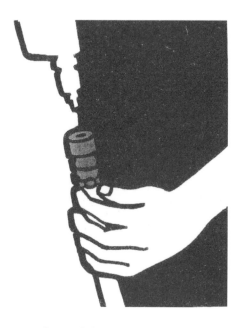

The quick disconnect connection.

● Hose connections. The two most common types of connection are the **threaded** and the **quick-disconnect** types. The threaded connection simply screws on, and is tightened with a spanner or wrench. The quick-disconnect variety has a spring-loaded system of complementary male and female elements for which no tools are required. Adapters are available to allow male-to-male or female-to-female connection with other parts of spray equipment.

Both types use a compression ring within a sleeve that is slipped over the end of the hose to provide a perfect seal.

The air compressor

The air compressor is perhaps the most important part of a spray system apart from the gun itself. Its purpose is to supply air at the correct pressure in the correct volume. Normal atmospheric pressure is about 14·7 pounds per square inch ($1·03 \text{ kg/cm}^2$) – a compressor typically delivers air at up to 200 pounds per square inch (14 kg/cm^2).

There are two major types of compressor: the piston compressor and the diaphragm compressor.

In the **piston compressor**, as its name implies, at least one piston moves back and forth within an enclosed cylinder. As it moves one way it draws in air

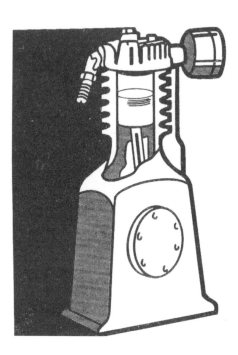

The piston compressor.

through an air intake; as it travels the other way it compresses the air and finally expels it through an exhaust valve into an airline. Piston-cylinders may be aligned vertically in relation to the crankcase (an upright compressor) or at an angle so as to form a V-shape in relation to the crankcase (a V- or Y-type compressor).

Piston compressors are available in single- or multiple-cylinder units, and single- or two-stage models, selection depending on the volume and pressure required. A **two-stage piston compressor** has

The "V" type compressor.

two or more cylinders of unequal size: the air is compressed first in the larger or largest cylinder, then transferred via an intercooler tube into the smaller cylinder which compresses it further before releasing it to an airline or to storage. A **single-stage piston compressor** has cylinders only of a uniform size, and in normal circumstances is limited to a maximum pressure of 100 pounds per square inch. This contrasts with the fact that two-stage piston compressors are generally found operating at minimum air pressures of 100 pounds per square inch. Two-stage compressors are usually more efficient, run cooler, and deliver more compressed air for the power consumed.

It is a piston compressor that is most commonly in service in a professional finishing operation.

The **diaphragm compressor** develops its air pressure through the reciprocal action of a flexible disc actuated by an eccentric cam. The design does not readily permit high pressures to be obtained.

● Displacement. The displacement represents the theoretical or calculated volume of air that the cylinder or cylinders discharge, expressed in cubic feet per minute (cu ft/min). It makes no allowance for heat, friction, or other losses in the compression cycle.

In relation to a two-stage piston compressor, the displacement is always reckoned on the first-stage cylinders only: this is because the second-stage cylinders merely rehandle the same air passed through by the first-stage – there is no increase in the quantity of air discharged.

The two stage compressor.

Calculating the Displacement of a Piston Compressor

The formula is:

the area of the cylinder base (in square inches)
times
the length of the piston stroke (in inches)
times
the number of strokes per minute
times
the number of cylinders
divided by
1728 (to convert cubic inches to cubic feet)
The result is in cubic feet per minute.

● Volumetric efficiency. The actual amount of air delivered by the compressor can be computed by multiplying the displacement by the volumetric efficiency, if the latter is known. A single-stage piston compressor with a displacement of 10 cu ft/min that was known to have 70 per cent volumetric efficiency, for example, would actually deliver about 7 cu ft/min.

Average volumetric efficiency rates for a single-stage compressor are:

max. operating pressure	volumetric efficiency
60 pounds	70 per cent
75 pounds	75 per cent
125 pounds	65 per cent
150 pounds	60 per cent

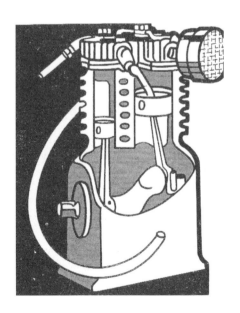

Average volumetric efficiency rates in relation to a two-stage compressor are:

max. operating pressure	volumetric efficiency
100 pounds	80 per cent
125 pounds	80 per cent
150 pounds	80 per cent
175 pounds	80 per cent

● The professional compressor outfit. For the professional, a fully equipped air compressor for use with a spray gun should have all of the following features:

    valve assemblies that are easily removable
    quick-acting valves
    multiple-ring piston assembly, involving both compression and oil control rings
    honed cylinders
    an efficient cooling system
    an automatic oiling system
    anti-friction main bearings

The compressor may or may not have any of several other extremely useful mechanisms that have precautionary effects.

One such is a **refrigerant air dryer**, which ensures that most of the water vapour in the atmospheric air does not enter the compressor's air intake and thus does not reach the point of use. This cuts down on the risk of rust in metal passages or as a contaminant in finished products. The unit generally comprises two main elements: a compressed air circuit and a refrigeration circuit. The compressed air circuit pre-cools the incoming warm and saturated compressed air; dry and cold, the air then proceeds to a heat exchanger where it is slightly warmed again; it then goes on to the refrigeration circuit (which works by continuous evaporation, just like a household refrigerator).

An **automatic unloader** is a device designed to maintain a supply of air within given pressure limits on electrically-driven or petrol-driven compressors, when it is not practical to start and stop the motor during operations. (If the demand for air is relatively constant at a volume approaching the main capacity of the compressor, an unloader is recommended.) When maximum pressure in the air receiver (the sealed tank in which compressed air is temporarily stored for use) is reached, the unloader pilot valve opens to let air travel through a small tube to the unloader mechanism and holds open the intake valve on the compressor, allowing it to run idle. Once the pressure drops to a minimum setting, the spring-loaded pilot automatically closes, air to the unloader is shut off causing the intake valve to close, and the compressor resumes normal operation. Maximimum and minimum pressures are set on a pressure-adjusting screw on the pilot – the maximum should obviously not exceed the pressure-rating of the air compressor unit.

An **automatic pressure switch**, operated by air pressure on a pneumatically sensitive diaphragm that makes or breaks an electrical circuit, may be used to start and stop electric motors at set maximum and minimum operating pressures.

To prevent motors from overheating through contant starting and stopping, **fuses** and **thermal overload relays** may be located on starting devices. There may also be a **centrifugal pressure release**, a device that allows a motor to restart and to gain momentum before the load of pumping air against pressure is engaged. This mechanism relies on the presence of steel balls that under the force of gravity wedge against a special cam at the centre of the crankshaft as the compressor slows down, opening a valve and bleeding air from the line connecting to the check valve. With the air pressure bled from the pump and aftercooler, the compressor can start up free of back pressure until some speed is reached. The steel balls then move out off the cam under centrifugal force, thus closing the valve so that air is again pumped into the air receiver.

It is evident from the foregoing that the standard practice in air compressor design is for the motor to work on a cut-in and cut-out basis. The average time a normally operating compressor outfit takes to pump from cut-in to cut-out pressure varies by compressor size and type and cut-in/cut-out pressures, as shown in the table below.

Cut-in and Cut-out Times in Relation to Compressor Outfits

type of outfit	cut-in h.p.	cut-out pressure (pounds)	from cut-in pressure (pounds)	pump time tank to cut-out (seconds)	air size (gal.)
1-stage	0·5	80	100	191	30
	1	80	100	83	30
	2	80	100	69	60
3		80	100	51	60
2-stage	1	140	175	284	60
	3	140	175	115	80
	5	140	175	75	80
	10	140	175	56	120
	15	140	175	42	120

A compressor should always be selected to supply more air than is required, to allow for reserve capacity for peak loads or for the addition of more equipment. Selection should follow reference to manufacturers' equipment catalogues and careful calculation of pressure and volume requirements. In an industrial paintshop, where the use of pneumatic

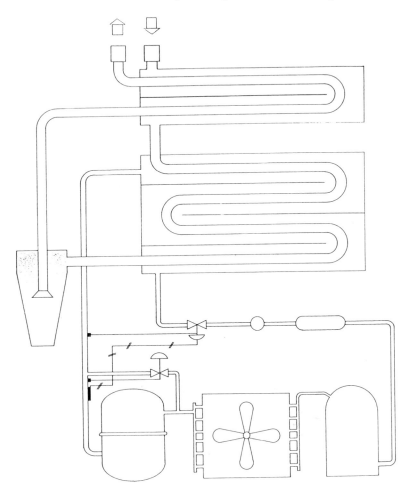

LEFT *Refrigerated Air showing a selection of refrigerated air dryers. The 'amateur' will probably not be able to justify the cost of this equipment. On smaller compressors, the filters cannot be cleared, and the drain taps opened, too often.*

RIGHT *Diagram showing the compressed air circuit and the refrigeration circuit.*

tools is continuous, the average correlation between continuous air output, cut-in/cut-out pressures and the power of the compressor may be represented by the following table.

Continuous Air Output in Relation to Cut-in/Cut-out Pressures

cut-in pressure (pounds)	cut-out pressure (pounds)	continuous output (cu ft/min)	compressor h.p.
80	100	up to 1·9	0·50
		2·0–3·0	0·75
		3·1–3·9	1
		4·0–5·8	1·50
		5·9–7·6	2
		7·7–8·7	2·50
		8·8-13·2	3
100	125	13·3–20·0	5
		20·1–29·2	7·50
		29·3–40·0	10
40·1–50·0	15		
120	150	up to 1·1	0·50
		1·2–2·1	0·75
		2·2–2·9	1
		3·0–4·3	1·50
		4·4–5·7	2
140	175	up to 3·4	1
		3·5–5·3	1·50
		5·4–6·9	2
		7·0–10·4	3
		10·5–17·0	5
		17·1-26·4	7·50
		26·5-35·3	10
		35·4-48·0	15

In planning to install an air compressor in a permanent location, several factors should be borne in mind:

a) the unit should be at least 30 cm (1 ft) from any wall so that air can circulate around to aid cooling, and to permit access from as many directions as possible for servicing or repairs;

b) the unit should be level, and on a flat surface;

c) the unit should be located as close as possible to where the compressed air is required, so as to cut down the length of airlines and so reduce pressure drop; and

d) the air intake must be sited so as to receive clean, cool, dry air, in quantity, and its outermost entrance must be protected from inclement weather.

● Routine compressor maintenance. For every individual air compressor, the manufacturer's maintenance schedule and sequence should be followed carefully. However, in general all outfits require regular attention to some specific elements.

Daily maintenance includes:
draining accumulated water
checking the oil level in the crankcase
Weekly maintenance includes:
inspecting the electric motor
blowing accumulated dust from cooling fins
Monthly maintenance includes:
checking the cleanliness of the air intake filter
checking the compressor's drive belt
Periodical maintenance includes:
changing the oil whenever necessary
checking that the safety valve will operate
checking the tightness of the flywheel on the crankshaft

Compressor problems and answers

● Compressor heating up. Generally caused by:
no oil in crankcase
valves sticking (check for dirt or carbon)
insufficient air through flywheel (perhaps caused by compressor being confined in too little space)
deposit of paint or dirt on cylinder and head
oil too heavy
broken exhaust valve
air intake filter clogged

● Compressor knocking. A knocking sound issuing from a compressor may be due to:
carbon on piston
loose or worn wrist pin
worn connecting-rod bearing
worn main bearings
loose flywheel
improperly installed valve assembly

● Motor failing to cut out and running on for longer than normal. Extended running of a compressor can be caused by:
air intake filter clogged
deposit of paint or dirt on cylinder wall
leak in airline
dirty or warped valves

● Compressor pumping oil. Oil issuing from the compressor may result from:
air intake filter clogged
worn or inferior piston rings
oil overfill
clogged oil intake valve

The air transformer.

Air control equipment

Between the air compressor and the point of use, any of a number of different devices may be installed that modify the nature of the air stream. A large proportion of these mechanisms are for cleaning or filtering the air, particularly of water vapour (which, as we have already seen, is highly deleterious in many ways to the commercial use of compressed air). Others monitor or regulate to a fine degree the pressure of air, perhaps indicating that pressure on a meter or dial. Yet others allow the use of the air to be spread across a number of different outlets to perform different functions at different pressures.

● An air transformer. An air transformer removes oil, dirt and moisture from the compressed air; it also acts as a regulator and indicates on a gauge the regulated air pressure; finally, it provides multiple air outlets for a number of air-operated tools. Air transformers are commonly used in spray refinishing workshops, especially in accurately controlling the fluid pressure of pressure-feed paint tanks that do not have their own regulators. In this, an air transformer's air-regulating valve is of prime significance, its positive control ensuring uniformly constant air pressure. A drain valve allows the elimination of oil sludge, dirt and condensation residues.

The size, nature and location of the pipe that connects the air transformer to the air compressor (or its air receiver/storage tank) should follow the transformer manufacturer's directions. A long pipe obviously makes for greater pressure drop and possibly larger amounts of condensation, yet the nearest a transformer should ever be to the air compressor unit is around 8 metres (25 feet).

An air transformer that has no regulation devices or attachments is instead called an **air condenser**.

A device conversely for simply regulating filtered compressed air, specifically to maintain mainline air pressure with minimum fluctuation as it comes from the compressor, is an **air regulator**. Air regulators are available in a great variety of volume and pressure capacities, and in differing degrees of sensitivity and accuracy, with or without pressure gauges.

● Certain types of air-operated equipment – grinders, chippers, hammer, pumps, and the like – require a very small quantity of oil mixed in the air that powers them. A device not unnaturally called a **lubricator** supplies this trace of oil to the system, and may or may not be combined with an air filter and an air regulator in a single unit. The lubricator has its own reservoir of oil, which must be kept topped up; a sight-glass may indicate the current oil level.

The spray booth

The installation, types and purposes of the range of spray booths is covered in detail in THE SPRAY BOOTH, pages 182–185. Application methods within an industrial spray booth are detailed on page 151 and Rolls-Royce, page 157.

Respirators

Even under ideal conditions, spray finishing inevitably creates a certain amount of overspray, hazardous vapours and toxic fumes. Anyone who works in or around a spray finishing operation should have the opportunity to wear some sort of respirator or breathing apparatus (see Chapter 1: SAFETY: Health precautions and Toxic Chemicals:

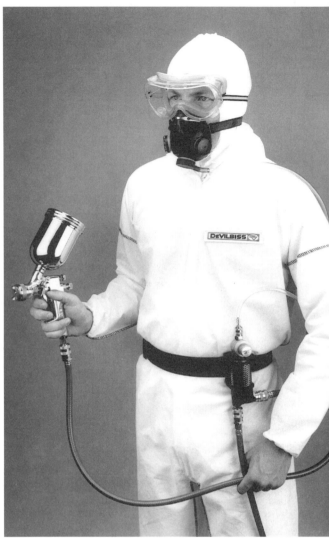

Poisoning, page 22). This is not only good sense, in Britain it is to a great extent the law (see Chapter 1: SAFETY: Health and safety: legal requirements, page 24).

Several primary types of respirator are available, notably the air-fed vizor respirator, the organic vapour respirator, the dust respirator and the air-fed half-mask respirator.

The **dust respirator** is the least form of respiratory aid, used mainly in operations such as sanding, grinding or buffing, and really rather unsatisfactory in any spray application. It covers the nose and mouth, and has a filter cartridge that removes only solid particles from the air breathed. It does not filter out liquids, vapours or gases.

The **organic vapour respirator** is the next step up

LEFT *The 'HLM' filter regulator.*

ABOVE *Air-feed half mask respirator.*

RIGHT *Air-fed full respirator outfit.*

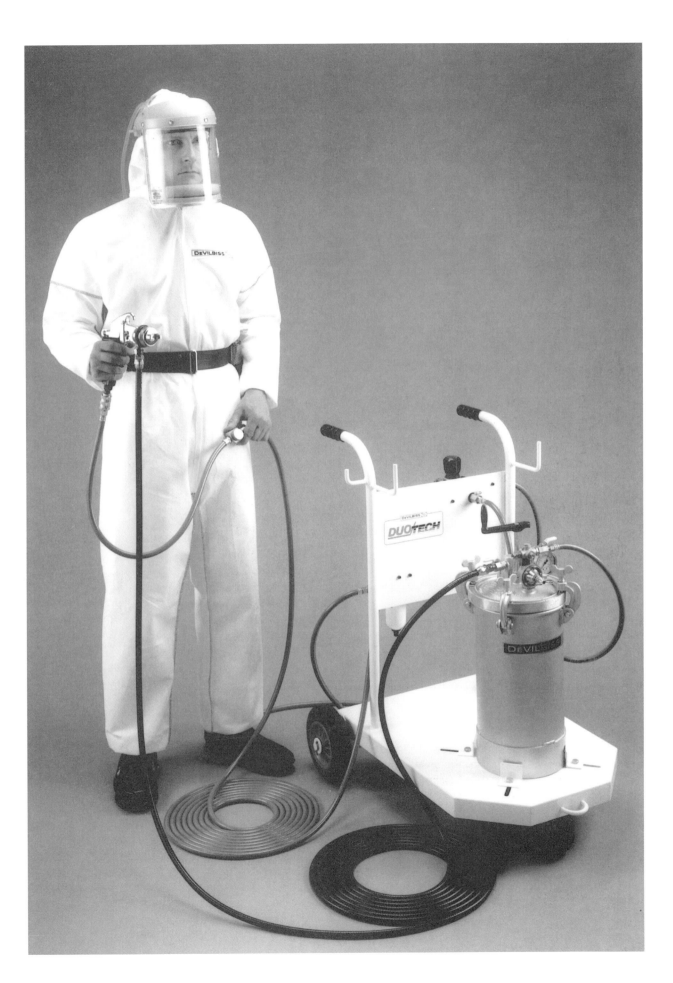

in respiratory precautions. It too covers the mouth and nose, but is primarily aimed at preventing penetration of vapours through the mask, for it has a cartridge over the breathed air that removes organic vapours by chemical absorption. Some respirators of this type, however, also have a pre-filter to remove solid particles before the air reaches the cartridge. This type of respirator is used in industrial refinishing spray workshops, but only in association with standard materials: it is not suitable for use with, for example, polyisocyanates.

The **air-fed half-mask respirator** operates with an external supply of clean, dry air through a low-pressure regulator from the main air supply. The piped air reaches the nose and mouth via an odour-removal cartridge filter at the front of the mask. Useful in circumstances where concentrations of vapour, fumes, dust and dirt might prove harmful to respiratory organs, this type of respirator nonetheless covers only mouth and nose, and does not provide protection against splashes on the surrounding areas of skin.

Protection against splashes on surrounding skin is, however, provided by the **air-fed vizor respirator**, the most protective type of respirator used in spray workshops. Again with an external supply of air passed through an odour-removal cartridge, the vizor in this case covers most of the face and is combined with a disposable paper hood and bib that additionally protect much of the head and the neck. These respirators are for use in relatively extreme situations, when other types simply do not provide sufficient protection.

The hot spray process

The hot spray process was first introduced in Sweden and Holland before World War II, primarily for the application of nitrocellulose lacquers on furniture. Since then the process has been the focus of considerable research and development, notably in the transport, heavy-agricultural and earth-moving equipment industries for which hot spraying with air-drying synthetic enamels gives higher build and greater durability on the rough metal surfaces. Today, many different types of coating are available using the process, applied by any of several different forms of equipment.

Recent decades have seen considerable legislative pressure put upon industry to reduce the adverse discharge of paints and solvents into the atmosphere: to keep the world green, the answer cannot be to paint it so. If Europe follows the lead taken by the United States, a minimum transfer efficiency – the percentage of solid content in a sprayable material left as a deposit on a product – performance level of 65 per cent will be established for spray finishing operations. This means that hot spraying will very much become the normal mode of spray finishing.

● The theory behind hot spraying. Atomization is the principle underlying any spray process: fluid paint has to be split up into a vast number of very tiny droplets. This atomization is possible only if the viscosity of the paint is sufficiently low – and with conventional cold spraying, the low viscosity is achieved by the addition of thinners.

In hot spraying, it is heating that produces the necessary reduction in viscosity. The viscosity of a finishing paint or lacquer at ambient temperature may be reduced by between one-third and one-quarter if it is heated to 60°–82°C (140°–180°F). To heat the paint any more does not usually cause any appreciable further decrease in viscosity.

Atomization results in a huge increase in surface area of the paint sprayed. The energy required to perform the atomization is derived from the high-speed air current. But in fact only about 1 per cent of that air stream's energy is utilized for the purpose. The remainder of that energy is used in spreading out the droplets to form the required fan pattern, in driving the droplets to the work surface (and beyond, in the form of overspray), and in evaporating off the solvents from the coating during the passage of the droplets to the surface. So around 99 per cent of the stream that emerges from the nozzle of the cold spray gun is no more than high-speed air. Moreover, the air rebounds off the surface being painted and takes away with it a large proportion of the atomized paint droplets, which never adhere to the work surface and form useless spray dust.

In the case of hot spraying, however, the higher temperature of the fluid means that less energy is required for atomization – which in turn means that less compressed air is required. Hot spraying in fact demands somewhere around half of the compressed air needed for cold spraying the same output quantity of atomized droplets.

In cold spraying, an average of about one-third of the total solvent in the coating evaporates during the spraying process before the wet paint reaches the work surface. The evaporation causes a drop in the

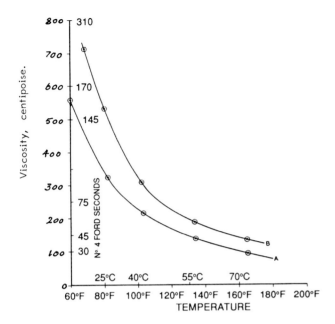

The effect of increase of temperature on viscosity.
(A) Cellulose lacquer. (B) Alkyd base synthetic enamel.

temperature of the fluid of some $5 \cdot 5°$–$11°C$ ($10°$–$20°F$) below the prevailing local (ambient) temperature. In the hot spray process, roughly three-quarters of the solvent evaporates by the time the atomized droplets reach the work surface, resulting in a correspondingly greater drop in temperature. Because of the high initial temperature of the paint, though, the final temperature of the paint as it reaches the surface is nonetheless still slightly above the ambient temperature.

And because the paint applied contains less solvent (is more viscous) in the first place, the superior evaporation rate of what solvent there is results in an applied film with a higher content of solids.

The principle of hot spraying has in recent years been commonly combined with other methods of application. Hot airless, hot electrostatic, hot automatic and hot two-component spraying are all now in relatively frequent use.

● The advantages of hot spraying over cold. A major advantage is improved adhesion and durability, resulting from the reduced level of flaws, pinholes and air-bubbles in the film due to the better wetting of the work surface achieved at the more conducive temperature.

It has been claimed that the temperature at

which the film is deposited is responsible also for improved drying times and baking schedules – but this claim is debatable, for in the formulations of nitrocellulose lacquers devised for hot spraying the solvents are relatively slow to evaporate and (despite the small quantity involved that does not evaporate during spraying) tend to remain wet in the film for a considerable period. This solvent retention is exaggerated by the extra thickness of the film of lacquer normally obtained by hot spraying, a thickness that reduces the through-drying rate. In general, it is better simply to say that the drying time of this type of surface coating depends to a large extent on the ration of surface area to volume of applied paint. As for the hot spray diminishing the baking schedules of stoving paints: that claim can only relate to the very short initial stage – the evaporation of the solvent – for the main part of the stoving schedule, the thermal polymerization of the vehicle, is completely unaffected by the method of paint application. (On the other hand, stoving enamels that cure by a thermosetting reaction within the film, and do not depend upon surface oxidation, naturally form a very suitable type of coating for hot spray application.)

But there is quite definitely a greater margin of error in application of hot spray as opposed to cold, with regard to the occurrence of sagging (caused by too heavy a coat) and 'orange-peel' (caused by a dry, thinnish film). Because errors are discernible so quickly, there are fewer rejects and less flatting, and the training of spray operators is easier than with the conventional cold spray guns, where the tolerance between sagging and orange-peel is more critical. Another potential surface defect is 'blooming', a condition that appears as anything from a light haze or loss of gloss to an area of opaque whiteness on surfaces to which nitrocellulose lacquers or enamels have been applied. It is caused by moisture condensing out on the undried film and precipitating the nitrocellulose polymer from solution as the solvent evaporates. That moisture may well be encouraged to form (at the 'dewpoint' temperature) during the drop in temperature caused by evaporation in the cold spray process. Because the drop in temperature is still above the ambient temperature in the hot spray process, there is less blooming.

The temperature change itself may be a factor causing different application characteristics in cold spraying: a $5 \cdot 5°C$ ($10°F$) change at an ambient temperature of 15·5°C (60°F) may cause a quite large change in viscosity, for example. It is evident that application characteristics remain more constant with hot spraying.

Because solids are present in the dried film to a greater extent, hot spraying achieves increased build when more than one coat is required, leading to **increased gloss**, increased durability and increased chemical resistance. These features are of particular commercial interest when the substrate to be coated is rough, because the smaller amount of shrinkage involved means that the film does not tend to reduce right down to the contours of the underlying rough surface. But even if normal film thicknesses are required, the hot spray surface with its higher level of solids means that fewer passes of the spray gun are necessary, thus also cutting down spraying time.

The reduced level of solvent in a hot spray film can also be useful when a surface has to be resprayed. If a quick-drying synthetic enamel containing a solvent such as xylol is sprayed cold over an old oxidized paint film, the xylol may cause the old film to swell up and wrinkle in a condition called 'lifting'. With hot spraying, much less xylol is present in the applied film, and there is correspondingly less risk of lifting.

The reduced atomization pressure needed for hot spraying leads to considerable economic gains in terms of reduced paint loss through overspray and through the formation of paint dust as droplets bounce off the work surface, and in terms of the electrical power that has to be generated to use the machinery (although of course this has to be balanced against the power required to heat the paint to the desired temperature in the first place).

In fact, the good atomization achieved by hot spraying allows the use of wider jet orifices on spray guns, leading in turn to more rapid application and again cutting down spraying time.

● The disadvantages of hot spraying. The main disadvantages are the machinery and power required to bring the paint to the required temperature, together with the slightly increased cost of maintaining the equipment. But there are other disadvantages too.

Hot spraying at temperatures higher than 93°C (200°F) can cause the top surface of the film to harden too rapidly, trapping pockets of solvent that rupture the surface when they subsequently evaporate through it. This is known as 'pinholing'. With nitrocellulose lacquers (in particular)

temperatures above that level are subject to poor flow and severe bubbling of the film. The hot spray process would therefore seem to cease to be satisfactory above specific temperature limits.

There is also a question-mark against the possible reaction over prolonged time of strong, hot solvents on the rubber from which paint hose-lines are made.
● Heating the hot spray. The hot spray units commercially available fall mostly into three types, according to the mechanism by which the paint or lacquer is heated. The alternative systems are:

> electrically heated by a surrounding water-jacket
> electrically heated by a metal block as central element
> heated by superheated air, itself heated electrically

From all these mechanisms, the paint hose carrying the hot paint to the spray unit is lagged or jacketed in a hot-water hose or hot-air jacket to conserve the heat.
● The heated-atomizing-air system. One innovative manufacturer has come up with a further modification to hot spray equipment that is forward-looking, economically useful, and also improves the quality of the final finish. The system uses the advantages of heated atomizing air. The air that atomizes the paint is not just warm, as it might be through friction under a turbine-based compressor outfit, but heated to a setting that positively increases the transfer efficiency by reducing overspray (the temperature difference between atomized paint and ambient air acts to restrict the spray to a constant pattern) and by promoting quicker evaporation of the solvent. The temperature of the output air from the wall-mounted air conversion unit can be regulated up to 115°C (239°F), to suit the material being applied.

The formulation of coatings for hot spraying

There are two types of coatings used in the hot spray process:
● lacquers composed of high-polymeric-chain molecules dissolved in strong solvents, which dry purely through solvent evaporation; and
● paints and varnishes composed of comparatively low-molecular-weight polymers dissolved in weak solvents, which dry either by surface oxidation or cure in a stoving oven by thermal polymerization.

We have seen that 75 per cent of the solvent in paint sprayed hot evaporates by the time the atomized droplets reach the work surface. In order to obtain optimal gloss and flow characteristics, therefore, it is imperative that the remaining 25 per cent is a true solvent for the binding medium used.

Nitrocellulose lacquers are examples of those lacquers that are composed of high-polymeric-chain molecules and that dry purely through solvent evaporation. Because nitrocellulose has a lower dilution ratio at the high temperature used for hot spraying than it has cold, an increased proportion of true solvent must be used. (The dilution ration can be defined as the amount of toluol/toluene that can be added to a solution of nitrocellulose of known concentration in a specific solvent before 'throw-out' or turbidity occurs.) Solvents and diluents that are fast-acting – such as methyl ethyl ketone, ethyl acetate, toluol and ethyl alcohol – should be kept to a minimum in any nitrocellulose formulation for hot spraying: excess causes a dry, dusty film with poor gloss. Similarly, solvents and diluents that have a high boiling point – such as diacetone alcohol and methyl cyclohexanone – should be kept down to a small percentage in nitrocellulose hot spray formulations, or severe solvent retention may lead to prolonged hardening times. The best results are obtained by using solvents and diluents that have a medium-range boiling point, such as butyl acetate, methyl Cellosolve, xylol/ xylene and butyl alcohol. These solvents are unfortunately among the more expensive. The greater quantity of solids and higher viscosity also add to the cost of hot-spraying lacquers.

In relation to those paints and varnishes composed of comparatively low-molecular-weight polymers dissolved in weak solvents, which dry either by surface oxidation or cure in a stoving oven by thermal polymerization, other factors have to be considered.

With paints that dry by surface oxidation in air, it is essential in any formulation for hot spray use to incorporate through-drying materials that can penetrate through the comparatively thick film deposited by hot spraying – materials such as phenolic resins and lead driers. Surface-drying catalysts such as cobalt driers should be avoided as far as possible, or wrinkling may occur on drying.

Examples of paints that cure in a stoving oven by thermal polymerization (thermosetting stoving enamels) are those based on a melamine formaldehyde resin/non-drying alkyd blend. Because the hot spray temperature is very close to the curing temperature of the resin, it might be expected that the material would be unstable and tend to solidify in the heating chamber. This does not normally occur, however, thanks to the presence of butanol, a strong solvent given off during the stoving cycle. Excess butanol in the enamel represses the thermosetting reaction in the heating chamber – the butanol cannot escape. Paints of this type are eminently suitable for hot spray application because their thick films cure satisfactorily.

However, two-pack coatings such as amine-cured epoxy lacquers, isocyanates, polyesters and acid-catalysed air-drying urea-formaldehyde lacquers should not normally be used in conventional hot spray apparatus owing to the possibility of gelation at the elevated temperature. Modern developments, particularly in the United States, have nonetheless been made in hot catalyst spraying equipment suitable for use with amine-cured epoxies and other two-component materials. Such equipment is used to apply high-solid products that result in thick films, and that exhibit good durability and resistance to chemicals and abrasion.

Other workshop application methods

In North America, the old, conventional methods of applying paint are now hardly used at all. Instead, paint is applied by electrostatic, airless, or high-volume low-pressure (HVLP) equipment.

Electrodeposition
Electrodeposition ('electrocoating') is used industrially for painting many articles. Perhaps its most important service is to apply priming coats to vehicular bodies and components, in which its major benefit – a film that is outstanding in its resistance to corrosion of many types, particularly that caused by salt on icy roads – is realized in the most practical manner. The resistance to corrosion is not just a property of the film but is partly due to the uniform coverage obtained by the process even on weld area seams, on high points on the base metal, and inside internal box sections.
● The theory behind electrodeposition. Like that of electroplating, the general principle behind the method relies on the presence of an anode and a cathode immersed in an aqueous medium through which a current passes. The surface to be painted takes the place of the anode.

One of the earliest paint media used in the electrodeposition process was an ammoniacal

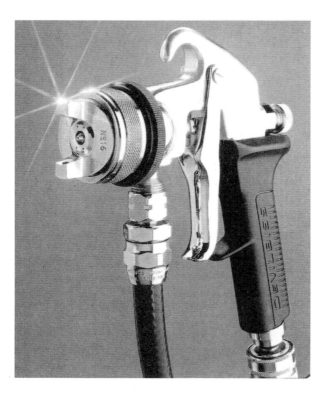

The duo-tech JGH spray gun which exploits the advantages of heated air.

solution of a drying oil that had been subjected to reaction with maleic anhydride to form a resin of high acid value. Dissolved in ammonia solution, such a material can be considered to be partly ionised, forming positive ammonium ions and negative resin-acid ions (or, more strictly, colloidal particles of resin acid carrying a negative charge). The passage of an electric current through the solution causes the charged particles to migrate. The positive ammonium ions pass to the cathode, and the negatively charged resin acids pass to the anode, where they are subsequently deposited.

But modern media are of a much higher molecular weight than the simple maleinized drying oil. In fact the negative particles that migrate towards the anode-surface are generally of colloidal dimensions: they can be in the form of an emulsion rather than a solution. This movement of colloidal particles under the influence of an electric current is known technically as **electrophoresis**.

Moreover, in the paint there are hydrogen and hydroxyl ions from the water, and ions from any other material present in the paint. The negative ions

discharged at the anode will generate protons – that is, produce acidity. This is just what happens in any electrolytic cell, and the process by which charged ions are transported across it is **electrolysis**.

All the paint media used in electrodeposition to date are acidic resins or polymers dissolved or dispersed in bases such as ammonia, amines, or potassium hydroxide. They are therefore stable only in solution in neutral or alkaline conditions: **electrocoagulation**.

Finally, the deposited film acts as a semipermeable membrane in a normal osmotic cell. Under the effect of the electric current, the water within the film is squeezed out – a form of osmotic dehydration that is described as **electro-endosmosis**, and is a bonus factor that improves the entire process. Because of it, the film leaves the tank with a low water content and is thus quite firm: it does not normally sag or run, shows no signs of solvent wash in corners or in box sections, and does not require any flash-off time before curing.

● The advantages of electrodeposition. One major advantage is that electrodeposition provides excellent and uniform coverage on sharp edges, high points, welds and joints – all areas in which conventional dipping processes tend towards a 'run-away' effect. Partly enclosed box sections also receive this uniform coverage and there are no runs or sags, no solvent wash in the oven or 'popping' of the solvent during stoving.

The result is the superb corrosion resistance already mentioned.

In addition, there is no fire risk with waterborne paints. And the fully automated and mechanised process is comparatively economical in paint consumption.

● The disadvantages of electrodeposition. The cost of installation is so high that the process is suitable only for the painting of truly large numbers of similar components. Even then, it is only a one-coat process: a further coat cannot be applied because the first coat is an excellent insulator and its presence foils the creation of an electric circuit. A full gloss finish is unobtainable using the process – there is no after-flow in the oven.

● The formulation of coatings for electrodeposition. The ammoniac solutions of maleinised drying oils used originally were soon replaced by alkali-soluble alkyd melamine and phenolics, which have given good service as a medium for corrosion-resistant primers. Amine solutions of epoxy resins are now favoured for car-body work.

Bases utilized in paint formulations for electrodeposition include ammonia (frequently used in the cathode compartment system), amines such as diethyl amine, dimethyl ethanolamine or morpholine, and potassium hydroxide (in the ion-exchange membrane system).

Flow coating

Where an article would be difficult to coat evenly, either by spray or by dipping, it can sometimes be uniformly covered by jets of paint issuing like a shower under pressure from strategically placed nozzles as the article passes by on a conveyor through a tunnel-like flow-coating chamber. The jets of paint are projected in all directions from nozzles fitted at selected points on header pipes that are coupled to a pumping centre. Excess paint drips off the article and flows back to a settling tank, where it is filtered prior to being repumped around the system. The system has advantages and disadvantages.

This method relieves a manufacturer of the need for a spray booth or a dipping tank, but requires its own plant. Solvent concentration in the flow-coating chamber must be carefully controlled by means of damper-regulated exhaust ducts fed by a low-velocity exhaust fan. If the solvent concentration is sufficiently high, the paint will remain wet until flow-out is complete (all bubbles have flowed out) and fat edges and tears have been eliminated.

The flow-coating chamber is generally incorporated into a multiple conveyor system that conducts a work article right through from rolling or pressing, through degreasing and pretreatment, to painting and stoving.

- The advantages of flow coating. Because the jet nozzles are so specifically located and aimed, smaller volumes of paint can be used than would otherwise be the case; flat sheets can be coated without runs, sags or air pockets; and the coat penetrates into the pores of the castings, giving improved adhesion. In a flow-coating chamber it is possible to coat an article that would float in a dipping tank. And the plant itself takes up less room.
- The disadvantages of flow coating. The rate of solvent loss is usually higher than with dipping. And there is greater difficulty in keeping the viscosity of the paint constant when using paints thinned with organic solvents.

Fire hazards are of the same order with flow coating as they are for dipping.

Roto-dip

The Roto-dip is a method of paint electrodeposition specific to the vehicle construction industry. Each vehicle is skewered on a spit that passes through it from front to back, and on which it rotates slowly forward, upward and downward as it proceeds through the various stages of degreasing, pretreatment, priming and painting. Rotation of the spit is effected by means of cogs at both ends engaged in an endless chain, and is continued after painting in a draining chamber, with the result that the final coat has no fat edges, no sags and no tears.

The method can in this way apply a slightly thicker than normal film of paint, which penetrates into all the nooks and crannies that are potential rust pockets if left uncoated.

A plant of this type naturally requires a very large dipping tank, and is generally used only with priming coats. The primer is waterborne primer (which is cheaper and non-inflammable in contrast to primers based on true solvents).

A similar system in which a vehicle remains the right way up as its lower half proceeds through a dipping tank full of waterborne primer is called the **slipper dip**. The method is intended to give a vehicle an extra coating of protective paint in areas that need it most. After the slipper dip, a coat of primer surfacer is normally applied by spray, and the two coats are then stoved together in the oven.

Airless spraying

Paint is fed to the airless spray gun by high-pressure pump (at up to 3000 pounds per square inch). The high speed of emission through a hard-metal wear-resistant nozzle atomizes the paint. The width of the fan spray pattern is governed by the user's choice of spray cap, which in turn has to take account of the viscosity of the paint.

Airless spray is used mostly in the commercial transport section of the refinishing market. The method is particularly suited to the application of heavy-bodied material to large areas: the emission rate of the spray gun is fixed, so that the fine adjustments possible with conventional compressed-air spray guns are not available. High paint throughput gives fast application of thick coats with low bounce-back and spray fog. Considerable time and effort is required for cleaning the equipment after use.

Recently, adjustable nozzles for use in airless spraying have become commercially available. It is

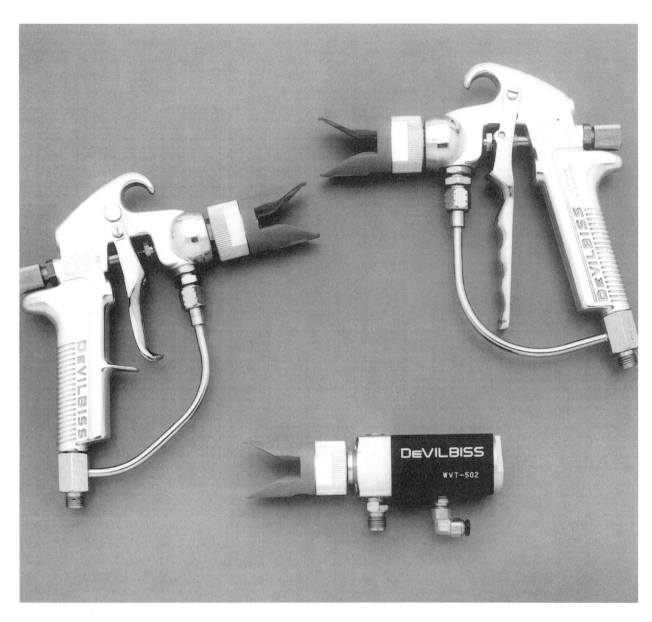

also possible now to rig up a system of compressed-air assistance to improve the atomization and spray pattern.

Air-assisted electrostatic spraying
Application of paint by air-assisted electrostatic spray gun is faster than with a conventional compressed-air spray gun. Moreover, the amount of paint used is substantially reduced because there is less bounce-back and overspray.

Like conventional spray guns, the electrostatic model has controls for both needle adjustment and spray pattern. The paint is fed to the gun under a

ABOVE *Air assisted airless pumps.*

RIGHT *The JGB 250 or 400 bar airless spray guns. Excellent for covering the ground, but without facility for fine adjustment.*

pressure-feed system. Time and effort is required for cleaning after use, therefore, with some attention being given also to the solvent used for the cleaning. This aspect makes the method less attractive for application on smaller projects.

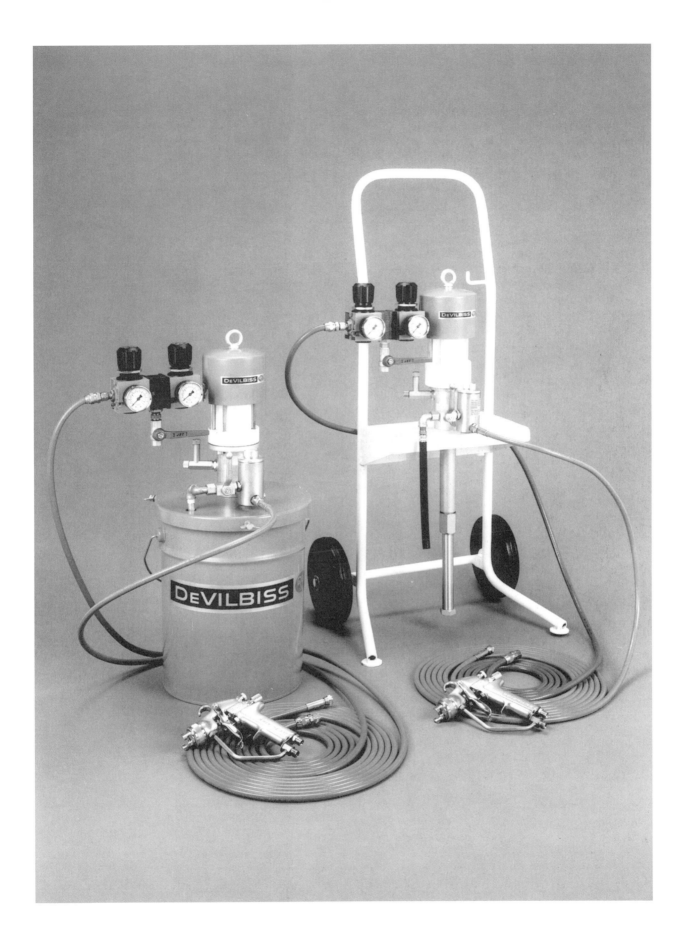

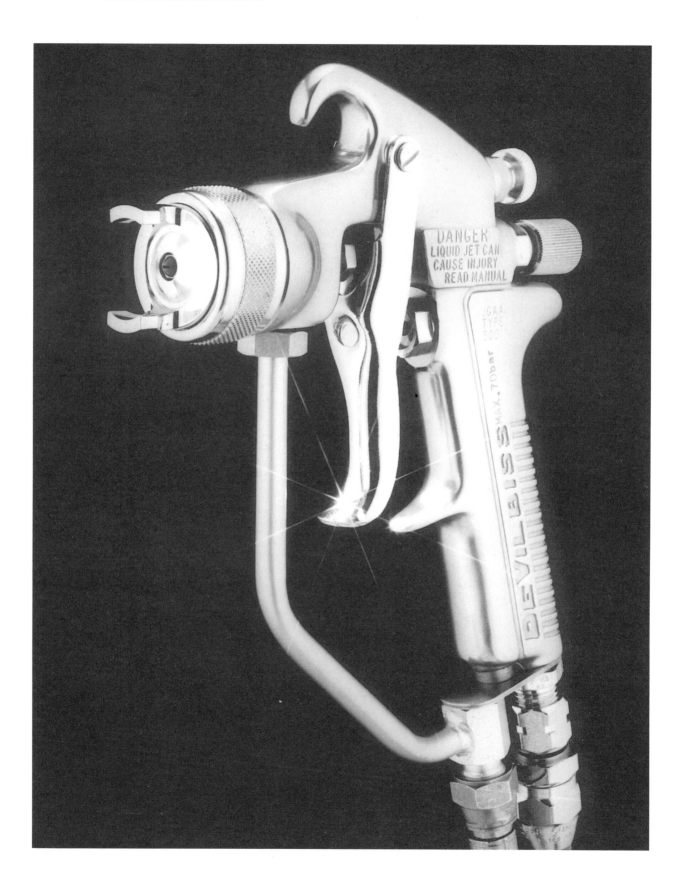

INHERENT DANGERS

The major dangers inherent in the application of surface coatings are those that affect the operator's health (in terms of inhalation, ingestion, or skin contact with injurious substances) and those that arise from the paint's inflammability or explosibility.

Dangers to the operator's health and safety have already been described in detail in Chapter 1: SAFETY: Health precautions and Toxic chemicals: Poisoning (page 22).

Inflammability: the flashpoint
The inflammability of a paint is initially governed by the flashpoint of its volatile constituents. As we have seen – in Chapter 2: PAINTS AND PIGMENTS: Solvents, diluents and thinners, page 49 – the flashpoint is the temperature at which a vapour that is combustible is given off, the lowest temperature at which the air-and-vapour mix will weakly explode on the application of a naked flame. (The flashpoint does not necessarily imply true ignition.) Most types of paint contain either solvents or diluents of high volatility that flash at relatively ordinary (room) temperatures.

When the flashpoint is known, the extent of its inflammability may be assessed. A liquid is said to be 'inflammable' if its flashpoint is below 65·6°C (150°F), for instance, and 'highly flammable' if its flashpoint is 32°C (89·6°F) or below.

The flashpoint of a liquid may be determined by using the specially devised Abel or Pensky-Martens apparatus. But it is possible to generalize the sort of flashpoints that are appropriate to specific types of paint:

cellulose-based spray paints	flashpoint
acrylic-based spray paints	below
some stoving spray finishes	23°C
some spray primers	(73°F)
msot stoving spray finishes	between
quick air-drying spray enamels	23°C and
quick air-drying spray undercoats	34°C
	(73°F and
	93°F)

The JGAA air assisted airless spray gun. The choice of spray cap dictates the spray pattern.

synthetic decorative finishes	above
synthetic coach paints	34°C
synthetic undercoats	(93°F)

The flashpoints of a number of different common solvents are listed in Chapter 2: PAINTS AND PIGMENTS: Solvents, diluents and thinners, page 49.

The flashpoint of a mixture of inflammable liquids is not necessarily identical with the lowest flashpoint of its individual constituents. The combined flashpoint may be higher, or it may be lower. If a liquid of known flashpoint is added to one of a higher flashpoint, the combined flashpoint might be expected to lie somewhere between the two. In fact, the usual result is that the flashpoint of the combined liquid is lower than even the previously lower flashpoint. The phenomenon results from the formation of an azeotropic mixture of higher vapour pressure (lower boiling point) than either of its constituents. A concentration of vapour sufficiently high to support ignition is therefore reached at a temperature lower than that required by either of its constituents.

In situations where a flashpoint may represent a genuine danger, there are five main precautions that can be taken:
a) not to use constituents of low flashpoint/high volatility;
b) to select solvents or diluents which, although of high volatility, do not form azeotropic mixtures;
c) to increase the proportion of constituents of low volatility at the expense of other constituents of medium volatility;
d) to replace non-associated liquids of high volatility with associated liquids of similar volatility (for example: ethyl alcohol might replace benzene/benzol); and
e) to use a small proportion of a liquid which, although highly volatile, is non-inflammable (such as methylene dichloride, ethylene dichloride, trichloroethylene or carbon tetrachloride).

The fire risk pertaining to a paint is determined more by its **ignition temperature** than by its flashpoint – the temperature at which the vapour not only ignites but continues to burn. This temperature is generally higher than the flashpoint, and is to some extent influenced by external conditions, such as the amount of free oxygen available, the heat evolved during combustion, and whether there are other materials present that might act as a wick or focus for the fire.

Explosibility

Another technical term for the flashpoint is 'lower explosive limit' – which is indicative that for any paint that has a flashpoint, temperatures above that flashpoint may cause not just fire but a true explosion. As the temperature and the concentration of vapour above the paint increase, the ease with which the vapour can be ignited increases, and the violence with which it does ignite also increases, up to a level of maximum explosivity. If the concentration of the vapour and the temperature is even further augmented, the violence of the ignition actually diminishes, the explosive force gradually decreases, until finally the paint will no longer support combustion at all: this is the 'upper explosive limit'.

Liquids that have a boiling point of about 113°C (235°F) and above do not form explosive mixtures with air at 25°C (77°F) because a sufficiently high concentration of the vapour cannot be obtained.

Upper and Lower Explosive Limits of Some Common Solvents and Diluents

	% volume in air	
	lower limit	*upper limit*
o-xylol	1·0	5·3
n-amyl acetate	1·1	—
n-amyl alcohol	1·2	—
toluol/toluene	1·3	7·0
benzol/benzene	1·4	8·0
n-butyl acetate	1·7	15·0
n-butyl alcohol	1·7	—
methyl ethyl ketone	1·8	11·3
acetone	2·1	13·0
ethyl acetate	2·2	11·5
ethyl alcohol	3·3	19·0

DEFECTS THAT OCCUR DURING PAINT APPLICATION

Acid Rain

It was once thought that at least the water from rain or snow could be depended upon to be pure and clean. But not any more! The many tons of nitrogen oxides and sulphur dioxide daily spewed into the air by emissions from automobiles, oil production facilities, coal-burning power plants and other industrial sources do not stay there. They come back down. They come down as dry acidic powder or they mix with moisture in the atmosphere to come down in rain, snow and fog as nitric or sulphuric acid.

These acidic deposits are the subject of a scientific and political storm that has state pitted against state, province against province, ideology against ideology.

Acid rain – or acid fog, which can be ten times more acidic than rain – is said to be responsible for a wide variety of harmful effects: dead lakes, sterile fish, decimated forests, lifeless soil, eroding architecture, marred finishes on motor vehicles, aggravated respiratory conditions and other health problems.

A characteristic of a non-metal is that it is an acid former. The basic laboratory experiment to demonstrate this is to burn sulphur in pure oxygen, collect the gas (sulphur dioxide) and dissolve the gas in distilled water. The distilled water is then tested with blue litmus paper and it turns pink, indicating an acid. Sulphur dioxide, though not as soluble as sulphur trioxide, is fairly soluble in water. It forms sulphurous acid (H_2So_3) not sulphuric acid (H_2So_4). But the sulphur dioxide in the atmosphere readily reacts with atmospheric oxygen to form the trioxide. Sulphur dioxide in polluted air reacts rapidly with oxygen to form sulphur trioxide in the presence of certain catalysts. Particulate matter or suspended microparticles, such as ammonium nitrate and elemented sulphur, act as efficient catalysts for this oxidation.

Most chemical reactions are more complex than the equations generally imply. But the reactants and the end products are all that most people are interested in and the reactant here is sulphur dioxide and the end product is sulphuric acid, a main constituent of acid rain. (Scientists have devised a method for attempting to decrease the acid rain effect by adding lime periodically to rivers, hopefully neutralising the acid rain and helping to prevent any further aquatic deaths.)

So what precautions can we take then, before preparing a vehicle for painting or carrying out a repair which may be effected by corrosion? As a precautionary measure, assuming a vehicle may be affected by acid rain, we can use a de-ironised water, that is to say, water which has had its hardness removed. Use a soft (de-mineralised) water for preparation purposes.

Whilst a mixture of cement dust and water is strongly alkaline, it will attack paint films. The attack may take the form of discoloured spots due to attack on the pigment (some reds will develop a blue tone if attacked by acids and a brown discoloration if attacked by alkali) or distortion of the paint surface may occur due to attack on the vehicle itself. Brunswick Greens are well known for their proneness to attack by alkali (yellow discoloration).

Some pigments are more prone to attack than others. The aluminium flake in metallic paints is particularly prone to attack by both acid and alkali. Basecoat and clear metallic finish has the advantage that the clear coat shields the aluminium from the contaminant. But even clear paints may be attacked, losing transparency and/or gloss. Air-dry paints, particularly when new, are more vulnerable than stoved finishes, but become more resistant to attack as they age.

Of the present range of refinish topcoats, best resistance to acid rain attack is shown by the polyurethane paints. I would further recommend that the vehicle be treated with a mixture of diluted oxalic acid before preparation.

Application problems and answers (in alphabetical order)
For defects that arise within a paint film after it has been applied, see the section later in this chapter entitled **Defects that occur after application**, page 144.

Adhesion poor In the paintshop, poor adhesion is most commonly noticed when masking-tape is removed.

Possible causes:
wax, silicone, oil, water, rust, solder flux, tallow soap, detergent, flatting residues, engine exhaust products, stearate powders from abrasive papers or discs, or other contaminants on the work surface undercoat incorrect for the metal or the topcoat
inadequate or no flatting
undercoat applied dry
primer allowed to harden days before further processing
use of cheap or incorrect thinner
incorrect or inadequate metal pretreatment
masking first colour of duotone system before properly dry
allowing colour to dry too far before removing masking-tape

Remedies: Normally the only thing to do is to strip the surface to the bare metal, use a phosphoric acid metal cleaner, and repaint. But when loss of adhesion is due to faulty masking technique, flat and feather-edge the affected area, and respray.

Bleeding A problem in red, maroon and yellow

Wheel arch of an MGB: the kind of horrors you can discover when you decide to give a car a 'quick' respray. Body filler in abundance. (Photo: Jim Tyler)

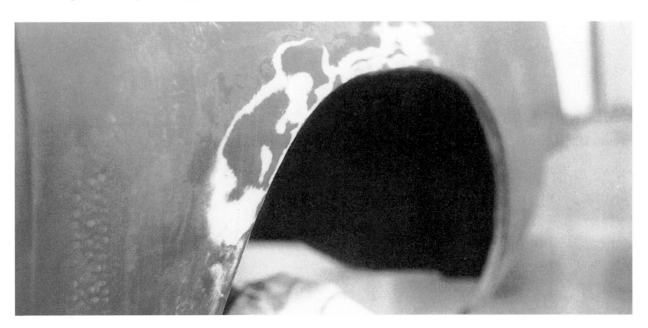

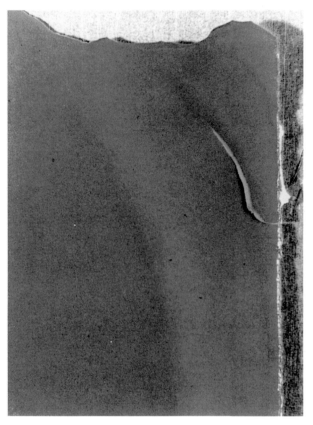

Adhesion Poor adhesion is most commonly noticed when masking tape is removed.

Blowing Bubbles spoiling the finish, as may happen if air is trapped under the paint in body filler.

finishes, in which pigment from an earlier finish dissolves in the solvents of the refinish material and discolours it.

    Possible causes:

        improperly cleaned equipment
        failure to seal prior finish adequately
        overspray from a colour prone to bleeding
        contamination of undercoat with material
    prone to bleeding

Remedies: Where bleeding occurs after the application of an initial coat of undercoat or finish, the fault can be sealed off with a coating of bleeding-inhibiting sealant (as directed by the manufacturer).

    But bleeding sometimes occurs only after several coats of undercoat and finish have been applied. In this case it is necessary to remove the affected paint altogether, and to refinish from bare metal.

Blooming A milky white cloudiness in work finished in gloss materials, varnish and enamels. (See also

Blushing below.)
Cause:

    moisture settling on the surface during drying

    Remedies: A mild case may respond to sponging down with lukewarm water and a brisk rub with a wash-leather. More obstinate cases may yield to treatment by polishing with a mixture of linseed oil, vinegar and methylated spirit in equal parts.

    If these methods fail, the work should be flatted down and refinished in gloss in properly dry conditions.

Blowing Bubbles spoiling the finish, as may happen if air that is trapped under the paint in body filler, solder or glass-fibre laminate, or in seams, expands and escapes through the paint film during low stoving or force drying. (See also Popping.)
Possible causes:

    poor application and/or sealing of body filler
    seams not adequately sealed

Blushing A milky dulling that occurs during humid conditions.

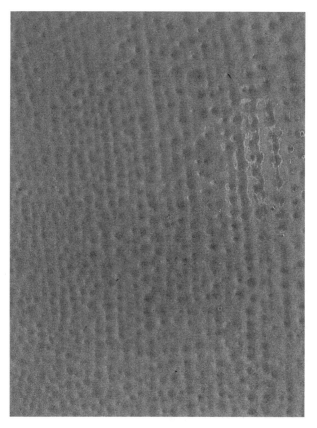

Cissing The defect occurs when the paint is repelled by some contaminant on the surface.

stone chips

scratches not adequately feather-edged

Remedy: Strip the work to bare metal, use a phosphoric acid metal cleaner and conditioner, refill and repaint.

Blushing A milky dulling of lacquer finishes that appears at the time of application during highly humid conditions. Condensation of atmospheric moisture precipitates the constituents of the paint film when the surface temperature is lowered by fast-evaporating solvents. It is not the same as 'blooming' (see above).

Possible causes:

conditions too humid or subject to temperature change

thinner is too fast or of poor quality

Remedies: In cases of slight blushing, it may be possible to remedy the defect by allowing the paint to harden and then polish over with polishing compound. In severe cases, try spraying the affected area with a slower or retarded thinner.

In the most severe cases, when water droplets are trapped in the finish, allow the paint to harden, wet-flat thoroughly and respray.

Bubbles in the finish See Blowing or Blushing.

Bonding poor See Adhesion poor.

Cissing Also known as 'cratering', 'saucering', 'crawling' or 'fish-eyes', the defect occurs when paint is repelled by some contaminant on the surface, and forms crater-like depressions that may vary in size, depth and density. Inspection with a low-power lens may reveal a small impurity at the base of each.

Possible causes:

wax, silicone polish, oil or grease on work surface

residue from surface preparation or pretreatment

overspray of different paint type

Cobwebbing A failure in the atomizing of the paint can cause filaments and threads that extend then break-up.

Crazing A crazy pattern that develops in one of the underlying finishes or in an undercoat film.

oil in the compressed air (check fluid hoses)
    Remedy: Remove the affected paint and respray.
    The use of additives that contain silicone in order to prevent cratering is not recommended. It is too easy for these additives themselves to contaminate the entire paintshop.

Cobwebbing A failure in the atomizing of the paint can cause paint to issue from the spray nozzle in filaments and threads that extend and then break up. Possible causes:
    cold paint that has thickened considerably
    incorrect spray pressure
    viscosity of paint too high
    use of cheap or incorrect thinner
    Remedies: Cobwebbing will disappear if the air pressure is corrected or the viscosity of the paint is reduced.
    Some heavy materials are difficult to atomize properly anyway, and require special equipment to be

sprayed successfully.

Contouring See Sinkage.

Covering poor See Opacity poor.

Cratering See Cissing.

Crazing A crazy pattern that develops in one of the underlying finishes or in an undercoat film. Possible causes:
    solubility differences over time in lacquer films
    lacquer stoved at too high a temperature before
      flatting and application of final coat
    paint repair over acrylic lacquer not brought up
      to paintshop temperature
    coat of a synthetic material between two lacquers
    first coat of synthetic enamel already curing as
      second coat applied
    second coat of synthetic enamel applied before

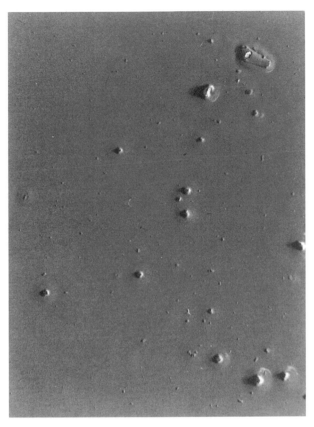

Dirt Particles This is usually caused by inadequate filtration of the paintshop and compressed air.

the recommended drying time of the first coat

use of a barrier sealer on a newly applied finish in order to rectify a defect without stripping

excessively heavy coats of lacquer with strong solvents on a synthetic primer surface over too little time

Remedies: Fine crazing in colour coats, particularly in acrylic lacquers, can often be rectified by flatting with P1200-grade abrasive paper, compounding, and polishing.

In severe cases, strip to bare metal, use a phosphoric acid metal cleaner, and respray.

Always check the state of a lacquer paint before refinishing. New lacquer films are completely soluble in their own solvents, but ageing and long exposure to sunlight may over a number of years bring about changes in the film that render it insoluble. Spray a small, well flatted area with the refinish paint. If crazing occurs it may be best to apply an isolating

(barrier) sealer over the whole repair area, or strip it right down.

Dirt particles in the finish This is usually because of poor paintshop practice.
Possible causes:

inadequate filtration of paintshop air
inadequate filtration of compressed air
spray dust allowed to accumulate in paintshop
work surface not properly prepared
paint tin lids left open, allowing dirt in
operator's clothing shedding dust or fibres
use of rusty containers for paint or thinners
high-velocity air turbulence in the spray booth
dust on spray booth floor not damped down
dry-flatting or grinding too close to paint area
poor-quality masking paper

Remedies: If the dirt particles are in the top finish only, it may be possible – once the finish has hardened completely – to wet-flat with P1200-grade abrasive paper and restore the gloss with polishing compound.

But in the case of particles that are deeply embedded, the only thing to do is to flat and respray.

Drying too slow Possible causes:

excessively heavy application leading to trapping of solvents in the paint film
wax, oil, grease or other contaminants on work surface
poor drying conditions (low temperature, high humidity, lack of ventilation)
insufficient drying time between coats
excessive use of retarder
use of cheap or incorrect thinner

Remedies: In general, slow drying may be overcome by improving the ventilation and temperature of the drying area, or by applying low heat. Caution is required in applying heat, however, for wrinkling may develop if the condition is due to extra-heavy coats. In the case of a contaminated work surface, strip to bare metal, use a phosphoric acid metal cleaner, and repaint.

Dry spray The paint from the spray gun arrives on the work surface in a powdery, friable condition.
Possible causes:

spray gun held too far from work surface
spray gun moved too quickly over surface
use of cheap thinner
compressed air pressure too high

Drying too slow Excessively heavy applications leading to trapping of solvents in the paint film.

Dry Spray The paint from the spray gun arrives on the surface in a powdery, friable condition.

thinner too fast-acting
    viscosity of paint too high
    incompatible spray gun fluid nozzle and air cap
    high-velocity air turbulence in spray booth
    temperature in spray booth too high
    Remedies: The paint has to be removed. With undercoats, remove by washing off with thinner and a rag, or allow it to harden and remove by flatting. With finishes, a dry spray of the final coat may be removed by flatting with P1200-grade abrasive paper, and the gloss restored by using a polishing compound.
    In the case of single-layer metallic finishes, a dry-spray coat must be flatted and resprayed.

Fish-eyes See Cissing.

Floating A non-uniform colour-change in the surface of a paint film; also known as 'mottling'. In brush-applied finishes, for example, a pigment float may

follow the line of the brush marks. In spray-applied metallic finishes, black edges may be seen in areas of high film thickness.
Cause:
    applying heavy wet films
    Remedies: If the film is still wet, application of a further thin coat of colour may rectify the defect. Alternatively, allow the affected area to harden; then flat and repair, using the correct spray or brush technique.

Flooding A uniform colour change over the whole surface of a paint film; also known as 'shadowing'. If a brush-applied paint film is allowed to dry for a few minutes, for example, a section that is then brushed over may show a different colour. In spray finishes, a colour difference may be seen between film sprayed at very low and at very high atomizing air pressures.
Possible causes:
    (brush:) working the paint after initial

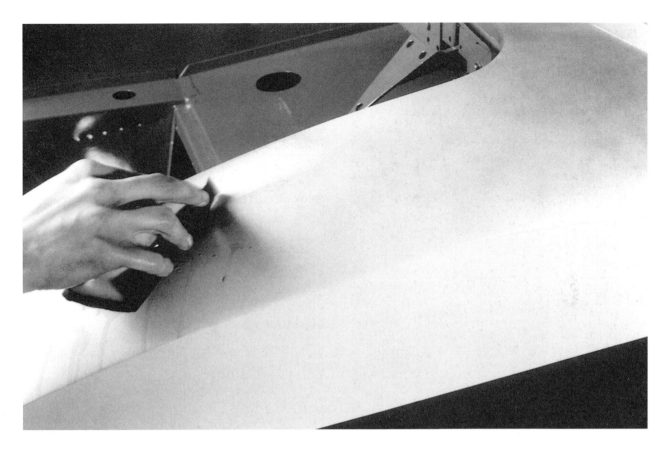

A guide coat, a light mist of colour, reveals any irregularities between coats during the flatting process.

application
   allowing runs to form
   (spray:) greatly changing spray atomization
pressure
   Remedies: If the film is still wet, application of a further thin coat of colour may rectify the defect. Alternatively, allow the affected area to harden; then flat and repair, using the correct spray or brush technique.

Gas fouling See Shrivel.

Gloss quality low Possible causes:
   use of cheap or incorrect thinner
   poor hold-out of undercoat (see also Sinkage)
   contamination of work surface before painting
   over-atomization of paint (air pressure too high
      or paint viscosity too low)
   overspray falling and drying on painted surface
   paint dried in the presence of industrial fumes

foul atmosphere in low-bake oven
   poor drying conditions (low temperature, high
      humidity, lack of ventilation)
   Remedies: Usually all that is required is to let the film harden and then restore the gloss with a polishing compound. But if contamination is suspected, strip the surface to the bare metal, use a phosphoric acid metal cleaner, and repaint. If the poor gloss is due to fine overspray in the surface, allow the film to harden, flat with P1200-grade abrasive paper, and polish with a polishing compound.
   In severe cases it may be necessary to flat the affected surface and respray.

Hiding power poor See Opacity poor.

Lifting Lifting is a severe form of crazing: see Crazing above.

127

Floating A non-uniform colour change in the surface of a paint film; also known as 'mottling'.

Gloss Quality Low Use of cheap or incorrect thinner, poor hold-out of undercoat.

Opacity poor The original finish, or perhaps a patch of undercoat, shows through the topcoat.
Possible causes:
    paint not stirred sufficiently
    paint overthinned
    use of cheap, incorrect or very slow-acting
        thinner
    too few coats applied
    Remedies: Allow the paint to flash off and then recoat. Alternatively, allow the paint to harden completely, wet-flat, and repaint.

Orange-peel The paint has a heavy mottled effect that resembles the peel of an orange. This defect is known alternatively as 'pebbling'.
Possible causes:
    faulty spray pressure
    spray gun held too far from work surface
    spray gun held too close to work surface
    drying uneven over-rapid evaporation of solvent

paint insufficiently thinned (viscosity too high)
use of cheap thinner
wide temperature difference between paint and
    surface
high-velocity air turbulence in spray booth
spray chamber too humid
    Remedies: After the paint is thoroughly hardened, rub out the orange-peel with P1200-grade abrasive paper and polish with a polishing compound. In severe cases it may be necessary instead to flat with P500- or P1000-grade abrasive paper, and respray.

Oven fouling See Shrivel.

Pebbling See Orange-peel.

Pinholing The finished surface has tiny holes or pits in it – the condition is known also as 'pitting'.
Possible causes:

Orange-Peel The paint has a heavy mottled effect that resembles the peel of an orange.

rapid drying of the top surface of a lacquer film when pockets of solvent beneath have still to evaporate through it (in turn mostly caused by a combination of high viscosity, low air pressure and hot, dry conditions in the spray booth)

application of colour coats over an undercoat or colour coat that has been dry-sprayed

pinholes in an existing finish not removed during flatting before repainting

poor application and/or sealing of body filler

Remedies: Minor pinholing confined to the colour coat may be removed by flatting with P1200-grade abrasive paper and polishing with a polishing compound. In other cases, wet- or dry-flat the affected paint to a depth that ensures the complete elimination of the holes, and then refinish. Alternatively, strip to bare metal and refinish.

On no account try to bridge pinholes with successive dry applications of primer surfacer.

Pinholes exposed after flatting body filler should be sealed off with a thin spread of filler applied with a knife held at about 90° to the surface. This technique ensures that the filler is forced well into the holes, and that it is not dragged out again as the knife moves on.

Pitting See Pinholing.

Popping Like 'blowing', this is a condition in which there are air bubbles in the finish. But in this case the bubbles are there because they were trapped during the application of the paint, unable to escape because of the speed at which the film surface formed.
Possible causes:

hot, dry conditions and/or air turbulence in the spray booth

compressed air pressure too low

insufficient flash-off time between coats

excessively thick films applied

use of cheap or incorrect thinner

Remedies: Minor popping confined to the colour coat may be removed by flatting with P1200-grade abrasive paper and polishing with a polishing compound. In other cases, wet- or dry-flat the affected paint to a depth that ensures the complete elimination of the bubbles, and then refinish. Alternatively, strip to bare metal and refinish.

Runs and sags An excessive amount of paint applied to a vertical or sloping surface fails to hold, and drips or runs down the panel.
Possible causes:

spray gun held too close to work surface

spray gun moved too slowly

incompatible spray gun fluid nozzle and air cap

compressed air pressure too low

paint viscosity too high or too low

poor application conditions (too cold, inadequate ventilation)

insufficient drying time between coats

excessive use of retarder

use of cheap or incorrect thinner

spray fan width reduced without compensating reduction in fluid delivery

work surface contaminated with oil

Remedies: Allow the paint to harden completely. Then wet-flat using P1200-grade abrasive paper and polish, or wet-flat with P500-grade abrasive paper and recoat.

On the other hand, if the sag is still wet and

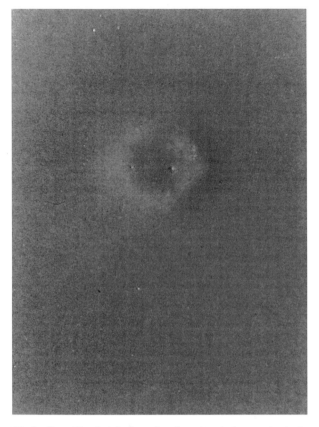

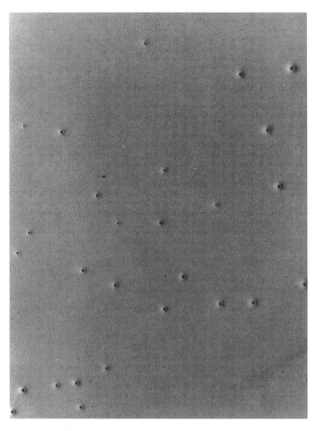

Pinholing The finished surface has tiny holes or pits in it – the condition is known also as 'pitting'.

Popping Like 'blowing', this is a condition in which there are air bubbles in the finish.

another coat can be applied, some success may be obtained by lightly stippling out the sag with a soft brush and respraying.

Sagging See Runs and sags.

Sand scratches See Scratch opening.

Saucering See Cissing.

Scratch opening Flatting marks that spoil the finish. The defect is known also as 'tramlining'.
Possible causes:
 heavy application of undercoat
 insufficient drying time before finishing coats
  applied
 use of abrasive paper that is too coarse
 colour on colour application when the original
  finish is soft, weathered or undercured, and
  sensitive to paint solvents

Remedies: If damage is minor, polishing with a polishing compound may be all that is required. Otherwise wet-flat using P1200-grade abrasive paper, and polish. Or allow the finish to harden completely, then wet-flat and recoat.

Scratches made when abrasive particles from a dirty paintshop are present on a surface being flatted are often incorrectly ascribed to be due to scratch opening. Insufficient thickness of colour coat can also give the appearance of scratch opening.

Shrivel During the paint drying process, the surface becomes wrinkled and furrowed in an irregular pattern. This defect is confined to materials that dry though oxidation or by a thermosetting process in an oven. Encountered in the latter context, the defect may alternatively be known as 'oven fouling' or 'gas fouling'.
Possible causes:
 applying heavy coats of paint

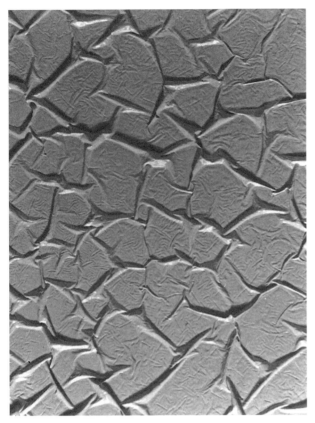

Shrivel During the paint drying process, the surface becomes wrinkled and furrowed in an irregular pattern.

poor air drying conditions (low temperature, high humidity, air turbulence)

foul atmosphere in the drying oven

Remedies: When the condition is slight, allow the film to harden through completely, either by air drying for several weeks or, in the case of stoving paint, by restoving under proper conditions. Then thoroughly flat to remove all traces of the defect, and respray.

If the condition is severe, strip the surface to bare metal, use a phosphoric acid metal cleaner, and repaint.

Sinkage As drying proceeds, the finish loses gloss: eventually underlying imperfections – the contours of filler patches, metal scratches and so forth – show through.

Possible causes:

excessively heavy application of one or all of the materials in the paint scheme

insufficient drying time between coats

undercoats dry sprayed, resulting in porosity

underlying filler not properly sealed

highly pigmented undercoat not stirred each time before use

use of abrasive paper that is too coarse

poor air drying conditions (low temperature, high humidity, air turbulence)

insufficient thinning of paint

undercoat flatted before entirely dry

insufficient weight of colour coat

Remedies: Allow the paint to harden completely – this may take several days or can be speeded up by applying low heat. Depending on the degree of sinkage, use P1200-grade abrasive paper and/or rubbing compound to level the surface, then polish with a polishing compound.

In severe cases, flat with P500- or P1000-grade abrasive paper, and respray.

Striping This is a defect of metallic finishes in which there are variations in the depth of the colour-shade, in stripes corresponding to spray gun strokes.

Possible causes:

inadequate overlapping of spray gun strokes

defective spray gun pattern

spray gun held too close to work surface

failure to hold spray gun at right-angles to work surface

Remedies: Either allow the finish to flash off, and apply a further coat using a correct spray technique. Or allow the finish to harden off, then wet-flat, and respray.

Tramlining See Scratch opening.

Wrinkling See Shrivel.

HOW PAINTS DRY

Paints dry in a manner that corresponds to how their binders dry. This is one of the reasons that the binder is often considered the most significant constituent of a coating material. So far in this book, we have often cited the evaporation of solvents as a major method of drying – as, indeed, for the vehicle refinishing industry and its use of nitrocellulose paints it is – but there are in fact no fewer than six different methods by which paints physically and chemically dry, all of which are relevant to specific types of paint and specific industries that use them.

The six are:

● Principally oxidative drying. Drying in contact with oxygen, and most commonly in atmospheric air. The process can be speeded up by using chemical catalysts. Binders of this type are mostly drying oils. Although drying-oil paints are easy to apply, they are now uncommon because the long drying times involved, and the low permanence of the result, make mechanical handling difficult.

● The evaporation of solvents. Previously the so-called cellulose paints were utterly dominant in this group. Now there are many other types.

● Combined evaporation and chemical reaction. The most important binder in this group is alkyd resin in its different variant forms, which now make up the binders in most air-drying primers and some stove-drying primers too.

● Polymerization. Polymerization is the chemical and physical process by which a large number of similar molecules (monomers) combine together to form a single multiple-molecule. The combination – a molecular chain – is then known as a polymer, or polymeride, and produces binders that may dry through heat (stoving, stove hardening) or through the addition of chemical additives, such as acids (cold hardening). Many modern binders belong to this group, including those used in polyurethane paints and polyesters.

● Heating a powder-dispersion binder in plasticizer. The binder is in the form of a stable powder dispersion in plasticizer, and when heated forms a homogeneous film. The group includes plastisols.

● The sintering of solventless powder-paint. The paint is in the form of powder that adheres to the work surface long enough for it then to be sintered into a film in an oven. The method is excellent for a large class of objects that require coating, and is in widespread use.

Of the above six methods of drying, the first four cover practically the entire range of the paint industry, whereas the last two belong in the border area between the paint and plastics industries.

Drying principally by oxidation

In general, paints for brush application are all air-drying. Stoving finishes formulated with aromatic solvents and comparatively little drying oil do not lend themselves to easy application by brush, for the solvents evaporate too rapidly. Most brush paints are based therefore on a fairly high ('long', more than 60 per cent, as opposed to 'short', or less than 45 per cent) drying-oil content with resinous media or alkyds, and with white spirit or similar as the solvent. Long-oil alkyds are most commonly selected as binding media in brush paints because they have very good flow characteristics (brush-marks are virtually eliminated) and the viscosity of the medium is such that it will still flow after most of the solvent has evaporated.

The proportion of oil contained in a medium is significant to solubility: the less oil there is ('the shorter the oil length'), the more solubility in white spirit decreases. For a shorter oil product it may become necessary to use more powerful solvents, such as the aromatic hydrocarbons xylol/xylene and toluol/toluene, or mixtures of hydrocarbons known as coal tar naphthas. In some resinous compositions alcohols such as butanol are added to the main solvent to aid the dissolution of the resinous complex.

In drying-oil paints, the oil dries by oxidation. The normally slow process can be accelerated by the addition of driers, or siccatives, which generally contain one or more of the metals lead, cobalt and manganese in the form of a naphthenate dissolved in white spirit. White spirit is a very suitable solvent, in that it is low in odour and has no effect on previous coats.

The actual oils used as drying oils are either vegetable oils or oil-modified alkyds. Vegetable oils are still extracted from the seeds and fruits of plants largely by crushing and pressing. Chemically, they are for the most part mixtures of triglycerides of fatty acids – and for those that need to know, a glyceride is an ester (a compound of an alcohol and an acid) in which the parent alcohol is glycerol/glycerine, an alcohol with three hydroxyl groups in its molecule. Oil-modified alkyds represent a chemical form of certain simple organic compounds which in reaction with vegetable oil make up an oil or varnish base.

● Linseed oil. Linseed oil is the drying oil in most general use. It is obtained by the pressing of flax (*Linum usitatissimum*) seeds, hot or cold. The raw linseed oil is refined and usually boiled at a temperature of around 300°C (572°F) in order first to remove gelatinous residues and second to provide higher gloss and better fluidity and weather resistance – although it is linseed oil in which driers have been incorporated by heat that is alternatively known as 'boiled oil'.

Linseed oil has a golden yellow colour and gives a yellow tint; boiled oil is almost colourless but dries with a yellowish tinge.

Made heavy and thick by heating under pressure, linseed oil (or tung oil) is alternatively called 'stand oil' and is used as a medium in some paints and varnishes.

● Tung oil, wood oil. Tung oil, or wood oil, is obtained from the fruit of several varieties of the Chinese tung tree, a member of the spurge family that because of its commercial importance to the paint industry is now grown in North America, Burma (Myanmar) and Zimbabwe as well as in China. The oil dries faster than linseed oil and is considerably more water-resistant. For this reason it is used extensively in marine varnishes and enamels. It is also more resistant to weak alkalis such as detergents and washing soda.

Its propensity to wrinkle in certain patterns when drying was once taken as a positive factor, in 'wrinkle finishes', but now the wrinkling property is generally removed by boiling. This requires great skill, however, for the temperature at which the change is effected is critical: one or two degrees less and nothing happens, one or two degrees more and the oil jellifies and is worthless.

Pale amber in colour, dull in appearance, unpleasant in taste and smell, tung oil also imparts a yellow tint.

Made heavy and thick by heating under pressure, tung oil (or linseed oil) is alternatively called 'stand oil' and is used as a medium in some paints and varnishes.

● Castor oil. Castor oil is derived from the castor plant, another member of the spurge family that grows wild in many tropical and subtropical countries, and that is cultivated in India, Brazil and East Africa. Untreated castor oil is a non-drying oil, and is used in some paints as a plasticizer. When polymerized and dehydrated it develops good drying properties: it remains liquid at low temperatures, it does not thin rapidly as temperatures rise, and it is notable for its high viscosity. It produces a paint film that is flexible yet durable, and when blended with synthetic resins gives good resistance to moisture and to chemicals. Castor oil is a common constituent in pigment pastes for use in nitrocellulose finishes. It has no yellowing capacity.

● Oiticica oil, cica oil. Oiticica oil is obtained from the nut of a South American tree of the rose family. It resembles wood oil, but produces a more brittle paint

film that is less wear-resistant and less water-resistant.

● Soyabean oil, soya oil. Soyabean oil is obtained from the soya bean plant that grows mainly in Asia and under cultivation in Europe and in North America. The oil has to be refined to remove non-drying constituents. It is used mostly in alkyd form and, because of its high weather-resistance and minimal yellowing tendency, for outdoor paints.

● Safflower oil. Safflower oil derives from the seeds of a thistle-like herb grown in India, Egypt, Asia Minor, Australia and the United States. It oxidizes at a slower rate than linseed oil, but is a useful material for the modification of alkyd resins, and is a common constituent in artist's colours.

A non-yellowing oil, it is particularly used in brilliant white enamels.

● Other drying oils. Perilla oil, made from a herb of the mint family, is similar in most respects to a mixture of refined linseed oil and tung oil.

Tall oil is a resinous liquid that is formed as a distilled and esterized byproduct of the pine wood-pulp industry. It is used mostly for less demanding indoor applications, but is included in certain alkyd formulations.

Poppy oil and walnut oil are light oils used primarily in white paints, especially artist's colours. They dry slowly.

Fish oil is sometimes used, and is cheap.

Sunflower oil is a semi-drying non-yellowing oil.

● Non-drying oils. Non-drying oils are important as a means of imparting flexibility to a paint film, particularly in compositions that depend on heat for their hardening properties.

Most used are coconut oil, cottonseed oil and untreated castor oil.

Drying by evaporation of solvents

Although cellulose products now occupy a niche in this group that is nothing like as central or dominant as once it was, cellulose in one form or another still forms a major factor within a great number of products of this type.

● Nitrocellulose paints. Nitrocellulose is obtained by treating cellulose with a mixture of nitrous acid and sulphuric acid. At that stage it is highly explosive, and to make it safe for handling it is moistened with alcohol. The result is then subjected to high-pressure steam treatment, in order to increase the 'fullness' of the product.

As a paint it is combined with different resins,

plasticizers and solvents. Although nitrocellulose paints have a low content of non-volatiles, they give good polishing properties, and are thus used for car body enamels, furniture paints, silver lacquers, and so forth.

- Cellulose acetate. Cellulose acetate represents nitrocellulose treated with acetic acid. Non-explosive and – even better – non-combustible, it is useful in fireproof paints as used on cables or in aircraft.
- Polyvinyl resins. Polyvinyl resins comprise a large group of presentday binders. Occurring in differing degrees of polymerization, they are frequently mixed with one another. Examples of such combinations include polyvinyl acetate (PVA) with polyvinyl chloride (PVC) and PVA with acrylates.

The vinyl compounds are available in both solid and dispersed forms. Solid types require strong solvents – which makes for a relatively high price, but which gives in return high chemical resistance, good adhesion, water-resistance and other similar properties. These types also combine well with other binding agents. The dispersed-base vinyl paints, on the other hand, are easy to apply, and during application are less sensitive to moisture. They are in addition non-flammable and non-toxic.

In pure form, however, some of these binding agents are too brittle to be used in paint. This includes PVA and PVC, among others, which must first be softened either physically with a plasticizer or chemically through co-polymerization. The physical plasticizers used in this way are organic esters such as dibutyl phthalate or tricresyl phosphate. Over the course of time, these plasticizers evaporate from the paint coat, eventually rendering the film brittle and possibly also causing some discoloration. Co-polymerization is therefore the preferred method. Acrylates are the plasticizers used, chemically incorporated into the polymer chain in such a way that every fourth molecule in the chain is a softener molecule.

- Chlorinated rubber. Obtained by chlorine treatment of natural or synthetic rubber, chlorinated rubber is highly resistant to strong acids and alkalis. For use in paint it is dissolved in xylol/xylene or toluol/toluene, and generally combined with a softener. It is most suited to heavy-duty applications, such as the painting of chemical factories or of road markings.
- Other solvent-evaporating media. Polystyrene can be dissolved in strong solvents, and is used particularly in quick-drying paints for industrial purposes.

Styrene butadiene is used for chemical-resistant paints, latex paints and similar.

- The application of solvent-evaporating media. A characteristic of these paints is that they are supremely adaptable to varying customer requirements. For spraying, a suitable solvent should be added to each individual binder, but only so much that sufficient fluidity is obtained. They can be applied using hot or cold conventional spray techniques (although of course the dispersion paints are not hot-sprayed). Other usable techniques include high-pressure spraying, electrostatic and ordinary dipping, flow coating, curtain painting and in some cases roller painting. Moreover, the drying time until the painted surface can be handled is short, depending somewhat on the solvent used, and can be still further abbreviated by force-drying. Stoving in an oven is required only for certain types that produce high film evenness and permanence.

There are nonetheless some potential disadvantages. Excessive dilution with a thinner lowers the covering ability and the filling ability, increases the moisture sensitivity, and causes a reduction in gloss. Their low solid content means that it may be necessary to coat an object up to five times in order to obtain a satisfactory finish. For several types, strong solvents are used that are not only toxic but severely affect mucous membranes and skin. Blisters and other evaporative problems may occur in the film when these paints are stoved. And the binders themselves, in all cases bar the dispersion paints, are relatively expensive.

Drying through combined evaporation and chemical reaction

Alkyd resin paints form the largest group of all the types of paint described in this section on binders and their drying methods.

The alkyd resin variants that are used as binders in paints are made from synthetic fatty acids, from dicarbon acids (which are resin-like chemical substances), or as a refined product from natural oils.

The precise proportion in each of fatty and resinous acids tends to affect in similar ratios the elasticity, hardness and drying properties of the film surfaces created. These binders are therefore often classified in four groups reflecting those proportions, from the most fatty to the most resinous: **fat**, **medium fat**, **lean** and **short**.

The fat type has the best elasticity, the longest drying time and the softest coat. All these properties gradually reverse as the binder combination becomes more resinous, so that the short type has the lowest elasticity, the shortest drying time and the hardest coat. Because alkyds have higher viscosities than natural oils, more thinner must be added – and a lean alkyd needs more solvent than a fat one. But because of the fatty acid content, alkyds have a lower yellowing tendency than natural oils, and the weather-resistance and permanence are generally of a higher order too.

One disadvantage of the alkyds is low alkali-resistance. For this reason they are not suitable for application on a concrete surface (or similar) without a primer based on PVC or chlorinated rubber.

Conversely, alkyd paints are used to great advantage in rust-protective coatings and in industrial and house painting. For home use, where simple handling is important, the **thixotropic** types of paint have been produced. These paints have two-stage motion-dependent consistency – that is, they are so thick that a stirring-stick will stand unsupportedly upright in them, but they turn liquid when stirred, and in that condition they are easy to work with. After application they regain their thick consistency, so reducing the risk of runs and sags.

Thixotropy is obtained by the addition of bentonite (inert lava-clay), certain specific iron hydroxides and various pigments, which together chemically and physically react to form molecular chains and networks that give the paint its jelly-like consistency. These bonds are not very strong, however, and can be broken by the simple mechanical action of stirring, and so the paint becomes liquid.

Thixotropic paints have a low solids content – they have little ability to fill holes or gaps in a previous surface – and are used mostly for do-it-yourself jobs in the household. A less thixotropic form of the identical paint may be used industrially for spray primers.

● The application of alkyd resin paints. Spraying and dipping are the methods most used; brushing and rollering are also employed in household circumstances. Industrially, the spraying of small surfaces with high accuracy is best effected with hot, high-pressure spraying, although with synthetic primers (as the alkyd-based primer types are generally but rather incorrectly known) the heat is not so necessary if a slightly lean paint is prepared or highly volatile solvents are used.

Electrostatic alkyd spraying is possible but requires the paint to be adapted: special solvents must be mixed in to provide the correct electrical resistance.

Finishing paints of the alkyd types are applied in largely the same way as the corresponding primers, but the spraying properties are a little different. Conventional hot-spraying yields the finest finish, with high gloss and good overlapping properties. Electrostatic spraying can be used in some cases, and gives a good result. Cold high-pressure spraying can, on the other hand, cause problems due to the double coats formed in the overlaps: the result with these highly fluid paints is all too often running and sagging. Yet hot high-pressure spraying makes it possible to use a lower working pressure, and gives higher viscosity (with reduced risk of runs) and a slightly better diffusion of the spray field edges than cold spraying, all together making supervision simpler for the operator and facilitating the application of the finishing coat.

Polymerization

The process of polymerization produces chemical structures that may be regarded as of several different types. Molecular chains may, for example, be described as unidirectional, as simple, straightforward, undeviating chains. Or the chains might have branches. Or a number of chains may interlink at specific points on each, to form a network – a network that may be two-dimensional or, in complex cases, three-dimensional, forming a sort of honeycomb structure.

The process by which chains, networks and honeycomb structures become interlinked is known as cross-linking, and substances used to promote cross-linking are therefore cross-linking agents.

As a matter of fact, the hardening of the drying-oil type of paint film is a cross-linking process that leads to a closely knit chemically bonded durable structure of large molecular size.

The use of multiple cross-linking is of considerable significance to the paint technologist of the present day. Many of the binders most used in industrial application belong to this group. They include:

  stoving enamels
  acid hardening (cold hardening) paints
  polyurethane paints
  polyester paints
  liquid epoxy and polyurethane resins
the composition and application of all of which are

described in detail below.

• Stoving enamels. Binders in these paints most commonly consist of alkyd and phenolic, urea or melamine resins. In a few cases the addition of acid allows for air-drying instead of stoving, if circumstances demand.

Phenolic resin in unmodified condition produces chemical-resistant and hard paints. The film is fairly brittle, however, and should be used only for thin coatings (as on the insides of tubes or preserve tins). Moreover, with unmodified or slightly modified phenolic resins adhesion is not particularly good, and work surfaces should be sand-blasted or phosphatized before painting. Temperatures at which phenolic resin paints are stoved are comparatively high – between 180°C and 220°C (356°F–428°F) – which reduces the possibility of using the more attractive full-toned colours.

Urea and melamine resins, in combination with alkyds, yield high film hardness and good permanence for full-toned colours as well as white, in spite of the use of temperatures again as high as 180°C (356°F). In general, melamine gives better weather-resistance than urea, although both have a wider register of ability than phenolic combinations. These resins are particularly used for high-quality applications, as on car bodies and refrigerators.

Epoxy resins also occur in stoving enamels, ordinarily in combination with one or more of the groups already listed here. At stoving temperatures of 180°C to 220°C (356°F–428°F), they produce extremely chemical-resistant coats that have good adhesion, good elasticity, good hardness, and several other beneficial properties. In combination with phenolic resins, epoxy resins yield extra-high chemical-resistance; in combination with urea and melamine resins they have unusually high resistance to yellowing. Main applications are on washing machines, laboratory equipment, equipment for the chemical industry, and the insides of tubes and preserve tins.

• The application of stoving enamels. Stoving enamels can be applied via practically all application methods except brushing and hand-rollering. Methods most commonly used are conventional cold and hot spraying, and hot high-pressure spraying.

One of the major problems with stoving enamels is to get the composition of the solvent just right. Some volatile solvents must be added in order to avoid runs – too much, though, and the surface becomes uneven: 'boiling' of the paint may occur. A very careful balance must be struck between solvents that evaporate rapidly and solvents that evaporate slowly.

• Acid hardening (cold hardening) paints. These are two-constituent paints in which the binder is similar in composition to those of the stoving enamels. After the addition of the hardener, however, they have a limited usable life – the time that they remain liquid in the container, or 'pot life'. At the end of the pot life they are unusable. The hardener ensures that they dry in air: no heat is required.

Because of the generally excellent properties available with these paints – high chemical-resistance, good resistance against degreasing agents, high mechanical strength, and so on – the range of use is wide. They are particularly employed where rust-protection is important, such as on ships and on outdoor tanks and factory equipment. Some are especially sensitive to impurities on the work substrate, however, particularly moisture.

Phenolic-resin-binder types are water-resistant: their hardener is phosphoric acid or some other organic acid. They are included in some artist's etching or wash primers but are otherwise used mostly in the wood industry.

Urea and melamine types also utilize organic acids as catalysts, give good light permanence, and are used mostly in the furniture industry.

Epoxy types provide good adhesion and hard, elastic coats with very high permanence.

• The application of acid hardening paints. Application methods are few: conventional cold spraying (with or without high pressure), curtain-painting and roller-painting. Manual brushing or rollering may occasionally be used.

These paints are easy to work with, but the pot life of only 24–48 hours after the hardener is added means that in most industrial contexts a certain amount of wastage is to be expected.

• Polyurethane paints. Polyurethane paints rely on isocyanate constituents to provide the hardening by chemical reaction. In Britain and elsewhere in Europe such paints are commonly known alternatively as DD paints, a name that represents an acronym of the Desmophen and Desmodur products of Bayer AG, in Germany. Desmophen is the trade name for the alkyd resin that carries the free hydroxyl groups on the molecular chain, and Desmodur is the name for the isocyanate constituent. When the two are mixed, the drying reaction proceeds rapidly because the hydroxyl groups of the polyester resin react with the isocyanate groups of the hardener to create high-polymer networks.

But the isocyanate group reacts not only with the hydroxyl group of the polyester constituent, but also with other free hydroxyl or amino groups. Great care must therefore be taken in the selection of solvents by composition: solvents and thinners that contain water and alcohol must be avoided, or they would react with the isocyanate to interrupt the reaction with the polyester. The consequence would be an insufficiently hardened coating, a complete waste of materials, that would have then to be washed off.

So in comparison with epoxy resin paints, polyurethane paints are more sensitive to moisture but less sensitive to low temperature during drying. The polyurethane paints normally have less adhesion on sheet metal than epoxy, but provide a greater diversity of useful properties.

The beneficial qualities of both polyurethane and epoxy paints can be obtained together, to some extent, by modifying them with each other. Used complementarily in this way, a correctly balanced mixture can produce good adhesion without excessive temperature-dependence. And the resultant combinations have in recent years greatly enlarged the range of uses open to both types of paint.

Single-constituent polyurethane paints with excellent film properties are now also available. For these paints to dry, the isocyanate constituent reacts with the moisture in the air. But the carbon dioxide that is given off during the reaction can be difficult to remove from thick paint coats.

Further comparatively recent additions to the polyurethane paints selection have succeeded in reducing the chalkiness to which these paints have a tendency when used out of doors. The new paints have superb external properties . . . but are rather more sensitive to chemical attack than the previous ones.
● The application of polyurethane paints. Application methods are as for epoxy resin paints.

But in a container from which small amounts of polyurethane paint is taken daily, small crystal-like formations may appear on the container walls. Worse, they may drop from the walls and create clots in the paint. The problem can ordinarily be overcome by recourse to the paint manufacturer, who should be able to supply appropriate rapid-acting solvents which, as they evaporate in the container, prevent the appearance of such formations.
● Unsaturated polyesters, liquid epoxy resins, liquid

polyurethane resins. These are lumped together here on the grounds that in all three types of paint the dry coat has almost the same thickness as the wet coat. The film density and permanence are accordingly excellent. But certain problems attach to the application of these paints. Solvents may simplify application, of course, but they almost inevitably ruin the very qualities that the paint might be used for: density and permanence. To use a solvent would also negate the possibility of spraying thick coats of about 500 microns with only two spray coats.
The target remains to avoid using solvents while yet achieving acceptable application properties.
● The application of liquid epoxy resins and polyurethane resins. The hardener is heated to a thin liquid consistency, although never at temperatures above 70°C (158°F), and stirred thoroughly into the paint. There is now 30–60 minutes of pot life – time before the paint becomes so thick as to be unmanageable. The mixture is then applied, after the addition of a rapidly-evaporative solvent such as acetone or methylene chloride, by means of spraying equipment of a special type. The solvent is assumed to disappear during application.

Once application is to the desired thickness, the paint should be evened (if possible, and as quickly as possible) by an assistant operator with a paperhanger's brush, or similar. Speed is of the essence because the paint quickly becomes more viscous.

The equipment used in application must be cleaned out thoroughly with thinner after every single session (at least at the end of every working day). If the paint hardens inside the equipment, both paint and equipment will probably have to be abandoned. It may certainly be more economic to abandon the equipment than to spend a considerable time trying to salvage it.

Paint consumption and coat thickness must be claculated in advance, and checked during the work with the aid of a wet-film thickness gauge. Coat thickness variations of around 200 microns are not unusual; a trained operator can achieve a variation limit of about 50 microns.
● Polyester paints. The principal constituents of a polyester paint are:
unsaturated polyester resin
    styrene (as both solvent and reactant)
    an organic peroxide (catalyst)
    an accelerator (assisting the catalyst)
It is the addition of the peroxide to the polyester resin

and styrene mixture (which may also contain the accelerating agent) that causes hardening in the form of gelling. Polyester resin, styrene and cobalt accelerator can be stored together for months, for example, but the moment the organic peroxide is added, hardening begins.

For this reason, polyester paints are normally delivered as two-constituent paints to be mixed on the job. It is possible to obtain styrene by itself, except that styrene is so volatile it is generally sold with a stabilizing agent. Similarly, organic peroxide catalysts are available but are labile (unstable at room temperatures) and sold with delaying agents. Moreover, the organic peroxides used as catalysts in polyester paints are extremely harmful to the cornea: protective glasses must be worn when mixing these paints. If peroxide is inadvertently splashed on to the cornea, water should be copiously applied to the eye as an emergency measure, and a specialist consulted as soon as possible. The accelerators are metal salts – salts of cobalt, lead or manganese usually – or tertiary (ternary) amines. The choice of accelerator depends on the organic peroxide selected. (Cobalt accelerators tend to cause a slightly greenish hue; tertiary amines a yellowing.)

There are two main groups of polyester paints: the air-drying glossy polyesters that dry in both room temperatures and elevated temperatures, and the polyesters that require paraffin wax as an extra constituent in order to dry.

The air-drying glossy polyester gives the more robust film. The hardening time can be shortened through forced drying. And the paint can be applied in thin coats, which is important for the open-pore technique of wood-finishing.

The polyesters that require paraffin wax for drying, on the other hand, give the best filling ability because the wax forms a cover on the surface and prevents the solvent-reactant styrene from evaporating. And although the surface is not as highly glossed as that produced by the air-drying polyester, the wax creates a surface that is evidently easier to polish.

There are many fields of use for polyester primers and finishes. Specialities include use on furniture and interior decor items produced in factories, on car bodies as a filler-refinisher, and on water-free concrete and cement. In thin coats, polyester can be used to paint marble (where thicker coats are required, a polyurethane primer is required). In thick coast for extra corrosion-resistance, a primer of the paraffin-wax type might be succeeded by a topcoat that is a combination of polyester and polyurethane. Many stoving finishes and metal surfacers are combinations of polyester resins and amino resins, which yield excellent results and a high gloss as a finishing coat.

● The application of polyester paints. The general method of application is cold spraying, under normal or high pressure. Curtain coating – formerly the major method for all applications – is still used for application on wood surfaces.

Primers for use in the vehicular industry have a pot life (time between adding the peroxide and the gelling of the paint to an extent that is unmanageable) of about one hour which, together with the small quantities sprayed, makes a conventional spray gun with gravity cup quite suitable.

Heating a powder-dispersion binder in plasticizer
Typical of this group is polyvinyl chloride (PVC) in plasticizer.

One means of application is with a 'doctor' – a knife-like blade of rubber or steel – and rollers, often used in combination to create a pattern. Another method is to coat the inside surfaces of hollow objects with the aid of centrifugal force.

The sintering of solventless powder-paint
The paint is produced in the normal manner, but for the purpose of application in this fashion it has to have two very precise properties:
a) it must be capable of being stored and used in powdered form with no physical or chemical change until heat is applied; and
b) when heat is applied, the powder must not melt to a thin liquid but must be sintered (fused) to a homogeneous film with an attractive surface.

The powder is sintered to the work surface in either of two very different ways:
a) the work surface itself is heated to a suitable temperature, and then introduced into a chamber in which the powder is kept suspended and in movement by air that enters from below; the temperature of the surface thus determines the amount of powder that adheres, and thus the thickness of the final coat when the powder has been finally sintered in an oven; or
b) the powder is sprayed electrostatically on to the work surface, where it adhere for sufficient time to enable the work surface to be put in an oven for

the powder to be sintered into a film.

Binders used for this kind of paint have so far been based on epoxy resin, nylon or polyethylene. The field is, however, developing at precocious speed.

The application and drying of special coatings

● Bitumen coatings. Bitumen coatings form a group of closely related types such as asphalt, pitch, coal and wood tar, all of which are originally black or dark brown in colour.

Air-drying bitumen paints are generally very low in oil content or oil-free altogether. They are extremely water- and chemical-resistant, and are commonly used in watertanks in arduous conditions to protect an iron undersurface. The principal drawback is that these paints tend to crack into a snakeskin pattern in sunlight.

Stove-drying bitumen paints, on the other hand, are combined with different oils and resins. Stoved in temperatures approaching 200°C (392°F), the resultant surface is elastic, hard, impact-resistant and has a deep black gloss.

Bitumen-epoxy combinations are presently increasing greatly in popularity. They produce chemical-, solvent- and water-resistant coats of appropriate hardness.

Bitumen paints may for some requirements be pigmented with aluminium powder, iron oxide red, or any of several other pigments.

● The application of bitumen coatings. The most usual methods of applying bitumen coatings are spraying, dipping or brushing. Spraying requires considerable judgement based on experience, however, because of the potentially quantitative variation in viscosity. The task is made more difficult by the necessity to heat the material.

● Zinc-rich paints. Although zinc-rich paints were introduced many decades ago, it is only in recent years that their potential as an important type of anti-corrosion paint has been realized.

Particularly different about these paints are the ratios of binder and pigment in their composition. Zinc-rich paints have a very low proportion of binder. In fact, the content of dry materials within zinc-rich paints varies between 60 and 95 per cent by weight, depending on the sort of binder on which each paint is based. The amount of pigment contained is even more significant. For every paint there is a volume of pigment concentration at which substantial changes in the properties of the coating occur, notably in relation to the hardness of the gloss, the elasticity of

the film, the chemical-resistance, and so forth. This critical pigment volume concentration is generally reckoned to be that at which the pigment plus any filler used is volumetrically equivalent to the binder. If the critical pigment volume concentration is exceeded, some of the pigment is superfluous, and the coat of paint becomes porous. This is true of all zinc-rich paints, and means in turn that it is essential to have the best possible binder for the zinc-rich coat, both for adhesion to the underlying surface and for providing an excellent surface for succeeding coats to key into.

The corrosion-resistance stems from galvanic principles: the less electropositive zinc in the coat dissolves, thus protecting the iron in the work surface. At this point, however, it may be as well to mention that in the unlikely eventuality that the painted work surface is subjected to water at temperatures exceeding 70°C (158°F), the iron becomes less electropositive than the zinc and it is the iron that consequently corrodes.

Zinc melts at around 420°C (788°F), and in the presence of oxygen converts to zinc oxide at around 350°C (662°F). At high temperatures, then, a zinc-rich coat inevitably loses its properties.

Zinc-rich paints in most common use include zinc ethyl silicate, zinc sodium silicate, zinc potassium silicate, zinc epoxy and zinc chlorinated rubber.

● The application of zinc-rich paints. Zinc-rich paints require a surface that has been extra-thoroughly cleaned, preferably by sand-blasting. To ensure optimum weatherproofing, an appropriate surface undercoating should be applied – one of the epoxy type, perhaps.

For the purposes of spraying, zinc-rich coatings can be classified in two main groupings: the organic and the inorganic. Organic zinc-rich coatings include zinc chlorinated rubber, zinc cyclo rubber and zinc epoxy. Inorganic zinc-rich coatings include zinc potassium silicate, zinc lithium silicate and zinc sodium silicate, in which the binder is an aqueous solution of these. Zinc ethyl silicate is additionally used in combination with organic solvents. Chemically, in each case an inorganic silicate is formed in combination with the zinc as the solvent evaporates.

Of the **organic zinc-rich coatings**, zinc epoxy is considered to give the best protection against corrosion and to have the optimum mechanical properties. Surface wear is negligible. A stirrer must be used. It is, however, the only one of the organic types to have a limited pot life. It can be sprayed using most high-pressure pumps, even with relatively small nozzles (of diameter, say, 0·381 mm); the most appropriate high-pressure paint pressure is 1,350–1,700 pounds per square inch (95–120 kg/cm²) through a hose 25 feet (7·5 m) in length. Through a conventional spray system, a suitable paint pressure is 14–21 pounds per square inch (1·0–1·5 kg/cm²), and suitable air pressure 45–70 pounds per square inch (3–5 kg/cm²). For electrostatic painting the following application values are recommended as a guide: specific resistance of paint 500 kOhms, paint pressure 11·5 pounds per square inch (0·8 kg/cm²), high tension 120 kV, air pressure of air shower 21·5 pounds per square inch (1·5 kg/cm²).

Zinc cyclo and chlorinated rubber are used mostly for repainting and touching up. Both have good applicability and good adhesion. A stirrer must be used, and the paint circulated. High-pressure systems can be used, but with nozzles no smaller than 0·457 mm; the paint pressure should be 1,990 pounds per square inch (140 kg/cm²) or higher. These coatings give no trouble in conventional spray systems – suitable paint pressure 14–21 pounds per square inch (1·0–1·5 kg/cm²), air pressure 45–57 pounds per square inch (3–4 kg/cm²) – but are more difficult to spray than zinc epoxy, and at lower pressures may give a striped spray pattern. Conventional spraying from a pressure-feed tank and bottom outlet similarly provides no real difficulty – paint pressure 14–28 pounds per square inch (1–2 kg/cm²), air pressure 50–57 pounds per square inch (3·5–4·0 kg/cm²) – although the paint must be constantly stirred, and there is generally a certain amount of wear on spray gun parts.

In certain cases, then, organic zinc-rich coatings are suitable for continuous automated spraying.

Of the **inorganic zinc-rich coatings**, zinc ethyl acetate is suprememly weatherproof, resistant to water only 30 minutes after application; it also has better resistance to solvents than zinc epoxy, although the coating may not be as hard as those of the other organic types. Spraying properties of zinc ethyl acetate vary between different commercial products, but in general it can be used in high-pressure pumps, but only for a limited time and with considerable wear on the parts that come into contact with the paint. To reduce wear, it is possible to use hard chromium-plated gun parts. A so-called solvent cup must be used. The high-pressure nozzle should be no smaller than 0·553 mm in diameter. Using a 0·660-mm nozzle, with the paint circulated

and a hose length of 25 feet (7·5 m), paint pressure of 1,350 pounds per square inch (95 kg/cm²) and above should suffice. If the hose length is, say, 75 feet (22·5 m) in length, the corresponding minimum pressure is of course 2,700 pounds per square inch (190 kg/cm²).

Zinc sodium silicate yields a very hard surface that is highly resistant to abrasive wear. The surface does, however, vary somewhat according to the weather conditions prevailing at the time of application. Thick coats show some propensity to crack. But the coating is comparatively cheap. It is suitable only for conventional spray systems with strainer cloths and water-wetting of the spray-head during standstills. Stirring is essential. Suitable paint pressure is 21–28 pounds per square inch (1·5–2·0 kg/cm²), air pressure 43–64 pounds per square inch (3·0–4·5 kg/cm²).

The inorganic group of zinc-rich paints evidently cannot as yet offer as many application possibilities as the organic types, but future developments are expectantly awaited in the field.

Drying ovens

Heat is transferred in any of three ways –
    convection
    radiation
    conduction
– and all three of these ways are employed in industry for the drying of paint coatings.

● Convection. In convection heating, it is the air surrounding the article to be stoved that is heated, and it is therefore possible to stove articles of any size, shape or thickness. The heat source may be electricity, gas, steam or oil. The temperature in the oven is normally controlled by a thermostat so that heat and fluid consumption is proportionate to the amount of working surface in the oven to be dried.

Convection ovens are used primarily to dry surfaces in batches rather than as a continuous operation – although continuous operation in a convection oven is perfectly practicable. Batches take longer to stove, because of the inevitable temperature drop between batches, but the extra time involved (20–30 minutes a batch) is not as much as that involved with infra-red (radiative) ovens.

Electric convection ovens have several advantages over gas- or oil-fired ones: they are cleaner, the plant is simpler and demands less in the

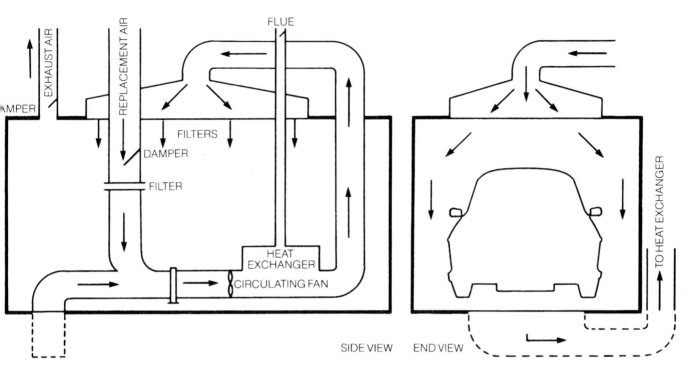

ABOVE *Diagram showing spray booth and stoving oven.*   BELOW *The basic operational principles of the plant.*

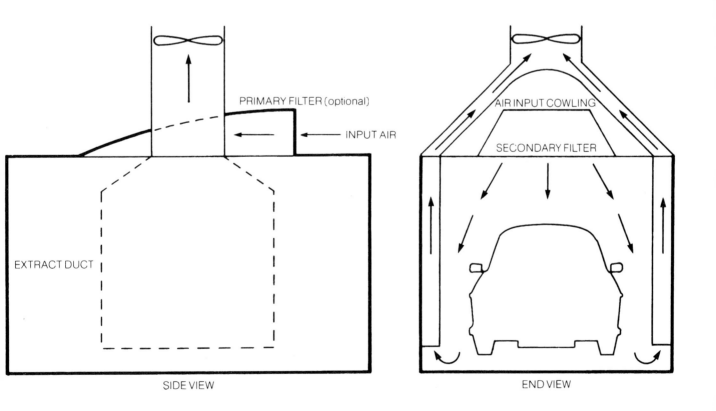

ABOVE *The refurbishment of railway coaches using a spraybake oven.*

LEFT *The refurbishment of an Aérospatiale AS.350 Ecureuil using a spraybake oven.*

ABOVE RIGHT *Railway stock gets the spraybake treatment at Brel in Derby, England.*

RIGHT *Spray booth using an infra-red drying arch.*

way of maintenance – and if anything goes wrong, cleaning or repair is less expensive.

● Radiation. Radiation heating for stoving painted work surfaces involves the use of infra-red emission directed from a substance heated by gas or electricity via suitably-shaped reflectors on to the work surfaces themselves. The reflectors are of a metal specifically chosen for its ability to reflect the radiation. The method generates considerable heat in the paint film; any heat that passes through to the underlying metal is in any case passed back to the paint film by conduction.

Some manufacturers use carbon filament lamps via internal reflectors to irradiate and dry repairs to car bodies finished in synthetic enamel. The radiative heat is generated by a range of special electric lamps housed in a suitable battery frame: bulbs may be anything from 250-watt to 400-watt in power. Radiation begins the instant that the lamps are switched on.

● Conduction. Conduction is the movement of heat along a solid from the hot end towards the cold end by a process of molecular vibration. Metals are in general very good conductors. In stoving ovens, conduction is usually a secondary means of heating a painted work surface.

● Indirect heat. In relation to stoving ovens, indirect heat refers mostly to an oil-fired type. The actual heating chamber incorporates a heat exchanger by which pure air only is circulated in the oven and the products of oil combustion do not enter the stoving zone.

The system has low thermal efficiency. Moreover, the working life of the heat exchanger is short in comparison with that of the oven.

● Direct heat. In relation to stoving ovens, direct heat refers mostly to a box-type oven in which articles are dried by convection in air heated by gas or electricity. Hot air is heated in a special chamber and then pumped through by a centrifugal fan into the oven. Air returned from the oven is split: some goes off as exhaust to the atmosphere via a damp stack, liberating some of the stoving fumes; the rest is heated once again and is recirculated.

The products of combustion are in this case circulated through the oven together with the hot air. In a well designed, direct-fired, forced-draught oven the paint film is unaffected by these products.

The low-bake oven

In vehicular finishing and refinishing, low-bake ovens are the general requirement. The complexity of the various drying processes in paint films, especially in combination, may demand a certain amount of experience in determining the amount of time that any specific work surface needs in the oven. Low-bake materials that dry by a combination of evaporation, polymerization and oxidation, for example, require slightly higher temperatures and slightly longer schedules. An important factor to remember when designing a low-bake oven, or when scheduling the flow of work through a low-bake oven, is that when a cold, painted car is wheeled into a hot oven some time elapses before the surface reaches the surrounding temperature.

Thermohardening or heat-curing coatings – coatings that dry without a chemical catalyst – have a critical minimum temperature below which curing is very slow. Above this minimum, on the other hand, the rate of reaction of a stoving finish is in general doubled with every 10°C (18°F) that the temperature rises. Stoving increases the size of the molecules of the medium by polymerization, while the evaporation of solvents (as well as the drying of other constituents) is vastly accelerated.

In the typical low-bake oven, many of these processes take place simultaneously – although the evaporation of the solvent is the dominant one.

DEFECTS THAT OCCUR AFTER PAINT APPLICATION

Post-application problems and answers (in alphabetical order)

For defects that arise within a paint film during application, or because of what occurs during the application, see the section earlier in this chapter entitled **Defects that occur during paint application**, page 120.

Alligator skin The surface cracks into coarse segments that together look like the pattern on an alligator's back. See also Checking.

Possible causes:
second coat applied before first dry
paint too thick
solvent evaporating too rapidly
use of cheap or incorrect thinner

Remedies: Flat the area thoroughly with abrasive paper until all traces of the defect have been

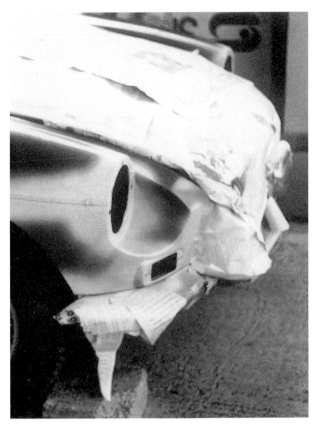

Is it clean? The masking on this MGB looks a little rudimentary; better to take off the bumper.

***Blisters** It happens to the best of us: practically all paint films are permeable to water vapour.*

eliminated, and then respray. Very careful cleaning and examination of the surface is essential to determine when all the traces have genuinely been removed.

An old surface exhibiting the defect can similarly be mechanically sanded down below the level of the defect before respraying, but it is better in this case to strip to bare metal and repaint.

Blisters (many) Even the best paint films are permeable to water vapour. When vapour penetrates the film it may set up forces sufficient to weaken the adhesion between the various coats, or to weaken the adhesion of the whole paint structure to the underlying metal. As a result, blisters containing water may form. But blistering may also be caused by contamination during the refinishing process or from failure to remove contaminants already present at that time. The source of contamination of this kind is sometimes easily identifiable, for the blistering may

follow the pattern of the contaminant – for example, fingerprints or wiping marks.

Possible causes:
  insufficient undercoat
  insufficient topcoat
  use of cheap or incorrect thinner
  use of inappropriate application method
  exposure to wet weather/humidity too early
  long exposure to wet, humid weather
  air leak in paint spray passages
  oil or water in compressed air
  paint atomization too fine
  work surface contaminated before painting
  insufficient cleaning/degreasing of surface
  handmarks on surface before topcoat
application
  overlarge temperature difference between
paint and work surface
  corrosion
Remedies: Flat thoroughly with abrasive paper

Blister (single or few) The presence of metal deterioration through corrosion.

Bronzing A problem with certain blue, maroon and black pigments.

until all signs of blistering have been removed – so that if blistering is confined to the topcoat, only that layer need be removed.

However, there are two dangers with this remedy. First: residues from the flatting process may themselves fill the bases of the blisters so that the blistered surface is not entirely removed, although it may seem to have been. Second: moisture within the blister may already have damaged underlying paintwork or metal.

The only certain cure is to strip to the bare metal, use a phoshoric acid metal cleaner in conjunction with steel wool, and repaint.

Blisters (single or few) The presence of a solitary blister or a group of blisters of varying sizes on the tops of a vehicle's wings or above headlight surrounds is usually indicative of metal deterioration through corrosion from the underside.

Probable cause:

    minute holes in the metal on the underside
Remedies: Temporary relief may be obtained by filling, stopping, and repainting. But failure may recur fairly soon. The only secure method is to replace the metal, give underbody protection with underseal, and repaint.

Bronzing A problem with certain blue, maroon and black pigments, by which a loosely adhering pigment layer in the surface is slightly different in colour from the original paint and imparts a metallic sheen.
Possible causes:
    with some pigments, may be unavoidable
    recommended mixing formula not followed
    hot-spraying of some reds or maroons
Remedies: In minor cases light hand polishing with a mild liquid polish should remove the bronze. Frequent washing and an occasional polish thereafter will maintain a good appearance.

In severe cases, wet-flat the colour, then respray.

Chalking, Chalkiness The ultimate cause is oxidation of the surface, the texture may be rather powdery.

Chalking, chalkiness Dulling of the gloss at an area where the colour also lightens and the texture may be rather powdery. The ultimate cause is oxidation of the paint film, leading to degradation of the surface. Possible causes:

    long exposure to sun and weather changes
    over-rapid oxidation due to application method
    over-rapid oxidation due to inappropriate paint

Remedies: Minor chalking may be removed by light polishing, which should also restore the gloss. More severe chalking requires polishing with a polishing compound.

Checking Fine cracking on the surface of the film, particularly if evident after a sudden and severe temperature change. Clear varnishes are more susceptible than paint to this kind of defect, known also as 'crazing' and 'crow-footing'. Alligator skin (or 'alligatoring' – see above) is a coarser form of the same defect. Ageing and weathering of all painted surfaces increase the likelihood of the defect's appearance.
Possible causes:

    use of cheap or incorrect additives to improve
      gloss or drying rate
    excess of clear varnish over colour coat
    insufficiency of clear varnish over colour coat
    application of refinish over already crazed coat
    excessive overall paint-layer structure
      (magnifying normal stress patterns)

Remedies: Flat the area thoroughly with abrasive paper until all traces of the defect have been eliminated, and then respray. Very careful cleaning and examination of the surface is essential to determine when all the traces have genuinely been removed.

An old surface exhibiting the defect can similarly be mechanically sanded down below the level of the defect before respraying, but it is better in this case to strip to bare metal and repaint.

In relation to an excessive overall paint-layer structure, a recommended guideline is that colour film thickness should not exceed 3 thousandths of an inch (75 microns), and the total film thickness, including the original and refinish paints, should not exceed 12 thousandths of an inch (300 microns).

Colour change Continuous exposure to sunlight inevitably causes a slight change from the original colour of any paint over time. This problem becomes a defect only when the change is more than slight.
Possible causes:

    recommended mixing formula not followed
    surface staining (yellowing) due to traffic fumes
    surface staining due to atmospheric chemicals
      (acid rain, industrial fallout, smog, etc.)

Remedies: The remedy depends on the cause, but there are only two possible courses of action. First use rubbing compound or polishing compound on a test area. If the colour is restored (as it may well be if traffic fumes are to blame), rub or polish the whole affected area. If the test area remains discoloured, wet-flat the colour coat, and respray.

Corrosion See Rusting.

Cracking A defect that extends below the colour coat, and is almost always the result of carelessness.
Probable cause:

    painting over an earlier defect, such as blistering

Remedy: Strip to the bare metal, use a phosphoric

Cracking A defect that extends below the colour coat i.e. painting over an earlier defect such as blistering.

Flaking Flakes of the topcoat and perhaps deeper layers erode away from the surface.

acid metal cleaner, and repaint.

Crazing See Checking.

Crocodiling See Alligator skin

Crow-footing See Checking.

Flaking Flakes of the topcoat and perhaps deeper layers erode away from the surface.
Probable cause:
    atmospheric attack at a point where one coat
      overlies an earlier, undetected defect in a
      previous coat or in the metal base
Remedy: Strip to the bare metal, use a phosphoric acid metal cleaner in conjunction with steel wool, and repaint.

Gloss low See Blisters (many), Checking, or (earlier in this chapter within the section **Defects that occur**

during paint application, page 131) Sinkage.

Peeling Peeling is a term that describes the after-effects of poor adhesion, when either the whole paint-layer structure or perhaps the colour coat can be readily detached in large strips.
See Adhesion poor, in the section **Defects that occur during paint application**, page 121.

Rusting, corrosion The ultimate cause is of course water reaching the underlying metal through breaks in the paint film.
Possible immediate causes:
    external injury to the paint film or paint-layer
      structure (especially if effected at a time during
      winter when roads have been dressed with salt)
    failure to remove rust completely before
      refinishing
    contamination of the metal surface before paint is
      applied (especially with grease or fingermarks)

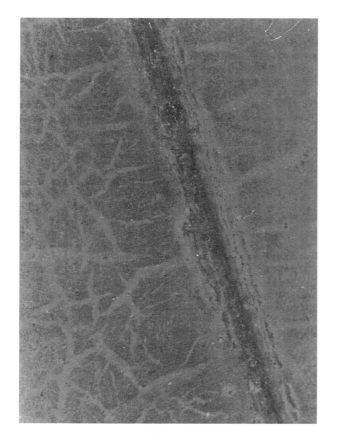

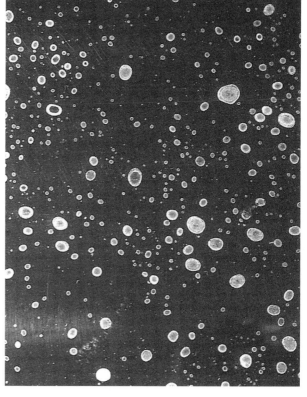

Rusting, Corrosion *The ultimate cause is water reaching the metal through breaks in the paint film.*

delay in painting after use of phosphoric acid metal cleaner

Remedy: Strip to the bare metal, disc-sand the affected areas to give a clean, bright surface, use a phosphoric acid metal cleaner and conditioner, and repaint.

Water-marking When a drop of water evaporates from a painted surface, the outline of the drop may still be seen and will not disappear on rubbing. Cause:

disturbance of the surface of the paint film

Water-Marking *This is a disturbance of the surface of paint film and is caused by drops of water.*

Remedies: If repeated polishing with a polishing compound fails to remove the outline or outlines, wet-flat the affected panels, and respray, using a rapid-drying thinner and allowing some 30 minutes in a suitably warm spray booth. After applying the final
finish coat, allow 36 hours' drying time before putting the vehicle into service, and arrange for the vehicle to be returned for buffing and polishing some two or three weeks later.

Wrinkling See Shrivel in the section **Defects that occur during paint application**, page 130.

4 · USING PRIMERS AND FINISHES

PRIMERS

There are many types of primers, some made specifically to overlie a certain material (wood primer, glass-fibre primer), some made conversely to key in colour coats above (metal primer surfacers), and some made in order to add protective properties that later coats might not have (rust-inhibitive primers for iron and steel).

A number of primers contain lead, especially white or red lead. The use of these is governed in England and Wales by the **Lead Paint Regulations Act, 1926** (and in other countries by similar regulations), which provides for the health and safety of all who handle such potentially toxic and injurious materials.

Primers for metals

● Oil-based primers. Zinc chromate is the general purpose metal primer. Very quick-drying, it also has rust-inhibitive properties when applied to iron or steel, and it is even more commonly applied to aluminium. It is available in its natural colour – a dull greenish yellow – or as red oxide or greyish green.

Red lead is used when application has to be by brush. It is slow-drying and the surface may form cord-like filaments – but if it doesn't, it is very hard and durable when finally dry.

Calcium plumbate has much better flow characteristics and a shorter drying time than red lead. It is the only primer that will adhere to galvanised steel that has not been pretreated.

● Cellulose-based materials. Fast-drying products, cellulose-based primer, primer-filler and primer-surfacer are applied to the bare metal or over sound

cellulose or stove-enamelled finishes. They must not under any circumstances be applied over air-drying oil-based paints, or cracking or lifting will undoubtedly occur.

● Two-pack primers – self-etch. Self-etch primer is suitable for all metals. The etching primer is mixed with an equal volume of spray activator, and allowed to stand for 10 minutes before use. The pot life thereafter is about 8 hours at normal temperatures. If used after this period the mixture has inferior adhesion and considerably reduced corrosion-resistance. Adhesion is also impaired if unduly heavy coats are applied. Spraying viscosity should be between 20 and 25 seconds in the BS/B4 flow cup at room temperature. Any viscosity adjustment should be made with an appropriate thinner. On no account should extra spray activator be added to adjust consistency.

The major constituents are zinc tetroxychromate in a solution of polyvinyl butral, and an alcoholic solution of phosphoric acid. Under good conditions a self-etch primer dries in 15–30 minutes.

Several high-build two-pack etch primers are available for use on road transport vehicles and containers.

● Two-pack primers – epoxy finish. Various epoxy finish primers are available. Selection is according to requirements and/or the surface to be coated. Most common are those suitable for fibreglass and metals where anti-corrosive properties are significant, for fibreglass and metals where anti-corrosive properties are not significant, and for steel only (with added zinc to give extra cathodic corrosion-resistance).

In every case the method is to mix 30 minutes before use in the ratio of two or three parts (as directed) of primer to one part of curing agent. For spraying, a very small amount of an appropriate thinner may be added, if really necessary. Normal epoxy primers should be allowed 30 minutes to dry before finishing coats are applied; zinc-rich primers require 3 to 4 hours.

Primers for wood
● Lead-based primers. Application of lead-based primers is by brush only. The primers – most often a mixture of white and red lead (and called pink primer) – are slow-drying but very durable. And poisonous.
● Oil-based primers. These primers are generally a mixture of oil and resin. Application is by any method. They are available in a range of colours.
● Other wood primers. Emulsion primers are very quick-drying, but tend to form cord-like filaments when brushed. Brushes and spray guns must be thoroughly washed out with water after use.

Aluminium wood primer, applied by brush, is very moisture-resistant and is particularly useful on resinous wood.

Primers for glass-fibre
Synthetic resin-based primers are ideally suited for use on glass-fibre surfaces. At least two coats are recommended. The first coat should be brushed to ensure penetration into pinholes and cracks.

FINISHES AND REFINISHES

Finishes used by motor manufacturers
The main motor manufacturing companies use four types of topcoat:

    acrylic lacquer (thermoplastic acrylic)
    high-bake synthetic enamel
    high-bake acrylic enamel (thermosetting acrylic)
    two-pack urethane acrylic enamel

By definition, any paint that hardens by chemical reaction is an enamel.
● Acrylic lacquer. Acrylic lacquers are used both for ordinary colours and for metallic finishes. They dry and harden by means of solvent evaporation only, which means they will air-dry, but they are usually stoved at between 150°C (302°F) and 160°C (320°F), at which temperatures the thermoplastic paint reflows, resulting in a high gloss. The reflowing

of the paint does not represent any kind of chemical change: the paint remains soluble in lacquer solvents, and when recoated with itself it is softened by the solvents of the overlying coat. The two coatings then fuse into one and are irretrievably bonded together. This property lends itself to spot repairs.

Acrylic lacquer is also known as thermoplastic acrylic (TPA).
● High-bake synthetic enamel. High-bake synthetic enamel is used for ordinary colours only. Despite its excellent filling properties, toughness and high gloss, it is unsuitable for metallic finishes because its metallic control and gloss retention are inferior to those of acrylic-based paints. It dries first by solvent evaporation and then hardens by chemical reaction which occurs at a temperature of 130°C (266°F) on a baking schedule of 30 minutes. When dry, the surface is resistant to solvents – any repair paint applied does not fuse in but just lies there, and can be wiped off (while still wet) without any effect on the finish.

To repair a defective surface on a high-bake enamel finish with the same original finish, a catalyst is added to the paint. This reduces the minimum stoving temperature to 90°–100°C (194°–212°F).
● High-bake acrylic enamel. Thermosetting acrylic (TSA) is used for ordinary colours and for metallic finishes. Otherwise in properties and application it is virtually identical with the high-bake synthetic enamels. It too dries first by solvent evaporation and then hardens by chemical reaction which occurs at a temperature of 130°C (266°F) on a baking schedule of 30 minutes. When dry, the surface is resistant to solvents – any repair paint applied does not fuse in but just lies there, and can be wiped off (while still wet) without any effect on the finish.

To repair a defective surface on a high-bake enamel finish with the same original finish, a catalyst is added to the paint. This reduces the minimum stoving temperature to 90°–100°C (194°–212°F).
● Urethane acrylic enamel. Urethane acrylic enamels dry and harden in much the same way as high-bake enamels do. The resultant surfaces have similar characteristics of durability and toughness. The reaction time is overnight at 20°C (68°F) or following stoving schedules ranging from 30 minutes at 60°C (140°F) to 15 minutes at 80°C (176°F). No catalyst is required.

Some motor manufacturers use urethane acrylic enamels for in-line repairs on defects in high-bake finishes.

Refinish paints

Refinish paints may also be classified in four groups according to the methods by which they dry:

    lacquers
    oil- and synthetic resin-based paints
    low-bake enamels
    two-pack paints

Within these groups the types most in use as refinish topcoats by small motor vehicle assembly plants and small specialist car manufacturers are:

    nitrocellulose lacquer
    air-drying acrylic lacquer
    air-drying synthetic enamel
    low-bake enamel
    two-pack acrylic enamel

● Lacquer paints. Lacquers dry through the evaporation of solvents: no chemical change is involved. They therefore have a high solvent content and dry rapidly at first.

The group includes cellulose- and acrylic-based car-repair paints, cellulose- and acrylic-based quick-drying primers, primer-fillers and sealers, and cellulose-based stoppers.

Nitrocellulose lacquers are a blend of nitrocellulose and synthetic resins. The nitrocellulose content gives rapid drying, the synthetic resins the high-build gloss-from-the-gun colour and gloss retention. The initial rate of drying is extremely rapid, but some solvent is retained for a longer period. For full hardness, around 16 hours' drying time is usually needed. Or the lacquers may be force-dried or low-baked at temperatures of up to 70°C (158°F). Adequate flash-off time must be allowed to avoid 'popping'.

● Oil- and synthetic resin-based paints. In these paints drying is initially by evaporation of solvent, but final hardening is due to chemical changes in the paint vehicle caused by the uptake of oxygen. While these changes are taking place, the paint vehicle gradually becomes less soluble in its own solvent, and there is a critical period during which lifting or shrivel will occur if another coat is applied.

The paints are characterized by high content of solids and a longer surface drying time than that of lacquers.

● Low-bake enamels. Low-bake enamels do not dry in air, they need a baking temperature of 80°C (176°F) or more to harden fully. Drying is initially by solvent evaporation, but final through-hardening is dependent upon a chemical reaction between two components of the paint vehicle. This reaction can take place only in a time period of 30 minutes once the appropriate temperature has been reached.

Low-bake enamels also have a high content of solids.

Once popular in continental Europe, low-bake enamels have largely been superseded by other paints that have shorter stoving schedules and do not require such high temperatures.

● Two-pack paints. When the two components of these paints are mixed together, a chemical reaction takes place that causes the paint vehicle to harden. A potential drawback is the limited pot life, the working time once the two constituent parts have been mixed.

Two-pack paints are characterized by a high content of solids and a low content of solvents: some are even solvent-free.

Typical of the group are two-pack polyurethane finishes, two-pack urethane acrylic finishes, two-pack spray primers and fillers, and polyester stoppers and spraying fillers with peroxide catalysts.

Metallic finishes

Metallic finishes were used in Britain on a small scale during the 1930s but quickly became unpopular because of the difficulty of matching an existing finish when repairs were necessary. They were later reintroduced on an enormous scale under the influence of the market in the United States.

That market was also responsible for the many and various descriptions of metallic finishes – 'polychromatic', 'opalescent' and even 'metallescent', among others – but the word 'metallic' remains the most apposite, in that metallic finishes contain a reflective metal or alloy pigment, and considerably less in the way of pigment altogether than ordinary finishes.

Metal pigments most in use include copper alloys, lead, zinc, aluminium and bronze.

The metallization of a lacquer is achieved by including in it minute flakes of polished aluminium. The paint manufacturer uses aluminium in a non-leafing form, as either powder or paste. This metallic content imparts a reflective quality to the lacquer. Colour variations are obtained by the addition of tinting pigments carefully selected for transparency or opacity.

● Colour matching. Metallic finishes cause much more trouble than solid colours when it comes to matching a colour. That is primarily because metallic finishes actually present more than one colour to the viewer – the face colour (or face tone), which is the

Metallic finishes: as the light penetrates the paint film, it is reflected back at a similar angle by aluminium flakes which have aligned parallel to the paint surface, when the coat is thin and has dried quickly.

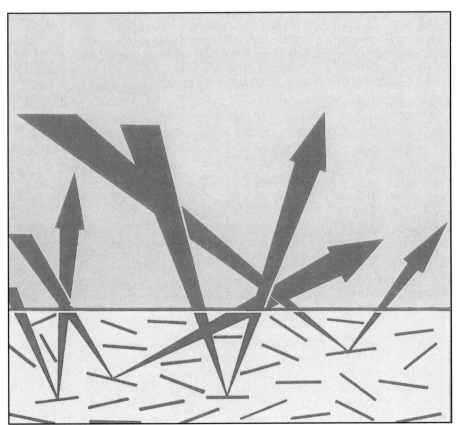

The light penetrating the paint film is reflected back by the flakes at various angles when a thicker, slower drying coat is applied. There will be less colour difference between the face and the side tones.

The light falling on a solid finish is diffused or scattered by the pigment particles, so that the colour will appear the same from any angle.

colour presented when the viewer sees it face on, and the side colour (or side or 'flip' tone), which is the slightly darker colour presented when the viewer is to one side and the amount of reflected light from the metal is therefore less.

Spraying methods and conditions that produce thin coats which dry rapidly favour an orientation of the aluminium flakes parallel to the paint film surface, so yielding the greatest difference between face and side tones: a silvery face tone, and a dark side tone. Thick, slower-drying coats conversely allow the aluminium flakes more movement, and therefore a more random orientation in the paint film, yielding less difference between face and side tones.

Quick-drying lacquers give greater control over face and side tones than slower-drying synthetics because of the wider range of application viscosities and film thicknesses at which lacquer can be sprayed while yet maintaining control over the aluminium orientation.

Another disadvantage is that both the original body colour and the refinish colour are very much influenced by the conditions under which they are applied. The refinisher has thus to reproduce the conditions of the initial application in order to match a metallic colour exactly.

Tinting may sometimes be required to colour match a colour on an older vehicle, or to tint a standard colour to match a 'special'. When tinting metallic colours, it is vital to remember that the tinting colours can affect either face or side tones, or both. It is necessary to discern precisely what colour change is required in both face and side tones. Tinting guides produced by the paint manufacturers supply detailed information that should help selection.

Tinters Affecting Mainly Face Tone

aluminium

Tinters Affecting Mainly Side Tone

oxide pigments
    white

Tinters Affecting Face and Side Tones

permanent blue
    permanent green
    permanent yellow
    red dyestuff pigments
    maroon dyestuff pigments
    black

Factors That Affect the Colour of Metallic Finishes

	colour lightens	*colour darkens*
Paintshop conditions		
temperature	warm, warming	cool, cooling
humidity	low	high
air movement	increase	reduce
Spray gun settings		
fluid nozzle	small	large
needle control	close up	open out
atomization	fine	coarse
fan width	broad	narrow
air pressure	high	low
Thinner		
fast-/slow-acting	fast	slow
effect	low viscosity	higher viscosity
Spraying technique		
gun distance	away	close up
gun speed	fast	slow
flash time between coats	long	short

Colour identification and colour matching of motor vehicles should always be carried out in natural daylight (out of direct sunlight). In the factory refinish paints can be colour matched by using colour-matching lamps designed to reproduce natural daylight.

● One-coat, or single-layer, metallics. In these, both opacity and the metallic appearance are achieved by relatively large aluminium flake pigments. After building up the required film thickness, the correct application technique is chosen for the final coat so as to give the nearest possible match in colour to adjacent areas on the vehicle. The correct technique can be judged by spraying small flexible test panels of metal or card and, when they are dry, shaping them to the contour of the vehicle where the repair is to be made.

Spraying to a break or trim line enables slight colour differences to go undetected. More effective still is the technique of spraying to an edge where the angle of the panel changes (and the viewing colour also automatically is different). This can be accomplished by the careful application of strips of masking-tape.

● Basecoat and clear two-coat, or two-layer, metallics. The colours are applied in a dual process consisting of a high-opacity basecoat followed, wet-on-wet, by a clear coat. The whole is cured in a single baking operation. This system gives maximum contrast between face and side tones, combined with high gloss – a feature not always possible with single-layer metallics.

Because the basecoat is a high-opacity paint, full-strength tinters should be used to adjust colour. The final coloration is visible only after application of the clear coat (which greatly changes the colour of the basecoat). Further applications of clear will again change the final colour. A guide to the final colour match may be obtained by first wetting up a suitable area of the basecoat with a fade-out thinner.

Alternatively, when applying metallic colour on a local repair, match it to a slightly lighter shade than the original finish on the vehicle, then apply two very thin coats of clear, the second faded out into the surrounding colour. This should produce a very close match indeed.

Colour mixing in the refinish shop

There are many advantages in mixing one's own colours. The main ones are instant availability of colour required, and in exact quantities, and the facility for accurate tinting where this may be necessary.

155

The gravimetric paint mixing scale with a sartorius electronic balance which is governed by the low flash regulations.

There are two main types of mixing systems: the gravimetric system and the volumetric system. In Europe, the more popular is the gravimetric system.

Characteristics of the Gravimetric and Volumetric Mixing Systems

Reading the formula and selecting the constituents
Gravimetric:
    formula displayed on microfilm/microfiche
Volumetric:
    formula displayed on microfilm/microfiche

Selecting the container
Gravimetric:
    paint poured into a container on a balance: no special container required

Volumetric:
    paint poured into container until level reaches preset marker, or until pneumatic warning device gives audible notification; container must have flat bottom and be of uniform cross-section along its length (a dented container must never be used)

Tareing or zeroing
Gravimetric:
    simple mechanical operation (although not required on most electronic balances)
Volumetric:
    simple mechanical operation (although not required on most electronic balances)

Stirring
Gravimetric:
    separate machines with mixing heads that fit on standard 2·5-litre and 1-litre cans; these heads

easily removed for hand stirring

Volumetric:

    separate machines with mixing heads that fit on standard cans, as above

Reaching the end-point for each constituent

Gravimetric:

    operator watches balance needle while pouring; skill in judging when to stop comes with experience; modern electronic balances are designed to make this operation easier

Volumetric:

    operator watches paint level, and stops when this reaches preset marker (this can be problematical if the marker is down inside a small can), or when pneumatic gauge gives audible notification

Whichever system is chosen, the installation of the equipment anywhere in Britain and in most other countries is strictly regulated by law. Equipment suppliers and installing engineers can advise in detail on safety and health precautions, but the installation should also be sanctioned by the local fire and factory inspectors.

The principles of mixing

The growing number of colour variations that have appeared in recent years (particularly in view of the growing popularity of metallic finishes) make the mixing scheme an invaluable means of overcoming colour-matching difficulties.

But there are some basic guidelines about the use of a mixing scheme:

1 All colour information must be kept up to date and in a system that is highly accessible for utilization.

2 The basic constituents must be thoroughly hand stirred before being placed on the stirring machine. Shaking the can or putting it in an agitator is not sufficient.

3 The scales/balance must be regularly serviced.

4 The equipment must be kept spotlessly clean. In particular, the pouring spouts of the stirring heads should be wiped clean after every pour to prevent build-up of paint residues

5 The mixing area should not be subjected to large variations in temperature: highs and lows can not only affect the performance of the equipment but may have a temporary effect on the viscosity of the paint. The mixing room might preferably be sited within the outer walls of a building, for example, where wide fluctuations in air temperature are less likely.

Where more than one topcoat is available, it is important to select the correct microfiche formula – and to ensure that it is the latest fiche available.

Before mixing, the stirring machine should be run for the correct period: 15 minutes in the morning, 10 minutes in the afternoon.

Zeroing or tareing of measuring equipment must be carried out with extreme care.

Virtually all mixing formulas indicate accumulated quantity values, eliminating the need for any calculations while mixing. In the case of overshooting the required amount of paint with any but the first constituent in the formula, do not attempt to adjust the amount poured. A fresh mix must be started.

Covering the scale pan with masking paper removes the need for cleaning off an occasional spillage.

When replacing an empty basic with a new one, fit the stirring head so that the spout is at the back of the can. This ensures that any paint which drips down the side of the can from the spout does not obscure the colour reference number.

Keep a supply of clean rags, a can of cleaning solvent, a paint brush, and some can openers by the mixing scheme.

OPERATIONAL SEQUENCES FOR VEHICLE REFINISHING

ROLLS-ROYCE

For fuller understanding of professional refinishing, it makes sense to look at the best. Though this section will not be of direct relevance to the individual, there are some general lessons to be drawn – not least about the importance of preparation – and the author hopes that the reader will find it of academic interest.

There have been periodical changes of a fundamental character both in formulation and application over the last 70 automotive years, from brush to spray application.

The industry has of course been revolutionised by computerised equipment and technology. Nevertheless, the computer, the memory bank, is only as good as the information fed into it.

Throughout manufacture the keyword is craftsmanship, a rare commodity and something that cannot and must not be hurried. Craftsmanship and attention to detail, the honing to perfection of every component have been a hallmark of Rolls-Royce and Bentley Products stretching back over eight decades. The same patience and care are as much in evidence today as ever.

In an age of robots, mass production and cheap synthetic substitutes, the time-honoured talents of craftsmen working with nature's finest materials, shine like a beacon.

Rolls-Royce and Bentley motor cars are built by a company employing a higher proportion of specialist craftsmen than any other motor manufacturer in the world, and where skills and attitudes towards quality are handed down from generation to generation. To sit inside a Rolls-Royce or a Bentley is a memorable experience, with rich walnut veneer from Italy, leather from Scandinavia, and carpets and cloths of pure wool, all brought together in perfect harmony.

Working with leather is part of the traditional craft of the coachbuilder. A Rolls-Royce or Bentley contains approximately 260 sq ft of the finest quality Connolly leather, hand-sewn and hand-tailored by one of more than 40 skilled coach trimmers.

The creation of the walnut veneer for the facia and door trims can take days. Cut by hand and matched by eye, the whorls and configurations are stopped out and stained, inspected, primed and then dried for 60 hours. Then they are sprayed with three coats of tough polyester lacquer, air dried for three days, hand-flatted, polished and finally inspected again.

Minor natural imperfections in the walnut veneers are corrected before the final application of lacquer and polishing. Into this interior veneer, sterling silver is carefully inlayed by hand into laser cut grooves.

Much the same meticulous attention to detail as paid to the passenger compartment is also lavished on the paintwork, and at times the quest for perfection can border on the obsessive.

The naked body shell can spend up to four days being cleaned, inspected, measured, and even brushed with wire wool. When the inspectors are satisfied with the condition of the body it is cleaned – not once, but five times.

After intensive anti-corrosion treatment and a three-stage priming operation, comes the actual painting. Several double coats of colour are hand sprayed on to the body. They are then stoved for one hour in an oven at 180°F and then rubbed down by hand. After washing, rinsing and degreasing, two more double coats of paint are applied.

The first applied coat of acid etch primer prepares the surface of the body for the primer and colour coats.

Rolls-Royce have recently completed a new £10 million paint plant at their Crewe headquarters. It is some 6600 sq ft, adjacent to the existing paint plant.

As their Chief Executive Peter Wood pointed out, the new plant would allow Rolls-Royce to combine the latest advances in finishing technology with traditional skills used in the manufacture of their cars.

The paint process of Rolls-Royce Motor Cars

Bodies-in-white are manually positioned at floor level in the body shop beneath the hoist unit, which is engaged by the operator into the roof of the body. He then initiates the automatic cycle which raises the body to roof level and lowers it on the waiting carrier on the 'inverted power and free' (IPF) conveyor. The hoist then automatically disengages and returns to its hover position ready for the next body.

Meanwhile, the carrier is released and the IPF transports it to the paint plant through the enclosed body transfer tunnel. The delivery conveyor is capable of storing 22 bodies, to act as a buffer between body and paint shop. The tunnel can be heated in the winter to guard against corrosion due to condensation.

The body ends its journey on the IPF adjacent to the pre-clean area, which is the start of the paint shop process. It is picked up by the overhead transporter system, undergoing pre-clean operations, both before and after this operation.

From here on, the pre-treatment process is fully automatic under the control of the central computer system, and in each zone under the specific control of the on-board computer mounted on each transporter unit. These on-board computers ensure that the body goes through the correct sequence of tilting, lowering and raising in each zone.

The first zone of the pre-treatment process is the alkali stage, designed for both spraying and full immersion of the body with hot alkali solution to

The magnificent 1907 Rolls-Royce Silver Ghost.

remove grease and dirt from the body.

Following a drain period over the alkali tank, the body enters the second zone of the pre-treatment process. This is a rinse zone which, again by a combination of spray and dip, removes the alkali chemical from the body.

The third zone is a spray rinse containing a titanium conditioner additive designed to improve the phosphate coating quality which is to follow in the next zone, and to ensure that alkali solution is not carried forward.

The phosphate process is full immersion combined with sprays and has a twofold purpose. In converting the metal surface to a zinc phosphate, it provides a key for subsequent painting operations, and also affords protection to prevent underpaint corrosion spreading should the paint film be damaged through to the metal. From phosphating, the body enters the next rinse zone where it is fully immersed and sprayed.

Following a drain period, the body enters the final spray rinse zone of the pre-treatment plant – the chromate and demineralised water rinse zone. A chromate solution is first sprayed onto the body and allowed to drain away. Diverter valves then change over, allowing demineralised water to be sprayed over the body to ensure that no chromate solution is carried on to subsequent stages.

The purpose of the chromate solution is to improve the previously-applied phosphate layer. It refines the crystal structure that has been created on the metal surface, ensuring that it is strong and adheres well, and consequently paint coats adhere strongly to it, and in turn to the base metal.

On leaving the pre-treatment plant, the body is tilted to remove excess liquid which might not be dried off in the oven and would otherwise be carried over its the Electroprimer paint dip tank. The body then enters the high-level dry-off oven where it is dried at a temperature of 115°C for 20 minutes.

From the oven, the body passes through two buffering stages which allow it to cool. These buffer stations, which occur throughout the process, are provided to ensure efficient operation, particularly when starting up in the morning and closing down in the evening, when it is necessary to ensure that no bodies remain in critical parts of the process such as the pre-treatment and electrocoat tanks.

The body next arrives on the fit-electric deck for electrical connection to be made using magnets attached to the body in preparation for cathodic dip painting. The body passes into the dip zone and is lowered into the electro paint. When fully immersed the current is switched on and ramped up over a period of about 40 seconds to full current. The body remains immersed in the paint for a period of four minutes, during which time it receives an even, all-over coat, with good penetration to box sections.

As it emerges from the paint tank, it receives a number of rinses. First is a spray of re-circulated ultra filtrate (U/F). The body then enters a dip rinse station where it is fully immersed in U/F solution. It is then sprayed with re-circulated U/F and indexes forward to a multiple spray rinse zone where it successively receives re-circulated U/F, re-circulated demineralised water and finally, as it exits this zone, clean demineralised water.

Following the rinse stage, the body is transferred from the overhead transporter unit back on to the main IPF conveyor. The body now moves into the electro-prime oven, where it remains for one hour at 185°C. The oven is designed so that the doors at either end cannot open simultaneously, thereby avoiding a through draught. In addition, a canopy is provided at each end to catch fumes where the doors open. Since electrophorectic paint produces rather heavy fumes when it is stoved, an incinerator is provided on the exhaust of this oven.

The body stands in an enclosure outside the oven to cool. Again buffering is provided following this stage. The body undergoes dry sanding and crack sealing operations before entering the first primer spray booth complex. Dust on the body is wiped off at a tack rag station using a varnish impregnated cloth. The next stage is to spray apply the primer paint. Just prior to the oven, a flash-off zone is provided to allow fast solvents to evaporate. An air replacement plant supplies heated and filtered air to the tack rag station, spray booth and flash-off area.

Water from the spray booths is collected in large underground recirculation tanks in the coagulation house. Chemicals in the water attack the paint particles to remove the stickiness from them and also encourage them to float.

Water is pumped from the recirculation tanks up to concentrator tanks, where a raft of paint gradually builds up on the water surface. Periodically the water level in these accumulator tanks is raised, allowing the raft to slide over a weir into a fabric bag where excess water drains back into the recirculation tank. The sludge is retained in the fabric bag and can be lifted out when full for disposal.

The paint plant's control room layout mimic with fault indication.

The automatic conveyor inverted power and free type system.

*A view of the high level storager prior to phosphating. The
(IPF) system.*

After priming, the body is stoved for one hour at 160°C. This oven is similar in construction to the electrocoat oven, having doors at each end with a canopy at the exit end.

On leaving the oven, the body stands to cool. At this time, grommet fitting, panel beating and inspection operations can be carried out. Dry sanding removes any nibs in the paint and ensures a smooth surface ready for the next coat of paint. Areas which have been sanded or repaired are spot-primed. Again, this facility comprises a tack-rag station, spray booth and flash-off area.

Paint application is followed by stoving at 160°C for one hour. The construction of the oven is similar to the first primer oven. A station is provided immediately after the oven to allow the body to be cooled, and for quick-fill operations to be performed if necessary. Dry sanding then takes place to remove excess filler and any defects in the paint film.

Buffer stations are provided for smooth operation of these processes, both at the start and finish. A deck for crack seal and fitting of sound deadener pads follows.

As in the previous spray booth complexes, the second primer spray booth system provides a tack-rag area, a spray zone and a flash-off. Stoving of the second primer is at 130°C.

At this point the body is picked up by the overhead system to transport it through the underseal operations. On the first station, grommets are inserted and sill boards are fitted to the body. A deck is provided for crack sealing of the underfloor.

On entering the underseal enclosure, masking is applied to prevent overspray contaminating areas where it is not required. Underseal is then applied. The next station allows the sill boards to be removed and transfer of the body back to the IPF conveyor. A further buffer station follows.

A dry sand enclosure prepares the body for colour application.

The main colour booth complex comprises tack-rag facility for removal of dust, spraying stations and flash-off. In this booth there are three spraying stations, although if clear-over-base is introduced in the future, there will be two spraying stations with an intermediate flash-off station.

The body is then stoved for one hour at a maximum temperature of 180°C and is allowed to cool. At this point, the body undergoes the final operations including wax injection.

The body is unloaded from the IPF and transferred to a yellow trolley for despatch to the trim and final assembly operations, via the airlock vestibule designed to avoid dirt entering the paint shop by allowing only one door at a time to be open.

In addition to the main process equipment, there are a number of supporting facilities provided within the paint shop. The ancillary block is the largest. It houses the control room, administrative offices, laboratory, as well as maintenance, stores, compressor and transformer rectification equipment.

The paint mix room is located in the final paint department which has been modified to accommodate the new paint mix and distribution equipment to serve both the new paint shop and final paint. This provides for nine colour lines, two primer lines, and one solvent line.

A vacuum system has been provided for the removal of sanding dust from the dry sanding booths, and breathable air is supplied by new air compressors. The latter will also be used to supply final paint spraying operations, thereby making the new paint shop independent of the factory compressed air system.

Other supporting facilities include the demineralised water plant, and the sub-station at the corner of the existing engineering block feeding the new paint facility.

Anti-Corrosion Measures

Body Shells
Body shell structure in steel; those areas particularly vulnerable to corrosion in zinc-galvanised heavy-gauge steel. Doors, bonnet, boot lid in aluminium.

Metal to metal contact surfaces of all spot-welded joints painted with zinc-rich primer prior to assembly to inhibit corrosion.

Paint Shop Processes
The sequence of operations undertaken on body shells is:–
(i) Body shells cleaned and checked.
(ii) Six stage immersion and spray. Metal cleaning and pre-treatment process chemically converts surface of metal into non-metallic zone phosphates. This surface coating has corrosion inhibiting properties and greatly improves paint adhesion.

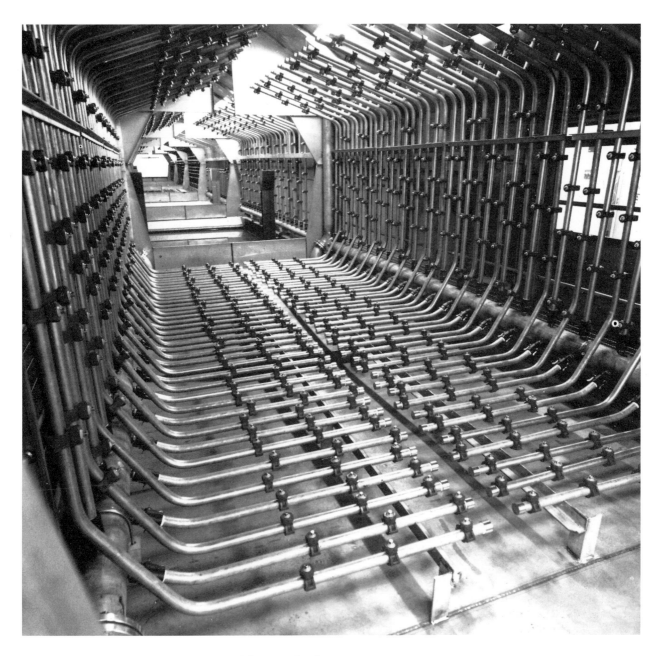

The pre-treatment tunnel for chromate and demineralised water rinsing after phosphating.

A body shell in electroprimer being 'dry sanded' to remove minor blemishes.

A body shell slowly emerging from the electroprimer dip tank.

(iii)   De-mineralised water spray and oven drying.
(iv)   Total immersion in water-borne cathodic electro-dip primer contained in 18,500 gallon tank (84,000 litres).
(v)   Twenty minutes stoving at 180°C (350°F).
(vi)   Thorough inspection and panel rectification.
(vii)   Body joints sealed with flexible plastisol compound.
(viii) Two coats of a polyester primer/surfacer applied by hand and stoved for twenty minutes at 160°C (320°F).
(ix)   Body flatted to eliminate any irregularities visible in the primer surface.
(x)   Another coat of polyester/polyurathene primer sealer applied by hand and stoved at 130°C (266°F) for 20 minutes.
(xi)   A coat of a water-based rubberised solution sound deadener/underseal applied.

ABOVE *An electroprimed body after leaving the electroprimer stoving oven on the (IPF) system.*

LEFT *Another automotive classic which undergoes many of the finishing processes described in this section – but the final effect is rather different. For the Lamborghini Countach, red was of course by far the most popular choice, with white second and yellow a distant third. (Photo: Chris Bennett)*

A car body leaving the underseal booth and about to be 'lowered' back onto the IPF conveyor.

(xii) Body sanded to eliminate any further paint blemishes.

(xiii) A coat of acrylic sealer and two colour coats of paint applied by hand and stoved for 60 minutes at 80°C (176°F).

(xiv) Wax injection of box section cavities.

After assembly of the motor car, the entire underbody surface and all fitted parts, which include brake pipes, painted items and machined faces, are coated with a wax-based anti-corrosion coating.

After Road Testing

(i) Underseal made good.

(ii) Entire underside sprayed with thixotropic black bituminous material forming fifteen thousandths of an inch thick.

(iii) Thorough inspection.

(iv) Two final colour coats of paint applied by hand and stoved at 80°C (176°F).

(v) Thorough inspection prior to polishing.

(vi) All painted surfaces polished.

(vii) Inspection of finished paintwork.

Sill Areas

The sill areas, excluding those on the Bentley Turbo R which are finished in body colour, are spray coated with an anti-stone chip coating which is a water based styrene butadiene copolymer. This forms a coating 0.006 inch thick and provides additional protection against flying stones.

Individual Components

(i) Sub-frames are fabricated from steel pressings and undergo similar phosphate and cathodic electroprimer processes as body shell. Interior surfaces are then sprayed with inhibiting oil before access holes are plugged with grommets.

(ii) Anti-corrosion protection is given to close tolerance ferrous parts by zinc cobalt plating; large components and pieces not required to be to such fine limits are protected by phosphating and black stove enamelled paint.

(iii) Components such as the brake actuator assembly, and the electric aerial mechanism, both of which are in vulnerable areas beneath the car, are protected by shields.

(iv) The dual exhaust system is austenitic stainless still with six austenitic stainless steel silencers. Resilient metal mounts ensure the system is free of stress.

Full system for top-quality car refinish

1 Remove as necessary bumpers, metal and plastic trim, badges, etc.

2 Wash the area to be painted, to remove dirt.

3 Clean with solvent-based water-miscible cleaner or mild detergent to remove contaminants.

4 Dry off and blow out seams and mouldings using compressed air at low pressure. Mask off as necessary. (It is not always necessary, however, to complete all the masking at one stage of the process.)

5 Remove paintwork from rusty edges by machine-sanding – or, if large areas are involved, use a chemical paint-stripper.

6 Feather-edge all damaged areas.

7 Sand down badly weathered or crazed paint until only sound finish remains.

8 Clean all bare metal with a phosphoric acid metal cleaner.

9 Apply two-pack polyester filler or stopper to damaged areas. Dry- or wet-flat to restore the body contours. Blow out seams and blow any dust from the surface. (The working time of the polyester stopper is only 5 minutes or so, so it is important to have the surface absolutely ready. It is best to mix enough for 3–4 minutes' working time.)

10 Wipe with a lint-free cloth and suitable spirit ('spirit wipe').

11 Apply primer to all bare metal areas, including any small cut-throughs. Pay particular attention to sills, doors and window frames. Etch primer is essential on aluminium, and has definite advantages on steel, promoting good adhesion and corrosion- and blister-resistance. But it is water-sensitive, and must be covered with a primer or primer-filler as soon as possible, especially in humid conditions when absorption of atmospheric moisture by the etch primer can lead to failure of the paint system.

12 Tack-rag wipe to remove dust and primer overspray.

13 Apply undercoat. Minor imperfections can be stopped up on the first coat with nitrocellulose stopper or nitrocellulose primer filler. After drying apply two further coats of primer surfacer. Or stop up on the last coat of synthetic primer surfacer after allowing the full recommended air-drying time or baking schedule.

14 Wet-flat using P600-grade abrasive paper and clean water. Clean and dry surface using sponge and wash-leather. Blow out seams and wipe up spatters.

15 Spot in any cut-through areas using the appropriate primer and primer filler. Allow to dry,

A phosphate body ready to leave the final spray zone of the pre-treatment plant.

and wet-flat to remove all dry spray using P600-grade abrasive paper. Clean and dry surface using sponge and wash-leather. Blow out seams and wipe up spatters.

16 Spirit wipe. (Some synthetic undercoats are sensitive to petrol. An alternative is a fifty-fifty blend of industrial methylated spirit and water.)

17 Tack-rag wipe.

18 Apply colour coats.

Certain lacquer systems require a flatting operation before the application of the final colour coat. This should be carried out using P800–P1200-grade abrasive paper and clean water. (If the finish causes clogging of the flatting paper, lubricate the paper with soap.)

19 Polish by hand or machine to remove any surface imperfections, and to improve the gloss of the lacquer.

20 Remove masking.

21 Replace bumpers, trim ,badges, etc.

22 Final polish, if necessary, using a liquid polish containing fine abrasive. (Never use wax polish on new paintwork.)

High-quality system using non-sand undercoat

1 to 13 As full system above.

14 Wet-flat using P320-grade abrasive paper and clean water. Clean and dry surface using sponge and wash-leather. Blow out seams and wipe up spatters. Alternatively, dry-flat with random-orbit sander, in which case the flatting paper should be of a grade equivalent to P320 wet or dry paper. Blow out seams and remove dust.

15 Spirit wipe.

16 Tack-rag wipe.

17 Apply non-sand undercoat.

In an air-drying system the non-sand undercoat must be allowed to dry before application of the colour coats. Minor denibbing may be carried out if necessary to remove dirt or insignificant imperfections. Then clean off, and tack-rag wipe.

In a low-bake system the colour coats may be applied wet-on-wet to the non-sand undercoat.

18 to 22 As full system above.

High-quality system using transparent fill-sealer

1 to 13 As full system above.

14 Wet-flat all filled areas with P400-grade abrasive paper and clean water. Clean and dry the surface using sponge and wash-leather, or dry-flat with random-orbit sander using flatting paper of a grade

equivalent to P400 wet or dry paper.

15 Scuff the original surface with ultrafine abrasive pad. Blow out seams and remove all dirt.

16 Spirit wipe, and then tack-rag wipe.

17 Apply transparent fill-sealer.

18 Apply two-pack urethane finish.

19 to 22 As full system above.

Cheap respray, without filling

1 to 4 As full system above.

5 Remove paintwork from rusty edges by machine-sanding. Thoroughly abrade any rusty metal.

6 Dry-flat all over with random-orbit sander using P180 stearate paper. Hand-scuff any areas inaccessible by machine. Blow out seams and remove dust.

7 Spirit wipe.

8 Tack-rag wipe.

9 Apply non-sand undercoat.

10 Apply colour coats.

11 Remove masking.

12 Replace bumpers, trim, badges, etc.

The painting of high vehicles showing the spray booth with heating unit.

ABOVE *Steam cleaning the bare metal Bentley R. See page 78. (Andrew Yeadon)*

BELOW *Two pack acrylics being applied. The isocyanates are kept at bay with masks and filters. (Duncan Wherrett)*

THE PAINTING OF COMMERCIAL VEHICLES AND TANKERS

Painting of new vehicles

The range of substrates is greater than in the car refinish market:
1 Steel – clean and scuff.
2 Aluminium – always etch prime.
3 Steel coated with electro-deposited zinc – thoroughly clean by solvent wash and scuffing, to remove oil, grease and contaminated zinc metal. Must be etch-primed.
NOTE: Due to the wider use of air-dry synthetic enamels in the commercial transport sector, a greater proportion of old paint systems may be susceptible to attack by strong solvents.

1. Paintwork in good condition
Prepare the surface as for car refinishing.

2. Paintwork in poor condition
Flat back to a sound substrate or remove with paint stripper. Paint stripper must never be allowed to creep behind overlapping joints and rivet-heads. These areas must be mechanically abraded.

Self adhesive transfers may be fitted, masked up and final coats of finished enamel butted up to them. Where lettering has been partly or wholly taken out on the side of the vehicle and it isn't possible to obtain the services of a sign writer, make a template by tracing the lettering on the opposite side of the vehicle, (lining paper which can be obtained from most decorative stores is suitable) rub the back of the template with whiting or chalk for a dark background or brown powder or charcoal for a light background.

Line the template up in the correct position, place a piece of masking tape over each corner to hold it firmly in position, and using a ruler and pencil, trace the marked out letters on to the panel, making sure not to apply too much pressure, to avoid marking the newly applied finish. That completed, remove the template, remove the loose powder with a badger brush or a piece of cotton wool, flicking over the panel lightly. Proceed to pencil in the lettering with a sable writer, using the appropriate colour.
Always pencil in with undercoat, followed by gloss for the best and long lasting results.

For manufacturer's Stoved Chassis Paints (as opposed to synthetic primers) – solvent clean and scuff where possible, etch-prime or use synthetic air-dry primer. Air-dried primer may be susceptible to solvent attack, synthetic undercoats are therefore most suitable. For galvanised steel, treat with mordant solution, dry off, etch-prime. For corroded, mill-scaled, heavy steel structure – blast clean to profile not exceeding 0.002–0.0025 in. Blow clean, then:
(i) Anti-corrosion blast primer or
(ii) 2 pack Epoxy Zinc Primer (followed by a water resistant etch-primer if in transit).
For wood, it is recommended that a coat of synthetic primer be brushed on so as to fill the wood grain. Subsequent coats may be spray applied.

Application by brush
Demanding only a well lit screened-off area of the paint shop, application by brush is suitable for vehicles where spray painting would demand a great deal of masking, e.g. multi-coloured buses. Considerable masking time may be saved by using brush application for small areas, e.g. flashes or narrow bands of colour along the sides. Brush application is limited to slow drying synthetic paints, so vehicles must stand in the shop during a long drying and hardening period.

Application by roller
A fast and easy method for the painting of roofs.

Refinish work
Dependent on the country of origin and the type of vehicle, painting may be over any of the following finishes:–

1   Synthetic resin air-dry coach enamel.
2   Fast air-dry synthetic enamel.
3   One-pack polyurethane enamel.
4   High-brake thermosetting acrylic enamel.
5   Two-pack acrylic enamel.
6   Manufacturer's synthetic chassic paints.
7   Low-brake synthetic enamel.
8   Chlorinated rubber finish (used where a degree of chemical assistance is required).
9   Cellulose lacquer.
10 Acrylic lacquer.

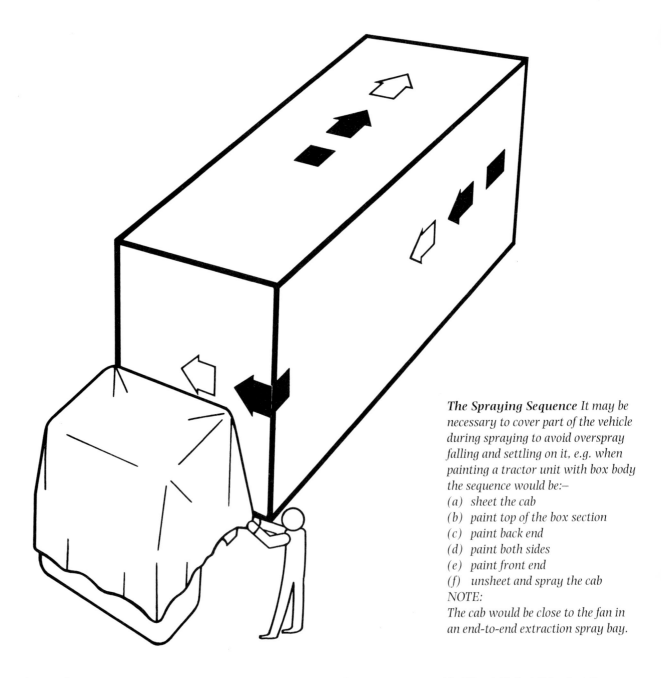

The Spraying Sequence It may be necessary to cover part of the vehicle during spraying to avoid overspray falling and settling on it, e.g. when painting a tractor unit with box body the sequence would be:–

(a) sheet the cab
(b) paint top of the box section
(c) paint back end
(d) paint both sides
(e) paint front end
(f) unsheet and spray the cab

NOTE:
The cab would be close to the fan in an end-to-end extraction spray bay.

Autocolour

Commercial vehicles and tankers

Product
Hi-gloss 383/ Hi-gloss 6.

Use Fast System (for 6 hour recoat, cold spray).

Thinning Hi-gloss 383, 6–8 parts + Hi-gloss 6, 1 part.

Spraying pressure 40–70 psi (2.8–4.8 bar) at the gun.

Application 2 single coats. Allow not less than 15 minutes and not more than 1.5 hours between coats.

Drying (20°C) Dust Free 1.5 hours. Handleable (light pressure) 4–6 hours. Recoat 6 hours.

Product
Hi-gloss 383.

Use Fast System (for 6 hour recoat, hot spray).

Thinning Use unthinned.

Spraying pressure 40–70 psi (2.8–4.8 bar) at the gun.

Application 1 mist and 1 full coat.

Drying (20°C) Dust Free 1–1.5 hours. Handleable (light pressure) 4–6 hours. Recoat 6 hours.

Primers and undercoats

Transport Primecoat P565–625:
An etching primer with good build for use over various bare metal substrates.
2-Pack High-build Etching Primer P566–4101,
Transport Zinc Chromate Corrosion Resisting Primer P540–303:
A high-build alternative to Transport Primecoat. For superb corrosion resistance over steel.
Transport Non-Stand Undercoat P545-line:
A traditional non-sand undercaot for use over sound old paintwork or works primer.
Transport QD Primer P540-line:
A faster drying alternative to Transport Non-Sand.
Transport Groundcoat P543-line:
For use where a coloured undercoat is required. Available in a wide range of colours.

Fast system (for 6 hour recoat, cold spray)

Where speed is essential, this system is ideal. When only one colour is required a vehicle can be taken from bare metal to final finish in one day. Where duotone work is involved, the first colour coat can be applied in the morning and the vehicle masked up and sprayed with the second colour coat 6 hours later.

Products
P383 – Hi-gloss 383 Basic and Ready-mixed Colours.
P850–1238 Hi-gloss 6 (additive for 6 hour recoat).
P850–1041 Slow Thinner 1041 (High-Flash).

Thinning
Stir paint well before thinning.
Thin to a viscosity of 40–50 secs BSB4 (29–35 DIN4). This will normally be achieved with the following thinning ratio:–
Hi-gloss 383 6–8 parts.

Hi-gloss 6, 1 part.
Where a high-flash system is required, use Slow Thinner P850–1041.

Overnight system

Product
Hi-gloss 383/Hi-gloss 16.
Overnight system (for 16 hour recoat, cold spray)

Thinning Hi-gloss 383, 4 parts + Hi-gloss 16, 1 part. Under cold conditions, warm paint to 20°C or add no more than 10% Thinner 930 to achieve viscosity.

Spraying pressure 40–70 psi (2.8–4.8 bar) at the gun.

Application 1 mist and 1 full coat.

Drying (20°C) Dust free 2–2.5 hours. Handleable (light pressure) 6 hours. Recoat 16 hours.

Hi-gloss 383

Hi-gloss 383 is a one-pack polyurethane topcoat specially formulated for use on commercial vehicles. It provides a finish with outstanding gloss and excellent durability, built to withstand the rigours of commercial use.

Hi-gloss 383 can be used as an original finish, or for respray and repair work. Although designed principally for spray application (conventional, hot or airless spray) it can also be brushed. There are two additives for Hi-gloss 383 – Hi-gloss 6 for fast dry and 6 hr recoat and Hi-gloss 16 for overnight dry. The Hi-gloss 383 mixing scheme provides instant access to around 4,000 colours, including a comprehensive range of fleet, BS and RAL colours.

Type of product Blend of polyurethane resins.

Substrates Well flatted existing paintwork in sound condition and primed and prepared surfaces.

THE RESTORATION OF THE HORSE DRAWN CARRIAGE

The growing interest in the renovation of horse drawn carriages and vintage cars has led to a revived

177

interest in one of the old crafts associated with coach building, that of coachpainting, which is the means of achieving entirely by hand the type of finish traditionally associated with passenger vehicles before mechanical mass production.

Several coats of paint were applied, anything up to eighteen coats. The type of paint did not have good covering power and each coat would take days to dry, which is why it took several weeks to paint a carriage.

The wood surface would be prepared by rubbing down with pumice stone. The primer was usually white lead and the filler coat was a mixture of zinc, lead and slate powder. The undercoat was usually white or grey, using stainers and a touch of charcoal.

The gloss would be of a spirit type (not the methylated spirit type), with of course an organic coating, using powdered pigments, linseed and pure turps. This would be mixed into a paste with either linseed or poppy oil on a slab of marble or glass.

The varnish was copal varnish and the dryer would probably be a paste dryer produced from the scum of blue lead or cobalt type dryer. The paint was wet flatted with pumice powder in a cloth pad or cuttlefish.

A typical full coach painting process

It was a lengthy operation, involving priming, stopping, filling, undercoating, two coats of enamel and two coats of varnish. High quality and long life were the primary considerations.

As has already been indicated, the adhesion of a paint system to its surface is the most important factor determining the life of a paint finish. If the adhesion is poor the paint film is unsupported, and a rapid breakdown will occur through peeling, flaking, blistering, splitting, cracking or chipping, according to the type of paint used and the conditions of service. The correct preparation of the surface was vital to the original coach painter, and is to the restorer today.

Before proceeding with the preparation of the carriage, the coach painter would first clean the

LEFT *The State Chariot 1860 in the middle of restoration, and* RIGHT, *restoration of Travelling Chariot of 1820. Rod Ousbey of Witty Brook Carriages and Harness Room is one of the few people capable of restoring these vehicles in the traditional way.*

entire surface to be painted, to remove heavy accumulations of dirt, grit, loose paint and rust. He would decide after carefully inspecting the carriage, whether old timber needed replacing or stripping or just the normal preparation and filling. In the case of new timber, then of course the woodworker sandpapered the replacements in order to take the paint or varnish, as the case may be.

However, for renovation work, it is more than likely that all the surfaces will have previously been painted with some kind of protective substance, all of which must be removed entirely before painting.

The stripping of old paint takes place before the insertion of new timber, for two reasons. Firstly, to prevent the new timber coming in contact with the paint remover and, secondly, to reveal the extent of the repairs required.

The restorer normally uses a spirit-type paint remover because it is less messy than the water wash type. His equipment includes paint kettle, paint brush, a broad knife and a putty knife and some coarse steel wool. He wears rubber gloves and goggles, and as always, carries out the operation in a well ventilated area. A heavy coat of paint remover is applied on one small area at a time. The painter draws the scraper downwards, as to push forward may result in penetrating the wood, making it difficult to remove the stripper afterwards and requiring more filling too. Any stubborn paint left on the surface is removed by a further application of paint remover, this time using steel wool. On any old carriage you will find that there is quite a heavy deposit of paint, so you need patience to get it off.

After all the paint has been removed all traces of paint remover must be wiped off using rags soaked in thinners or white spirit.

A selection of artist brushes. There is still work to be done with them in carriage restoration.

After the wood had dried out it is rubbed down with 180 grade wet-or-dry paper, dry, paying particular attention to brass hinges and mouldings to ensure a 'key' for the primer coats. Aluminium doors are rubbed down with 400 grade paper using white spirit as lubricant.

After removing dust, and ensuring that the working area is clean, as an added precaution, using clean rags and white spirit, the entire surface is wiped over and dried thoroughly, and tack-ragged for the primer coat. It is important that wood or metal is not left exposed to a damp atmosphere longer than is necessary. Priming is a very important part of the painting operation, since the entire paint structure depends on it: the primer is the only part of the paint system in actual contact with the surface being finished.

The primers for metal surfaces are formulated to prevent corrosion, and for wood, to prevent warping and rotting. These primers were originally based on white and red lead, titanium oxide, zinc chromate and toluenated alkyds.

After overnight drying, an oil based knifing compound is applied in thin layers over rough or minor surface defects. This is similar to filler only with more extender added to it, produced from white limestone or chalk.

For deep screw holes the painter makes a mixture of whiting and linseed oil to form a stiff putty with a touch of goldsize to harden it. This would be followed by two or three coats of oil based filler allowed to dry for as long as two or three days.

A very thin contrasting colour is applied, its purpose being to guide the craftsman in the even rubbing of the entire surface, using 220 grade wet-or-dry paper with plenty of clean water to wash away the residue, a rubbing block being used on flat surfaces.

By using these fillers on the wood surface, it is possible to obtain a mirror like finish.

Ensuring the surface is perfectly clean and

thoroughly dry, the appropriate undercoat is applied. Although each coat of paint is applied separately, each coat has a special function in the build-up of the complete paint film. The undercoat provides a suitable ground with the correct adhesion, absorption, hardness and tension for subsequent coats of finishing materials.

The undercoat would originally be based on an oleoresinous phenolic or alkyd vehicle, perhaps with the addition of boiled or bodied oil, barytes, blanc fix and china clay.

Soft undercoats under hard gloss finishes cause cracking; absorbent undercoats cause lack of gloss and possible flaking; undercoats which are glossy have a tendency to cause fretting and lack of key; overpigmented undercoats lack flow and are ropy with a tendency to powder; thin undercoats lack opacity and give insufficient build. All of these problems faced the original coach painters and face the contemporary restorer in exactly the same way.

The undercoat is allowed to dry for a period of about sixteen hours in suitable conditions before being de-nibbed, dry, with 600 grade paper, wiped over with the tack-rag and the first full gloss coat of enamel is applied; added to which would be in the region of 10% of white spirit to help the flow and ease of application.

This is left to dry for two or three days before wet flatting with 600 grade paper, washed and dried thoroughly, wiped over with the tack-rag and the second coat of gloss applied.

The brushing viscosity is in the region of 138 to 167 sec in a B.S.B.4. cup and covers a surface area of approximately 13–15 sq metres per litre. This paint is based on either fairly long oleoresinous media or long oil alkyds and generally white spirit or turpentine.

Long oil alkyds are normally chosen for the binding mediums of brushing paints: Because they have good flow, join-up is still possible after the bulk of the solvent has evaporated and white spirit is suitable because it is low in odour and has no effect on the previous coats. The carriage stands for some three or four days before the next stage in which the flatting of the entire surface is carried out, using 600 grade paper. Soap is used as a lubricant which not only prevents the paper from getting clogged up with particles of paint, but helps the cutting action when flatting.

At this stage, the whole carriage is washed down thoroughly, dried, wiped over with the tack-rag and the first coat of varnish applied. Some two to three days would elapse before the next flatting operation, using 600 grade paper. At this stage some craftsmen preferred to use the cuttlefish for flatting. All lining is carried out at this stage. (Writing this brings such wonderful memories flooding back to me. I was fortunate enough to spend a considerable amount of time during my career on just this kind of work.) The lines are applied by hand with a lining brush, a knot of long hair, the filling of which is sable or a mixture of sable and ox hair, inserted in a quill. Lining brushes are available in a variety of sizes and shapes, from 'whip', or exceedingly fine, to a full line, which is some half an inch across. The sizes are named according to the quill used, lark, crow, duck, small goose, goose, extra goose, small swan, medium swan and large swan.

When running a line freehand, the eye is fixed some distance ahead of the brush, which is swept across the panel in one steady stroke. When following a chalk line, the brush may be held between the finger and the thumb, using the little finger as a support.

With the lining completed, the carriage is once again washed down and thoroughly dried.

At this stage, great care is taken by the painter to ensure that his brushes, varnish pot and the surface and surroundings are perfectly clean, before applying the final coat of varnish, after which the carriage stands for several days before being lightly washed down with cold water, leathered off ready for collection.

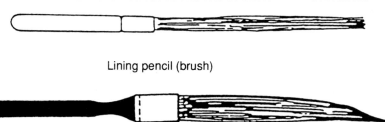

Lining pencil (brush)

Sword liner or dagger brush

The lining brush (above) and sword liner as used by the coach painter.

Varnishing is never carried out in very cold or damp conditions, because the surface would tend to bloom, turning it milky. Varnishes are made by cooking resins with oil and driers. These oils are chiefly linseed and tung oil and the resins are both natural and manufactured. Natural resins, termed copals, are either dug from the ground or tapped from living trees. Synthetic resins are manufactured. They produce varnishes which are paler, but when mixed with natural resin varnishes, they produce varnishes of finer quality than those made with only one type of resin.

Use and care of brushes

Brushes should not be dipped in more than half their length of filling and should not be left standing in the pot of paint at any time; and they should not be stood or left in water, since bristles are open-ended tubes and water will swell and distort the handle and rust the ferrule. It is better to rinse the brush in white spirit or brush cleaner. On no account should soda, strong alkali or acids be used for cleaning. After cleaning out the brushes, remove the cleaning solvent by twirling the brush between the palms of the hands, making sure that the splashes do not fall on newly-applied paint work, then place the brush suspended on a wire in a brush keeper in a mixture of linseed oil and turps, so that the bristles remain supple and free from dust.

For re-use, simply scrape the linseed oil mixture from the brush on the side of the keeper, rinse out in white spirit and twirl the brush between the palms of the hands to remove the cleaner. Some varnishes do not take kindly to linseed oil so it is advisable to pay particular attention to the cleaning of brushes before using these materials.

Always rinse out writing pencils and liners in white spirit after use and work vaseline into the hair to keep them in shape and place them in a long metal case for protection.

This craft is still continued today. My friend Rod Ousbey of Warwickshire still paints his carriages in the traditional way. Why? Because his customers demand it.

THE SPRAY BOOTH

The spray booth is a compartment, room or enclosed space built to confine the overspray and fumes resulting from spray paint finishing. It is constructed either of galvanised steel in sheets bolted to each other or on to a frame, of aluminium sheets similarly bolted, or of masonry (brick, breeze-block, or the like) rendered and sealed to give a smooth dust-free surface. In every form of construction there are various models, designed for different spray applications. Some are in addition either joined to or combined with a low-bake oven facility. Such combined units have become more attractive since the required minimum baking temperatures have come down from 80°C (176°F) to 60°–70°C (140° –158°F).

Ideally, however, the spray booth segregates the spraying operation from other operations, rendering all activities therefore the cleaner and safer. By containing the overspray and fumes fire and health hazards are much reduced. And a booth equipped with adequate and approved lighting also allows better control of the finish quality.

There are two major types of spray booth: the **dry spray booth** and the **wet spray booth** or air-washer. It is the wet spray booth that is found in industrial applications, the dry booth that is most used for vehicle refinishing.

The dry spray booth effectively acts as a large vacuum cleaner, drawing from the spraying area contaminated air containing overspray and fumes through replaceable filters before venting the air to the outside. Some also filter the incoming air to ensure cleanliness in the paint zone. Available in a wide range of sizes and styles, they are used for the spraying of most finishing materials.

To ensure the sufficient velocity of air through the spray booth to keep the booth free of overspray and fumes, exhaust fans are located at strategic points, each with its own motor and fire-resistant metal blades. Air input through the spray booth roof with extraction at floor level is preferred, because stagnant areas are more easily avoided and there is less danger of overspray contaminating horizontal surfaces. For each bank of air filters or arresters a draught gauge or manometer indicates when overloading takes place.

The volume of air exhausted by a spray booth is often enough to produce three or more complete air

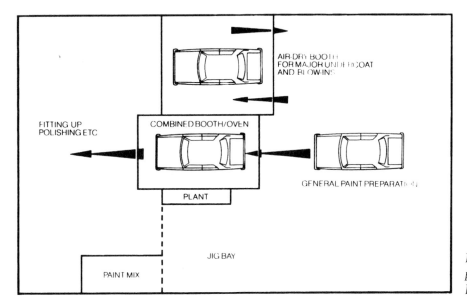

AIR-DRY BOOTH
FOR MAJOR UNDERCOAT
AND BLOW-INS

FITTING UP
POLISHING ETC

COMBINED BOOTH/OVEN

GENERAL PAINT PREPARATION

PLANT

JIG BAY

PAINT MIX

Paintshop layout showing one possibility for optimum use of a large rectangular area.

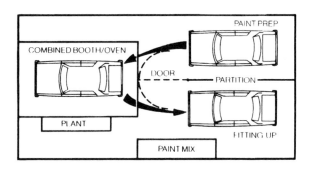

PAINT PREP

COMBINED BOOTH/OVEN

DOOR

PARTITION

PLANT

FITTING UP

PAINT MIX

How preparation and fitting up can be separated in a narrow area with no vehicle turning problems.

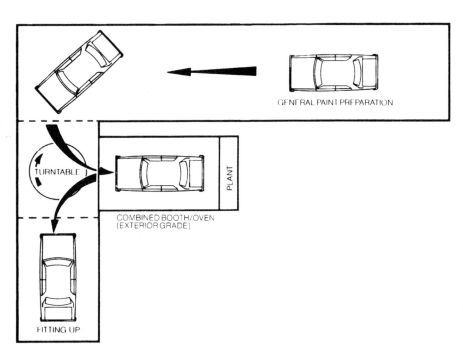

GENERAL PAINT PREPARATION

TURNTABLE

PLANT

COMBINED BOOTH/OVEN
(EXTERIOR GRADE)

FITTING UP

How an external booth/oven can extend the available space; a turntable is also a useful, if expensive, space-saver.

183

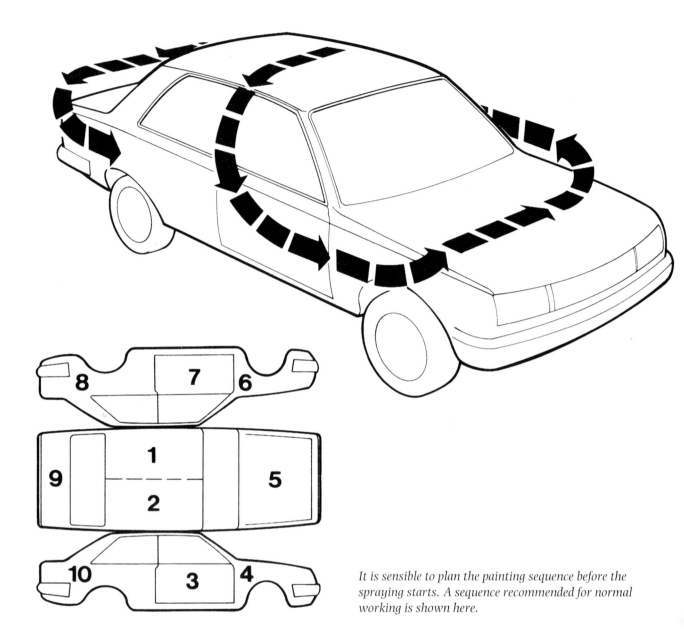

It is sensible to plan the painting sequence before the spraying starts. A sequence recommended for normal working is shown here.

changes per minute in the booth. Under such conditions the temperature may become irregular and uncomfortable. Excessive dust may also become a problem. To prevent these conditions, 'make-up' air may have to be introduced into the booth to compensate for the exhausted air. A machine that can do this automatically – and supplies air that is both filtered and heated – is an air replacement unit.

The booth may be pressurized: air may be forced in at a greater rate than it is extracted. This creates a positive pressure within the booth which prevents any dirt entering it from outside.

A control panel enables the spray booth operator to select the required spraying and drying times at the touch of an electronic dial. Where there is a water-wash facility, the control panel will also take charge of regulating and monitoring that program. And on combined units the low-bake conditions can additionally be dialled in. All main control functions are provided by one printed circuit board that can be quickly replaced if necessary, but which is generally guaranteed to last the life of the booth.

● Routine maintenance of a dry spray booth.
a) Filters should be periodically inspected and replaced with the multi-stage filters specifically designed for the booth.

b) Manometer readings should be monitored daily and checked against a 'normal' reading.

c) Keep the booth clean. Floors and walls should be wiped down after every job. Scraps and leftovers should be tidied out.

d) Coat the inside of the booth with a strippable spray-on covering. When the overspray on it becomes too thick, strip and recoat.

e) Periodically check the lighting inside the booth, and replace weak or burned-out bulbs. Improper lighting can cause bad finishes.

● Booths for spraying high-sided vehicles. Both spray booths and combined spray-booth/low-bake oven units are available that accept high vehicles such as double-decker buses and box wagons. Extra booth equipment normally retained within booths of this type include tall stepladders with upper platforms and knee-rails, mobile scaffold towers or pairs of towers with linking walkways, raised mobile catwalks, and mobile cranes to lift the sprayer over tank vehicles. Some booths are fitted with lifts that allow a tall vehicle to be lowered into a well in the floor.
A well of this type may at other times allow a sprayer access to paint a vehicle's underbody and chassis.

REFINISHING OPERATIONS

Touching up: spot paint repair

Before beginning work on any spot repair it is important to determine the condition of the area surrounding the repair that is to be integrated with the repair. This will in turn determine the technique of repair to be employed (and possibly save a costly rectification at a later stage).

All too often, what seems to be a small, localized area of deterioration turns out to be just the worst in a catalogue of defects requiring much more radical efforts to patch up than was first envisaged.

There are four major methods of spot repair.

Simple compounding or polishing can restore some surface defects such as dust and light orange-peel.

Sometimes just the colour coat can be applied to a clean, sound, flatted, existing colour.

A spot-to-bare-metal repair is necessary when a localized defect affects primer or filler coats as well as the colour coat. Local flatting to bare metal is called for at the affected area, but attention must also be

paid to surrounding areas with a view to ensuring that the new paint system blends in with the old. This method lends itself to stone chips and local blister repairs.

Bare metal repairs are necessary when the film is suspect over a whole area (a door panel, perhaps, or possibly the entire car body). The method refurbishes extensive blistering, flaking, or areas that require repainting simply through old age.

Operational sequences for local repairs

In all the following cases, damage has been made good and the paint repair system brought up to the surfacer stage. The techniques may be varied slightly according to the topcoat being used.

But before any refinish work is begun, the colour should be carefully identified. Refer to the vehicle manufacturer's colour code and country of origin – both indicated on a plate affixed to the vehicle. Other useful details include the paint manufacturer's colour register, colour pack and microfiche formulas. The colour can then be obtained as quickly as possible, a test panel prepared for checking against a thoroughly clean section of the original paint work, and any necessary tinting carried out before the vehicle is ready for the colour coats.

A spot repair is a highly localized repair that is not intended to be integrated with the existing finish, merely invisible within it. A fade-out repair, however, covers a wider area than the apparent damage and is specifically intended to blend in with the existing finish.

Spot repair of an ordinary solid colour

1 Wet-sand with abrasive paper not coarser than P600-grade wet or dry paper.
2 Wipe clean.
3 Remove all overspray of the primer surfacer from the surrounding area. At the same time improve the feather-edging of the primer surfacer by wet-flatting with P1200-grade abrasive paper. Compound a further 8–15 cm (3–6 in) around the repair area.
4 Clean off.
5 Spirit wipe. Tack-rag wipe.
6 Apply colour coats. Extend each coat beyond the previous coat but keep within the compounded area. Extra thinner may be added for the final coat. Air pressure should be about 30 pounds per square inch (2 bars) at the gun. The paint may be applied by

moving the gun in a circular motion, or with short strokes from the centre of the repair to the perimeter.

7   As soon as possible after the application of the final colour coat, mist-coat the edge of the repair with fade-out thinner or a 1:9 mix of paint and thinner respectively. This may be applied in several passes at 35–40 pounds per square inch (2·5–3·0 bars) to achieve even wetting-out.

8   After allowing it to harden, burnish with rubbing compound and polish.

The polishing should be related to the gloss of the surrounding original finish. In the case of the repair of a synthetic enamel with a lacquer, too much polishing would produce a flat mirror-like spot surrounded by the original finish of lower gloss.

Fade-out repair of an ordinary solid colour

This sequence is especially useful when applying synthetic enamel.

1   Wet-sand with abrasive paper no coarser than P600-grade.
2   Wipe clean.
3   Extend the flatted area further by some 7–10 cm (3–4 in), using P1200-grade abrasive paper.
4   Wipe dry.
5   Use compound on a further 23 cm (9 in) beyond the flatted area. Remove any overspray of the primer surfacer.
6   Clean off. Spirit wipe. Tack-rag wipe.
7   Apply two or three single coats of colour to obliterate the surfacer. Air pressure should be 30–35 pounds per square inch (2·0–2·5 bars) at the gun.
8   Add fade-out thinner to the paint to a proportion of approximately 25 per cent. Reduce air pressure to 20–25 pounds per square inch (1·5–2·0 bars) at the gun, and apply one or two fade-out coats using a distinctly arcing motion of the spray gun, but keeping within the compounded area.
9   As soon as possible after the application of the colour coats, apply fade-out thinner to the edge of the repair. Make several light passes with the gun, at an air pressure of 35–40 pounds per square inch (2·5–3·0 bars) at the gun.
10   Allow to harden. Polish.

Polishing on air-dry synthetic enamel should be restricted to light burnishing with either polishing compound or liquid polish. Alternatively, burnish with gentle pressure from a high-speed lamb's wool mop.

The success rate in fade-out repair using synthetic enamels can be very high in certain areas – notably below the waist-line of the vehicle – but repairs on horizontal areas tend to be more difficult.

Fade-out repair of a metallic finish

1   Wet-sand with abrasive paper no coarser than P600-grade.
2   Wipe clean.
3   Extend the flatted area further by some 7–10 cm (3–4 in), using P1200-grade abrasive paper.
4   Wipe dry.
5   Use compound on a further 23 cm (9 in) beyond the flatted area. Remove any overspray of the primer surfacer.
6   Clean off. Spirit wipe. Tack-rag wipe.
7   Apply two or three single coats of colour to obliterate the surfacer. Air pressure should be 30–35 pounds per square inch (2·0–2·5 bars) at the gun.
8   Mix the thinned paint with blending-clear, in the ratio 2 parts paint to 1 part blending-clear. Reduce the air pressure to 20–25 pounds per square inch (1·5–2·0 bars) at the gun and apply one or two fade-out coats, using a distinctly arcing motion of the spray gun and extending into – and keeping within – the compounded area.
9   Increase the proportion of blending-clear in the mixture to 1 part thinned paint to 1 part blending-clear. Apply a fade-out coat as before. Extra blending-clear may be added in successive coats up to the maximum proportion recommended by the paint manufacturer.
10   As soon as possible after the application of the colour coats, apply fade-out thinner to the edge of the repair. Make several light passes with the gun, at an air pressure of 35–40 pounds per square inch (2·5–3·0 bars) at the gun, until all dry spray has been absorbed.
11   Allow to harden. Polish.

It is possible to use a variant of this technique in relation to a repair of an ordinary solid colour, notably a colour that has a pigment of a transparent quality. Where there is a definite difference between original colour and repair colour, the technique relies on lowering the opacity of the repair paint, so allowing the original colour to 'grin through' and influence the colour of the repair.

Colour of normal opacity is sprayed over any areas of dissimilar coloration until those areas are completely obliterated. Then a blending-clear of a type recommended by its manufacturer is added in the quantity also recommended. The whole panel is then sprayed with the number of coats normally used. Increased amounts of clear may be added to successive coats, but must never exceed the maximum proportions cited by the manufacturer.

The use of this technique often avoids colour tinting for minor repairs, and is useful too for carrying out spot repairs.

Fade-out repair of a metallic basecoat and clear finish

1 Wet-sand with abrasive paper no coarser than P800-grade.
2 Wipe clean.
3 Extend the flatted area further by some 7–10 cm (3–4 in), using P1200-grade abrasive paper.
4 Wipe clean.
5 Use compound on a further 23 cm (9 in) beyond the flatted area. Remove any overspray of the primer surfacer.
6 Clean off. Spirit wipe. Tack-rag wipe.
7 Apply two coats of basecoat to obliterate the surfacer. Air pressure should be 30–35 pounds per square inch (2·0–2·5 bars) at the gun.
8 Reduce air pressure to 20–25 pounds per square inch (1·5–2·0 bars) at the gun, and apply one or two fade-out coats using a distinctly arcing motion of the spray gun, being careful not to trigger off at the end of each stroke, and keeping within the compounded area. (Triggering off at the end of each spray stroke tends to produce a silvery edge.)
9 Mist-coat the edge of the repair with fade-out thinner. Make several light passes with the gun, at an air pressure of 35–40 pounds per square inch (2·5–3·0 bars) at the gun.

Mist-coating is optional, but a check on colour while the basecoat is still wet from the fade-out thinner gives a fairly accurate indication of the colour match. Any colour adjustment necessary should be carried out before the application of clearcoat.
10 Flash off.
11 Apply clearcoat, extending beyond the basecoat and fading out within the compounded area.
12 Mist-coat the edges of the repair with fade-out thinner.
13 Allow to harden. Polish.

It may be advantageous to apply clearcoat over the whole panel, in which event the necessary surface preparation should take place at operations 3 to 6 above.

Touching up: equipment and materials

Sanders and sanding
Various electric devices are available to assist the refinisher.

What is known simply as a **sanding machine** is used by panel-beaters to sand damaged areas that require body filler, and by refinishers to sand out rust. The most common variety takes a 180-mm (7-in) sanding disc, on a spindle thread at about 1,800 rpm.

An **orbital sander** includes both circular and square pads, and a dust-collection bag. The most common variety sands a 1·5-mm (1/16-in) diameter orbit at 13,500 orbits a minute.

An **oscillating sander** is used by a refinisher for rubbing large panels, body fillers and woodwork. Its vibrating action moves in straight lines backwards and forwards. A metal clip at each end holds the abrasive paper in position. The most common variety has a rectangular rubber base pad that measures 180 x 90 mm (7 x 3½ in).

The **dual-action sander** is a popular and much-used machine that operates by electricity or by compressed air. Excellent for feather-edging paintwork and repairs, the business end comprises for the most part a 15-mm (6-in) abrasive disc fastened with rubber solution on to a rubber backing pad. A worn disc can be peeled off without difficulty and replaced with a new one. The compressed air versions are particularly useful for use with water when flatting. (Electric versions should not be used with water at all.)

● Abrasive papers. Abrasive papers used by refinishers are relatively complex in composition. Technically, they are made up of a backing, a 'make-coat', a 'size-coat', and the abrasive mineral. The backing is often paper but may equally well be cloth (cotton or polyester) or some fibrous material (such as treated cellulose). The minerals involved are usually either aluminium oxide or silicon carbide, both of which are manufactured synthetically.

The resultant papers are available in various grades, ranging from 80 (coarse) to 1200 (very fine). The grades reflect the number of particles of abrasive mineral grit in one linear inch of paper. Produced in sheets of standard sizes, the papers can be used either wet or dry – and are therefore often called 'wet or dry abrasive paper' – but in refinishing are mostly used with water and hard soap in order to avoid a build-up of paint particles on the paper.

● Sanding discs. The discs produced for sanding

TOP LEFT *The Black and Decker half sheet orbital finishing sander.*

LEFT *The Desoutter random orbital sander.*

ABOVE *The Desoutter Air operated orbital sander.*

machines generally use variants of the minerals used in abrasive papers, especially aluminium oxide.

Polishes and polishing

Rubbing and polishing compounds are formulated carefully from materials that cause no harm to a finish. The refinisher should steer well clear of alternatives such as the metal polishes that contain strong solvents, alkalis, and ungraded abrasive particles.

● Rubbing compounds. Rubbing compounds are like flatting papers: the coarser grades cut fast but produce deeper scratches. The finest grade capable of doing the job should therefore always be used.

● Polishes. The surface to be polished must be free from dust and dirt, and the compound applied to a small area at a time, using a soft open-mesh cloth easily impregnated with the compound. The cloth may be damped before use, or the compound thinned with water before application, but solvents or petrol must never be used.

Applied by hand or by mechanical polishing mop, application should be at a greater pressure initially, easing up as the compound dries and the desired effect is achieved. Machine polishing actually requires a fair degree of skill: the mop must be kept on the move to prevent friction from causing localized heat that can soften or burn some finishes. Sharp edges and awkward curves must be avoided so as not to remove the finish altogether.

Newly applied lacquer finishes should never be compounded or polished until they are thoroughly hard and a substantial proportion of the solvents have evaporated. Compounding too early may result in loss of gloss (hazing) and the finish may be permanently impaired. Wax polish should not be used until a finish is at least four weeks old, by which time all the solvents will have evaporated from the film. Any earlier, and the wax may migrate into the finish, causing softness, loss of gloss, and a tendency to watermark.

On the other hand, burnishing, applying gentle pressure with a high-speed rotary polisher at a speed of between 5,000 and 6,000 rpm with a lamb's wool mop, can remove dirt nibs from stoved finish paint films when other methods fail. (You might first try drawing a razor blade held vertically across the surface, or wet-sanding with P1200-grade abrasive paper.) Sufficient heat will be developed to reflow the sanding marks or other such imperfections, giving a high-gloss finish that is unlikely to haze back. But this

operation still requires minimum initial drying times according to the paint type –

nitrocellulose lacquer	3–4 hours
acrylic lacquer	2–3 hours
two-pack acrylic enamel	overnight air-dry (or cold from stoving oven)
air-dry synthetic enamel	overnight air-dry (or cold from stoving oven if used with hardener-thinner)

– and if the paint is allowed to dry for longer than these times, a hand polish after the flatting operation (using a suitable grade of polish) will give the extra assistance required by the polishing mop.

Polishing mops must be kept clean. Compound and paint residues in a mop increase friction and the tendency to burn the finish. Lamb's wool mops used with a machine polisher can be washed with warm water and soap, and returned to the machine to be spun dry.

A polishing cloth remains clean between jobs if it is kept in a sealed plastic bag.

Sealers

A sealer is applied to fill flatting scratches and to improve colour hold-out, so giving improved uniformity and gloss to the final colour coat. The emergence over the past few decades of undercoats with far greater hold-out properties has seen a corresponding diminution in the need for sealers. However, a sealer can also be used as a groundcoat to aid a final colour match.

A normal sealer is not the same as a bleeding-inhibiting sealer (or indeed an isolator).

● A bleeding-inhibiting sealer. The use of a bleeding-inhibiting sealer is intended to prevent the bleeding through of a previous colour coat. The disadvantage is that these sealers have a much poorer hold-out than conventional sealers: they cannot be flatted – application must be followed by a primer surfacer before any flatting operation is carried out.

Isolators

An isolator is used to prevent the wrinkling of an old paint film under the action of strong lacquer solvents. Two coats of isolator are normally applied. As with the bleeding-inhibiting sealer, a primer surfacer must then be put over it before any flatting operation.

An isolator should not be used indiscriminately –

and not at all in a system of high film thickness, or adhesion failure or cracking may occur.

Fade-out thinners

Fade-out thinners are special blends of solvents designed to assist in the blending in of dry spray at the edge of a spot or fade-out repair area.

Other touching up equipment and materials

● Spray mask. An essential part of the refinisher's equipment, it protects an operator from inhaling the material being sprayed. As the saying in the profession goes: Wear the mask at all times, and you will live longer.

● Splinter-proof goggles. Every refinisher should be equipped with these, to protect the eyes when sanding or when stripping paint or when washing down with solvents.

● Electric fan paint stripper. This type of paint stripper is especially useful for removing coach lines and mouldings that have been stuck on or ironed on. But remember to use it only in a flameproof zone.

● Touch-up brushes (or one-stroke brushes). A set of these is vital to a refinisher for touching in door edges, wing edges, door shuts, and bonnet and boot channels. The most useful sizes are 18 mm (3/4 in), 12 mm (½ in) and 5 mm (3/16 in). Wrapping cleaned paintbrushes in brown paper preserves their shape and keeps out dust and other contaminants.

● Filling-/stopping-knives or plastic spreaders. The very pliable knives are used to apply cellulose stopper

The (7") 180mm Polisher, 750 watts, 1800 rpm.

A range of filling knives from Hamiltons as used by the refinisher.

and polyester filler. Sizes most popular with refinishers are 32 mm (1¼ in) and 89 mm (3½ in).
● Stirring sticks. Use plastic, wooden or non-ferrous metal rods to avoid sparks when stirring cellulose materials or other materials containing highly inflammable solvents.
● Scrapers. The refinisher uses these to remove loose and flaking paint or rust when burning off or chemically stripping.
● Window scraper. This is extremely useful for its set purpose – removing paint from windows.
● Rubber or cork blocks. These are essential to the refinisher for all kinds of rubbing down and flatting operations.

● Synthetic sponges. These are used for all washing-down operations. Never wring out: always rinse and squeeze out after use.
● Chamois leather, wash-leather. A refinisher uses this to dry a surface off prior to painting. After use, rinse in clean cold water and squeeze it out – do not wring it out. Lay it out to dry before storing.

Touching up: some handy tips

● Removing residual masking tape adhesive. To remove residual adhesive, apply a fresh piece of tape over the residue, and then pull it off.
● Pouring from 25-litre thinner cans. Coffee cups/mugs of proofed paper or plastic with their bottoms removed will fit into the aperture of certain 25-litre thinner cans, and provide excellent pouring spouts.
● Mixing lacquer and thinner. When thinning lacquer paints to simple mixing ratios (such as 1:1, or 2:3), pour the thinner into the container first. This makes stirring easier.
● Paint in the gun cup running very low. To use the last few drops left in a gun cup, detach the cup, turn the gun upside down, and pour the last of the remaining paint down the fluid tube. Then spray with the gun held in the upside-down position. This should give you an extra few square inches of coverage.
● Styling line ends with no convenient fade-out point. Where a styling line ends and there is a short distance with no convenient break line, raise the masking paper and support it to enable a good fade-out to be achieved, at the same time preventing a wide area of overspray on the original finish.
● Avoiding bridging. Remove styling line tape before the paint dries: this avoids bridging, which may cause the styling line colour to pull away from unflatted body enamel. The colour will also flow to a finer edge.
● Spraying the front end of a vehicle. Always mask off the engine when spraying a front end. Dirt from the engine compartment cannot then blow up on to the bonnet, and paint cannot get on to the mechanical parts either.
● Rivets and runs. When spraying commercial vehicles, avoid overlapping on rivets. This reduces the risk of runs at these points.
● Removing runs and sags. Gently press masking tape on to a sag while the paint is still wet. Remove the tape, and with luck you remove the sag. Alternatively, gently stipple with an 18 mm (3/4 in) one-stroke brush. Sags or runs in synthetic paints

may also be removed by stippling. (Even if not successful, it leaves a reasonably thin film to rectify.)
● Masking tape adhesive sticking to window rubbers. To reduce the risk of this after stoving, remove the tape while it is still warm.
● Obtaining flexible test panels. Use a thinner to wash off the ink printed on old microfiche films. The clean film then itself represents ideal test surfaces.

The care and maintenance of the finish on a vehicle

Modern vehicle finishes are resistant to most forms of atmospheric pollution. Provided a simple maintenance procedure is followed on a regular basis, the protective capacity – and indeed the colour and gloss – of a finish should last the entire life of the vehicle.
● Washing. Many potential contaminants that attack paint film are water-soluble, and can be removed before harm is done simply by thorough washing with plenty of water and a few drops of detergent. Frequent and regular washing also removes the accumulated dirt, dust and traffic film.

Warm water, rather than cold, with detergent should remove gummy deposits exuded by some trees in the summer months.

Stains made by tar and bitumen or grease can be removed with petrol or white spirit.

Airborne pollutant particles from industrial sources may sometimes become attached to a painted surface into which they gradually penetrate, possibly causing discoloration and pitting. Rubbing with a rubbing compound and polishing should remove light contamination of this kind. But in extreme cases, a 10-per-cent solution of the highly poisonous oxalic acid may be used, taking care not to let the solution run behind mouldings or into other inaccessible places. Several applications within a 15–20 minute period are preferable before all traces of the solution are washed off, and thorough drying. Polishing may be required afterwards. All contact between skin and eyes and the solution must be very carefully avoided: goggles and gloves must be worn. Contaminated clothing must not be reworn before laundry.
● Polishing. Liquid polish of good quality should be used, and will normally restore any loss of gloss through accumulation of traffic film.

Wax polish provides high gloss and added

protection, but should be applied only on a clean surface. Any residue from previous applications should first be removed with white spirit or a liquid polish cleaner. Polishes that contain silicone are also effective, but must be kept away from a paintshop to ensure that the silicone does not contaminate any new paint surface.
● Ventilation. Water lying on a painted surface eventually penetrates the paint film. The effects may not be visible immediately, but the water will in fact have caused a deterioration in the film's protective properties. If a car is garaged, good ventilation is essential. Storage outside on a hard ground or under a carport may be prefereble.

BODY REPAIRS

Major structural repairs are outside the scope of a vehicle refinisher, and therefore outside the true scope of this book. But the refinisher may well find himself or herself expected to carry out minor repairs – repairs on dents and the effects of corrosion – that require attention to a local area on a vehicle's body.

The least technical form of such repairs is in beating ('roughing out') a section of body damage back into its original shape, or as near to it as possible. Abrasions and small holes may be repaired with glass-fibre or similar materials ('sanding and filling'), for later painting over following operational sequences already outlined above. Welding where metal joints have sprung apart or snapped under strain may also be necessary, and likewise requires painting thereafter.

Roughing out

In the case of damage in which the vehicle body is distorted, the temptation is very much to use brute force to restore some semblance of shape. But although brute force may give the appearance of speeding up the first stages of repair, it is all too often found instead actually to cause additional work. If the metal has been permanently marked or stretched by the force applied, more time and effort will be required in completing the work to a satisfactory finish.

The golden rule is: assess the damage first, and

devise a method of repair involving the least amount of force possible. Damaged panels should be restored by *relieving* the stresses that have been set up in them by the force of impact.

The skill of all body repair techniques lies in the correct handling of the basic tools. Roughing out is the basic operation of minor repairs, representing the reshaping of the damaged area by hand with the aid of a heavy dolly, which prises the disjointed section back into its original shape. When repairing collision damage, the normal method of repair is to try to reverse the process that caused the damage in the first place. Vehicle body panels and wings are generally covered with a sound-deadening material, however, that must be removed before starting work.

The point of impact is generally the most displaced point on any damaged panel. To reverse the process, then, this same point on the underside of the panel should be struck using the same force that was originally applied against it. If this spot is hit accurately with a roughing out dolly using the same force, the panel may well spring back almost to the contour it had before impairment.

Larger repairs may require several blows. Hold the roughing out dolly lightly in the hand, strike the first and hardest blow at the centre of what seems to be the most displaced point, and then direct further blows around the first one, gradually working outwards and decreasing the force of the blows, until all the damaged area has been roughed out.

● Roughing out tools. The following tools suffice for the average job:

> standard bumping (planishing) hammer
> pick and finishing hammer
> round boxwood mallet
> flat hammer-file
> utility dolly
> toe dolly
> general purpose dolly
> general purpose spoon
> flexible panel-file
> half round radius file
> tin snips
> centre punch
> cold chisel
> welding goggles
> flat steel rule
> panel puller

The planishing hammer is used more than any other tool. Designed for use only with a dolly, it must never be used for chiselling or other operations, and must be kept clean and free from spots of underseal or paint. Delicate planishing can be effected as well or better with a body spoon. (Some craftsmen make their own spoons from old, flat files.)

Dollies are made of cast steel or drop-forged iron, heat-treated for hardness, and are used to support a surface as it is being smoothed or forced back into shape by the planishing hammer. They are prone to becoming coated with underseal or paint, and must be regularly cleaned and polished for the best results. An air-chisel, although noisy can be a useful extra tool.

Sanding and filling

A vehicle's wing section under repair may be covered in a double skin, through which access for roughing out is impossible. In these circumstances it may be necessary to use a disc sander to remove loose paint and rust, in preparation for filling and repainting.

● Using a sander. Before using an electrically operated sander, make sure that the device is properly connected and earthed. If the machine is not earthed, the operator may receive what could be a fatal electric shock while using it. Always wear goggles to protect the eyes from flying particles of metal from the panel and abrasive dust from the disc. Relpace sander discs as soon as a tear is noticed. Hold the sander so that the disc meets the panel as flat as possible, although of course the central nut retaining the disc must never come in contact with the sanded surface. Tilting the sander may cause gouges and scratches in the metal. Use the sander over an area quite a lot wider than the area to be filled.

● Using a filler. The area to be filled must be clean and dry before the filler is applied. Refinishing fillers are based on the polyester group of thermosetting resins. They require a catalyst or activator to cure them, and are therefore sold in two-pack form comprising the polyester paste and its hardening agent. The two constituents mixed together, the resultant catalysed chemical reaction takes place very quickly.

In the old days – and in some circumstances even today – filling was with solder under heat. Refinishing fillers of the polyester resin type do not require heat during application, and therefore eliminate both the problem of fire risk and the potential problem of heat distortion which can occur when soldering flat body panels. They are also cheaper and easier to use than solder.

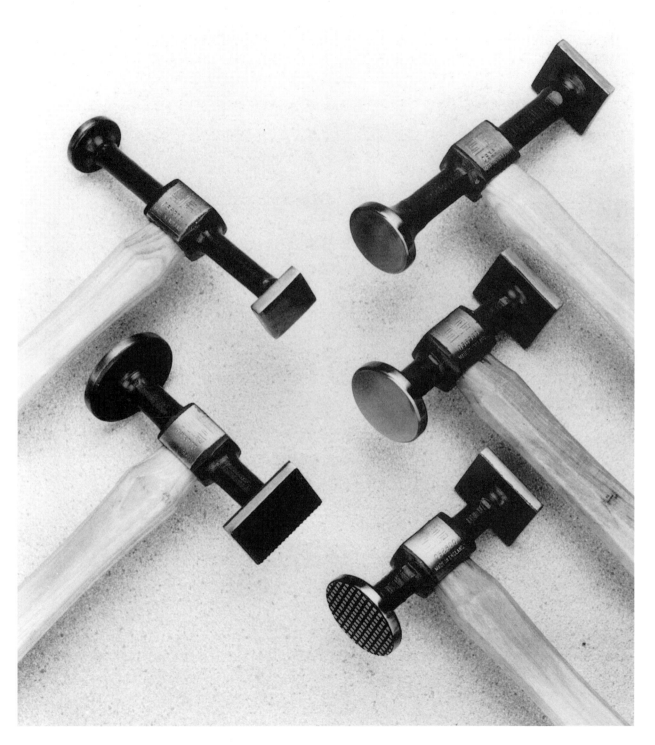

A range of finishing hammers, by the Sykes Pickavant Group.

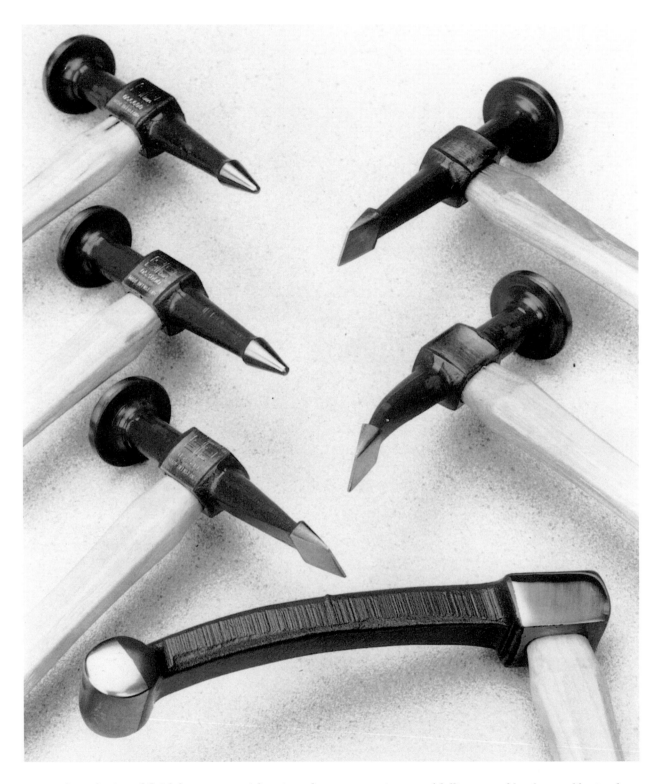

ABOVE *Curved pein and finish hammer, straight pein and finish hammers, pick and finishing hammer, and fender bumping hammer.*

RIGHT *A range of dollies as used by the panel beater, by the Sykes Pickavant Group.*

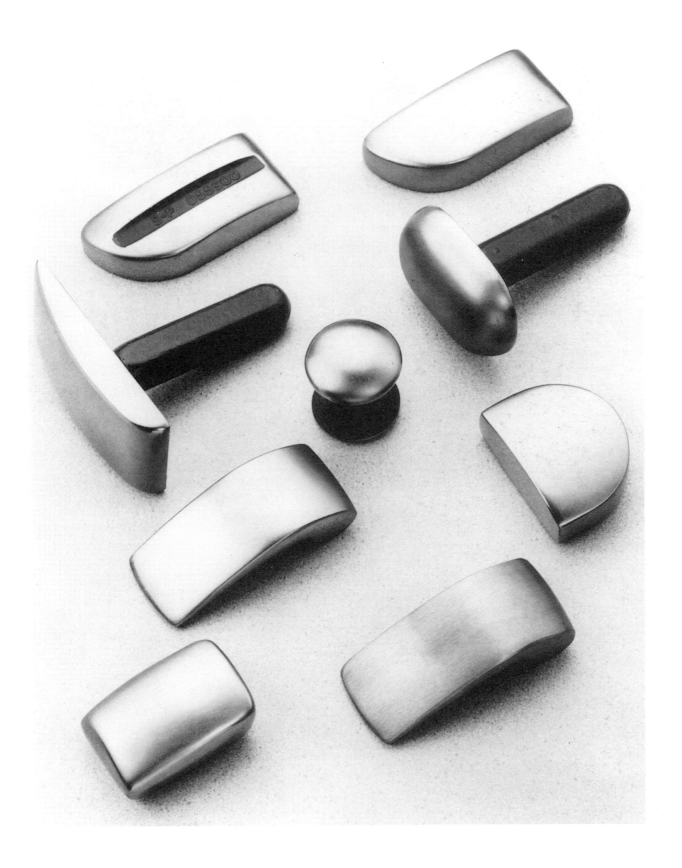

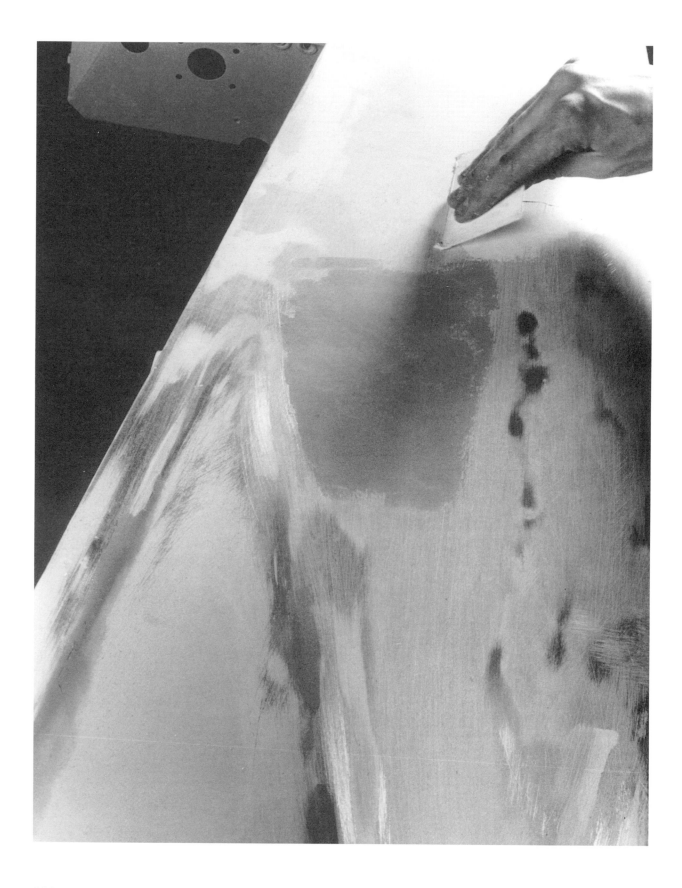

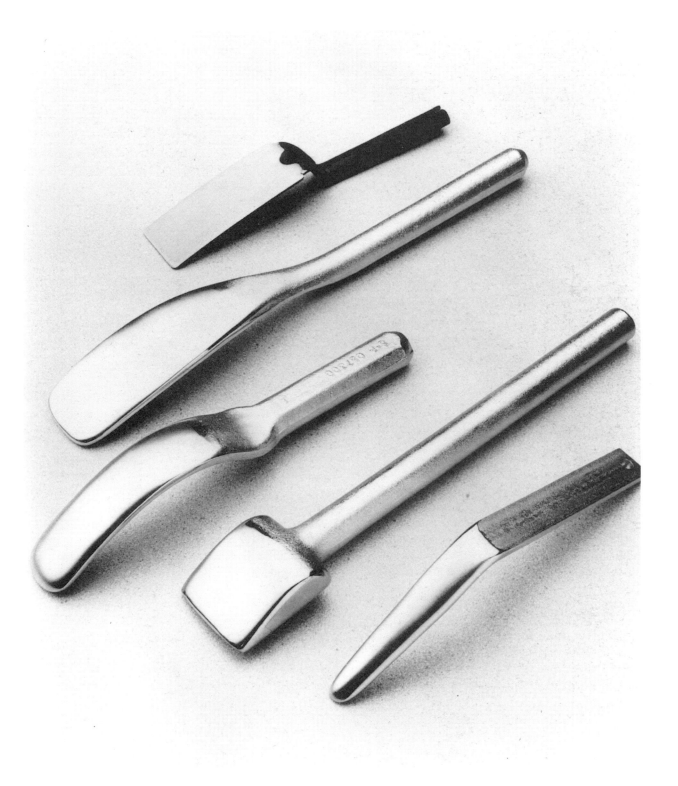

LEFT *Preparing the surface with a sliver of polyester filler and fine emery paper. (Photo: Duncan Wherrett)*

ABOVE *A range of spoons as used by the panel beater from the Sykes Pickavant Group.*

LEFT *A selection of flexible body files.*

RIGHT *Traditional coachmaking tools like these are used most often by the individual restorer, or, as here, for refinishing of luxury automobiles such as the Bentley Continental R. (Photo: Andrew Yeadon).*

Always mix the materials according to the manufacturer's instructions. Apply the paste filler with a stopping knife or flexible spatula. The filler should harden in about 10 minutes, provided that the two constituents have been properly mixed. Such fillers have excellent bonding qualities, and feather out to a fine smooth edge.

After the filler has set, its upper surface can be shaped to the contour of the panel using an abrasive file followed by rubbing down with abrasive paper. A superlative finish can ordinarily be obtained by finishing off with P220-grade wet or dry abrasive paper.

Once filled, the panel can be prepared for repainting.

Gas welding

Gas welding processes are so called because the welding heat is provided by a flame produced by the combustion of a mixture of gases. A variety of gases are used commercially for gas welding, but **the mixture of oxygen and acetylene** is by far the most common because of its high flame temperature and because both gases are relatively easy to handle.

Oxygen is produced industrially either by an electrolytic process or by separation from atmospheric air (in a process described as the liquid air process). Acetylene is a totally synthetic hydrocarbon gas produced by the action of water on calcium carbide. A colourless gas that has a distinctive (and nauseating) odour, acetylene is highly combustible when mixed with air, giving a luminous smoky flame. But in pure oxygen, acetylene burns with an intensely hot non-luminous flame.

For the purposes of welding, acetylene is dissolved in a liquid chemical, acetone, which is capable of absorbing up to 25 times its own volume without changing the nature of the gas itself. When oxygen and acetylene from their separate pressurized

cylinders are mixed and ignited, the flame that results reaches a temperature of 3,480°C (6,300°F) at an intensity that is enough to melt all commercial metals, and so thoroughly that the metals actually flow together to form a complete bond. On very thin materials, however, extra metal in the form of a wire or rod is added to the molten metal to strengthen the seam.

In a body repair shop, welding is carried out using **high-pressure welding equipment**. The dissolved acetylene is supplied in cylinders at a pressure of 225 pounds per square inch (15·75 kg/cm^2). The cylinders are maroon in colour, and contain 60, 100, 150 or 200 cubic feet (1·70, 2·83, 4·25 or 5·66 cubic metres respectively) of gas when fully charged. The oxygen comes in blue (formerly black) cylinders containing 80, 100 or 220 cubic feet (2·27, 2·83 or 6·23 cubic metres respectively). To prevent potentially lethal mistakes from being made, oxygen and acetylene cylinders have valve outlet

fittings with opposing threads.

The full set of high-pressure welding equipment consists of:

- a cylinder of oxygen
- a cylinder of dissolved acetylene
- a high-pressure welding torch, with separate oxygen and acetylene controls, and with tips of different sizes
- an oxygen regulator, with gauges
- an acetylene regulator, with gauges
- two 10-foot (3·048-m) lengths of 3/8 in (9·525 mm) high-pressure rubber/canvas hose, with clips, coloured red for acetylene and blue for oxygen
- keys for cylinders and spanners for all fittings
- a pair of welding gogles/a welding mask
- a cylinder trolley

The cylinder trolley ensures that the equipment is mobile and can be brought close to the work. Both cylinders must be securely fastened to it, but should

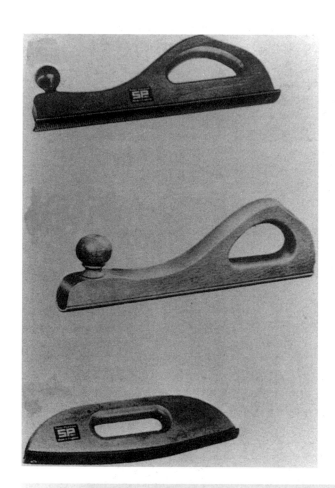

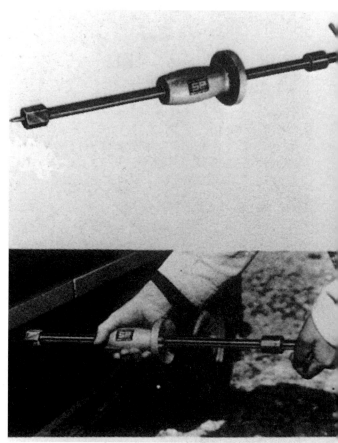

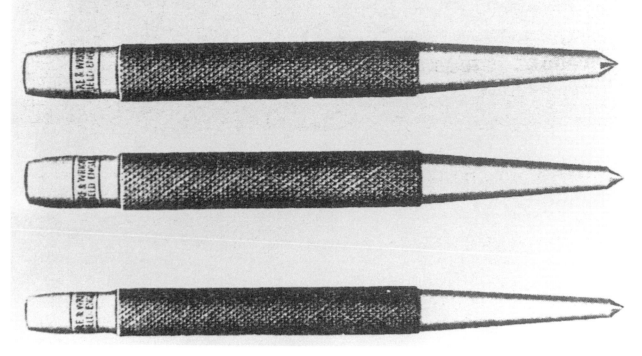

ABOVE FAR LEFT *A selection of files, as used by the panel beater.*

ABOVE LEFT *A panel puller, as used by the panel beater.*

LEFT *Centre punches, as used by the panel beater.*

ABOVE *Turn the page sideways to see the Bentley Continental R body panels more clearly. Hands and eyes check the naked body shells for the tiniest flaws. The Continental R body is actually painted before going through production, a departure from the norm at Crewe. (Photo: Andrew Yeadon).*

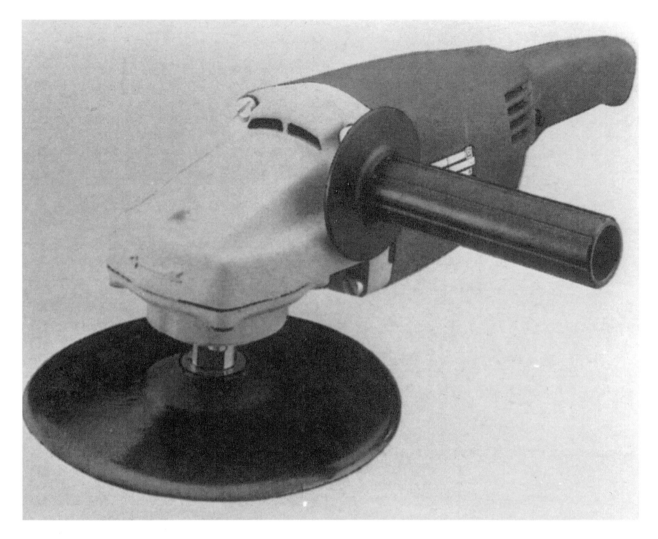

also be quickly replaceable. Of sturdy construction, the trolley should also be narrow in order to travel through the restricted space of paintshops and body repair shops.

● The welding torch. The welding torch has two needle valves – to regulate either oxygen or acetylene – a mixing chamber and an interchangeable welding nozzle, all incorporated in a shank. The torch (or 'blowpipe') mixes oxygen and acetylene in the correct proportions and causes the mixture to flow to the end of the nozzle or welding tip, where it is burned.

To enable the welding of metals of different thicknesses, an assortment of tips of different sizes is supplied.

● Ventilation. When welding, always ensure that ventilation is adequate: a suction fan is essential, preferably with a fume hood. For long jobs, breathing apparatus may also be necessary. These precautions

The (7″) 180mm Sander, 900 watts, 3200 rpm.

are especially necessary when welding hollow vessels.

Operational sequence for oxyacetylene welding
1 Before fitting the regulators, blow out the cylinder valves to remove any dirt or obstruction.
2 To ensure gas-tight connections between each cylinder valve outlet and regulator, first screw down the hexagon or wing nut by hand, then give the regulator a twist to bed it down on its seat, and finally tighten the nut properly (but without excessive force).
3 Any new hose in service for the first time should be blown through to remove possible grit.

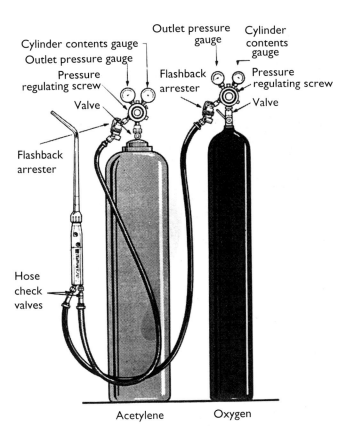

Cylinder contents gauge
Outlet pressure gauge
Pressure regulating screw
Valve
Flashback arrester
Hose check valves

Outlet pressure gauge
Cylinder contents gauge
Flashback arrester
Pressure regulating screw
Valve

Acetylene   Oxygen

A high pressure welding outfit manufactured by Murex Welding Products Ltd.

4 Attach the appropriate hoses to the regulators and the welding torch, and fit the welding torch with an appropriate tip or head if such is supplied independently.
5 Slacken off the pressure-regulating screws, slowly open the regulator outlet valves, and slowly turn on the gases with the cylinder key: the slow speed prevents damage to the regulators. The cylinder valves must be opened at least two full turns in order to ensure that the flow of gases to the regulators is unrestricted.
6 Set the regulators to the required pressure.
7 Open the acetylene control valve on the welding torch, and check working pressures when

pure acetylene is coming out of the end of the nozzle.
8 Light it. Reduce or increase the acetylene supply by the welding torch valve until the flame just ceases to smoke.
9 Turn on the oxygen via the welding torch control valve until the white inner cone is sharply defined. Check working pressures again. The welding torch is now ready for use, and is burning with a neutral flame that can be used for most welding operations.

Operational sequence to shut down oxyacetylene welding equipment

1 On completion of the welding operation, first turn off the acetylene via the welding torch control valve.
2 Turn off the oxygen via the welding torch control valve.
3 Close the cylinder valves using the cylinder key.
4 Open the welding torch valves one at a time to release the pressure in the hoses, shutting the first before opening the second.
5 Unscrew the pressure-regulating screws on the oxygen and acetylene regulators.

Technical Terms in Welding

The material of the parts to be welded is the *parent metal*. Any material that it is necessary to add to complete the weld is *filler metal* and, if in wire or rod form, is obtained from a *welding rod*. The surface to be welded is the *fusion face*, and the part of the weld where the parent metal has been melted, provided that filler is used and *interdiffusion* has occurred, is the *fusion zone*, the depth of which is the *weld penetration*.

A single longitudinal deposit of weld metal laid on a surface by fusion welding is a *bead*, and a series of overlapping beads forms a *pad*. Small local welds used to hold parts in their correct positions for full welding are *tack welds*.

Most welded assemblies comprise *butt joints* (a technical term borrowed from carpentry) in which edges are adjoined end-to-end. At *edge joints*, however, two metals are put together to form a corner.

The different parts of a weld have their own terms. The exposed surface of any weld is the *weld face*; the fusion face of a fillet weld is a *leg*, and the *toe* is a border line where the *undercut* – or wastage of the parent material in the form of a grooving – occurs. The zone at the bottom of a space provided for or

205

occupied by a fusion weld is the *root*, whereas the *throat* is the minimum depth of the weld measured along a line passing through the root.

Backfiring and flashbacks

A welding torch is said to backfire when it goes out with a loud pop, and then relights itself immediately (provided the heat of the job is sufficient to ignite the acetylene).

Backfires result from defective equipment, incorrect pressures, incorrect lighting up, or careless use of the welding torch in permitting the nozzle to touch the work, overheating the nozzle-tip, or working with a loose nozzle. Usually a backfire is arrested at the welding torch's mixer or injector. If prompt action is taken – turning off first the oxygen and then the acetylene valve – no damage occurs, and the welding torch may be relit provided that the cause of the trouble has been diagnosed and eliminated.

Sometimes a backfire may pass beyond the injector and travel back into either the oxygen or fuel gas hoses. This is a flashback, and is more serious altogether in that damage to hoses and regulators may be immediate, with risk also of injury to the operator. A flashback should be suspected at once if

Blowpipe and cutting torches; Murex Welding Products Ltd.

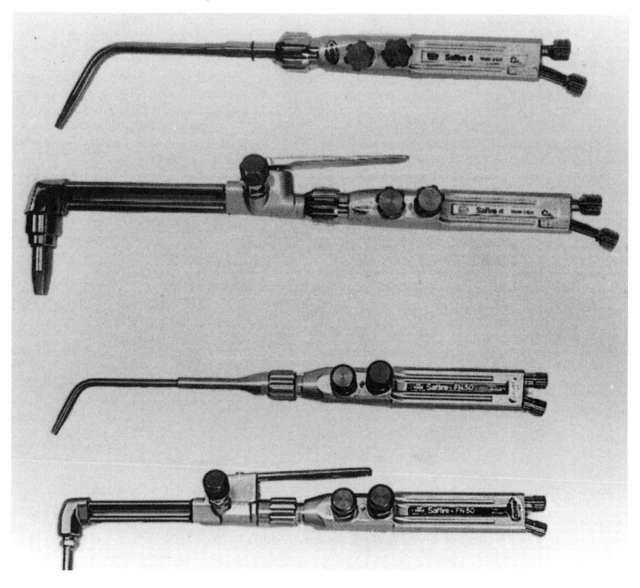

there is a squealing or hissing noise, if sparks issue from the nozzle, if there is heavy black smoke, or if the welding torch itself becomes hot. If the flashback flame burns back enough, it may burst through the hose.

Persistent backfires indicate that the blowpipe should be replaced.

Welding rods and fluxes

Good welding rods are designed to deposit metal of the correct composition, with an allowance also for the chemical changes caused by the welding process. Rods used in oxyacetylene welding are available in the following metals:

mild steel
wrought iron
high carbon steel
alloy steel
stainless steel
cast iron
copper
copper alloys
aluminium
aluminium alloys
hard-facing alloys
zinc-based die-cast alloys

Rods are obtainable in sizes ranging from 1/32 in (0·794 mm) to ¼ in (6·35 mm) in diameter. Some have a copper coating to keep the surface free from oxides or rust, but uncoated rods are equally efficient provided that they are clean.

Fluxes are de-oxidizing agents, chemical compounds used in combination with welding rods in order that all elements necessary to overcome oxidation are present. A flux must be of a specific composition in relation to the parent metal to ensure a perfect weld.

A flux must be used with:
cast iron
(high) carbon steel
stainless steel
copper
copper alloys
aluminium
aluminium alloys
magnesium alloys

The methods of use are also specific to the flux and the parent metal. For further information consult the literature available from welding equipment manufacturers or a welding manual.

Gas cutting

Oxyacetylene is widely used for actually cutting through metal, especially in the major body repairs side of the vehicular industry. Special nozzles have been developed for cutting away damaged parts of sheet metal body sections. The cutting is done by means of a hand cutting torch.

The cutting torch differs from the regular welding torch in that it has an additional lever to control a further supply of oxygen, extra to the conventional oxygen and acetylene valves that are used to control the flow of oxygen and acetylene in heating the metal.

The cutting tip has an orifice in the centre of the oxygen flow surrounded by several smaller holes for a preheating flame that generally uses acetylene, propane or hydrogen.

Brazing

Brazing, or braze-welding, is one of the easiest ways of fixing two pieces of steel together – beginners usually get it right within a very short time. As in fusion welding two pieces of steel are held together and heated up, but this time instead of steel from both pieces being made to flow into the joint, a rod of bronze alloy is pushed into the heat of the flame so that when it melts it adheres to both metal pieces. The adhesion is particularly good – in effect something between gluing and the total fusion obtained with a proper weld – because there is molecular bonding between the braze and the steel, although the steel itself does not melt. Moreover, because less heat is required for brazing, there is less distortion of the steel. But it is essential that the steel to be brazed is utterly clean: cleaning the steel first may make all the difference between successful and unsuccessful brazing.

A brazed joint cannot be as strong as a welded joint. Joints that represent structural integrity on a job (especially on a vehicle body) should be welded, not brazed.

● Brazing method. Set up the equipment as if for welding, but turn the oxygen on the torch up a little higher than normal: what is wanted is an oxidizing flame.

To minimize distortion, lightly preheat the panel. Note points at which any initial distortion takes place, and tack it down at these points. On long welds, keep the heat as low as possible by making a series of short braze runs at intervals – spaces can be filled in later.

Heat the end of the brazing rod in the flame. Then dip it into the flux (unless a pre-fluxed brazing rod is being used). Heat the workpiece, and at once feed the end of the rod into the flame. The flux will melt, and after a little more heating the braze will run into the weld. In this way, the flux coats the workpiece before the rod melts.

Arc welding

Electric arc welding is easy to set up and cheap to buy – but, unfortunately for vehicle refinishers, it is not suitable for welding thin steel. It can, however, be adapted to carry out brazing. It also takes quite a lot of practice to get it right.

The equipment consists essentially of a transformer which modifies mains electric current into the type of current suitable for safely welding steel. The electric circuit made causes a bright electric arc to jump between welding rod and workpiece. The arc melts the steel at the point on the surface, and melts the end of the welding rod too, the molten metal being thrown in liquid droplets into the weld

pool. The melting process is pretty well instantaneous, so heat distortion is minimal.

Brief as the heat is, it is really fierce – so much so that it is virtually impossible not to burn right through thin steel. For brazing, the initial method of arc welding required carbon arc equipment by which the arc was created within an inert gas that prevented oxidation of the weld while also determining the heat characteristics of the arc. This system is known as **metal inert gas (MIG) welding** or **gas metal arc (GMA) welding**, and is still sometimes employed. In fact, if the metal involved is tungsten – tungsten inert gas (TIG) welding – it is possible not only to braze using a filler rod but to weld properly two pieces of steel directly together.

But the only true inert gases used in welding are argon and helium – both rather expensive – and so for many applications, gases containing chemically active constituents are used. The gases most used for today's **metal active-gas (MAG) welding** are carbon

The principle of plasma arc welding; Murex Welding Products Ltd.

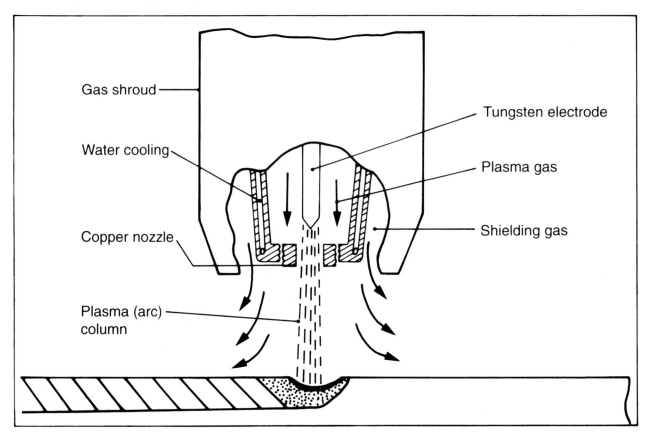

Gas shroud
Tungsten electrode
Water cooling
Plasma gas
Copper nozzle
Shielding gas
Plasma (arc) column

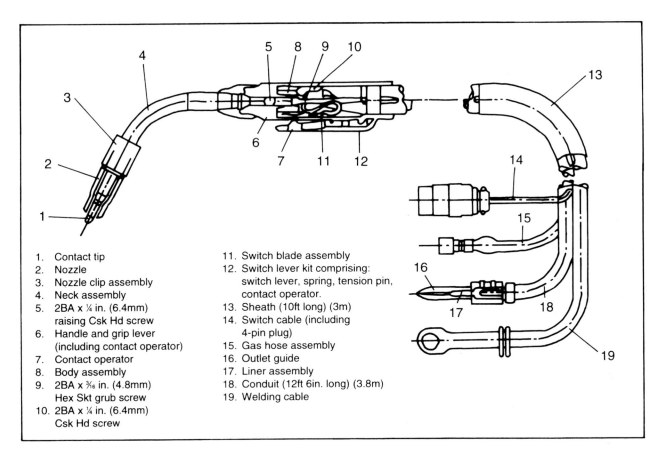

1. Contact tip
2. Nozzle
3. Nozzle clip assembly
4. Neck assembly
5. 2BA x ¼ in. (6.4mm)
   raising Csk Hd screw
6. Handle and grip lever
   (including contact operator)
7. Contact operator
8. Body assembly
9. 2BA x ³⁄₁₆ in. (4.8mm)
   Hex Skt grub screw
10. 2BA x ¼ in. (6.4mm)
    Csk Hd screw
11. Switch blade assembly
12. Switch lever kit comprising:
    switch lever, spring, tension pin,
    contact operator.
13. Sheath (10ft long) (3m)
14. Switch cable (including
    4-pin plug)
15. Gas hose assembly
16. Outlet guide
17. Liner assembly
18. Conduit (12ft 6in. long) (3.8m)
19. Welding cable

ABOVE *How the MIG welding torch is constructed;
British Oxygen Ltd.*

BELOW *The principle of TIG welding; Murex Welding
Products Ltd.*

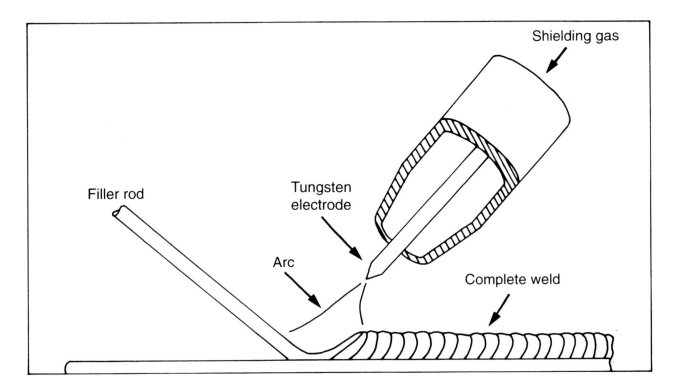

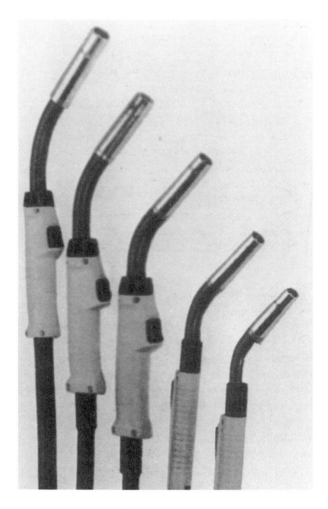

The formulation of polyester resin – glass fibre panels and lay-ups

The use of glass fibre panels, corners, wings and even complete front and rear domes has proved very attractive to the vehicle builder and repairer over the years, and there are very few constructors or operators who do not employ this type of material at some stage.

Glass fibre components are very strong, do not dent and are free from drumming. They can easily be made by the user to suit his or her requirements and dimensions, and should they suffer damage by extremely severe impact, the resultant hole can be repaired with the same material laid-up in situ.

Basically, the principle involved in reinforced plastics is the combination of polyester resin and reinforcing fibres to form a solid structure. Glass reinforced plastics are a family of structural materials which utilize a wide range of thermoplastic and thermosetting resins.

Phenol formaldehyde is a hard material; Polystyrene is a hard, brittle thermoplastic: polythene and plasticized polyvinyl chloride are soft, tough, thermosplastic materials. All plastics have one important common property. They are composed of macromolecules, which are large, chain-like molecules consisting of many simple repeating units. These are called molecular chain polymers. Not all polymers are used for making plastic mouldings. Man-made polymers are called synthetic resins until they have been moulded in some way, when they are called plastics. Most synthetic resins are made from oil or coal. The resin is an essential component of glass fibre reinforced plastic. The most widely used is polyester resin. Polyester resins are formulated by the reaction of organic acids and alcohols which produces a class of materials called esters. When the acids are polybasic and the alcohols are polyhydric they can react to form a very complex ester which is generally known as polyester. These are usually called alkyds and have long been important in surface coating formulations because of their toughness, chemical resistance and endurance.

In order to mould or laminate a polyester resin, the resin must be cured.

Catalysts for polyester resins are usually organic

dioxide or a mixture of carbon dioxide and argon. Controlled reactions take place between the gas or gases and the liquid weld pool.

Spot welding

All modern vehicles are put together with thousands of spot welds. Some years ago, motor manufacturers' advertisements made a feature of the awe-inspiring efficiency with which electrically-operated spot-welding robots danced and twirled rapidly from one set of welds to another. A spot welder gives the cleanest weld of any system.

The weld is produced by an electric arc between two electrode arms, the pressure between which can be adjusted. Some models also have a timer on which to preset the desired duration of weld.

When spot welding a vehicle body, it is important to remember that unless a repair weld is of the same high quality as the original manufacturer's, the structural safety of the vehicle may be jeopardized.

peroxides. These are supplied as a paste or liquid in a plasticizer or as a powder in an inert filler. The cure of a polyester resin will begin as soon as the catalyst is added.

A master mould of the required part is necessary and this may be made of aluminium, steel, chromium plate or of polyester resin/fibre glass itself. A 'gel' coat is first prepared by mixing the resin and activator in the required proportions and applying a coat by brush to the master mould which has already been coated with 'release agents' so that parting will be easy when the lay-up is finished. When this is partly set, a further coat of freshly mixed resin is applied and then a sheet of glass fibre is laid on and rolled into the resin by means of special serrated rollers until impregnation is complete and all air bubbles expelled. The process may be repeated if required. The lay-up is then set aside for several hours to allow it to 'cure' completely, whereupon it may be extracted out of the mould by flexing the mould all round the edges. Compressed air directed down the gap between the mould and moulding will help to effect release, and after any edge trimming which may be found necessary, it can be fitted into its respective place in the vehicle body. The operation may then be repeated again and again, merely by applying fresh release agents to the mould and making successive small mixes of resin. Once mixed with resin and accelerator the 'pot life' of polyester resin is very short and after some 15–30 minutes, it becomes useless and must be thrown away. It is perhaps worthwhile to mention here that the resin and activator should never be mixed together as they react violently with explosive force.

The polyester resin is available in both clear and thixotropic forms, the latter being required for lay-ups having vertical surfaces, as it will stay put instead of running down to form a pool at the bottom of the mould. Clear and thixotropic are intermixable to give the user the right consistency.

A variety of coloured pastes are available for adding in the proportion of 1–5% to the mixed resin, either clear or thixotropic so that the lay-up can be self coloured in order to exactly suit the ultimate colour scheme of the finished vehicle.

The preparation of the surface before painting is most important for this type of material, because the moulds in which the glass-fibre laminates are manufactured are lined with the parting agent; if all the traces of it are not removed from the surface to be painted, it will of course affect the drying and durability of the paint.

It can be effectively removed by thorough cleaning with water or a hydrocarbon solvent, such as white spirit, depending on the type of parting agent used. After the surface has been thoroughly cleaned, a flatting operation with 320 or 220 grade wet or dry paper is necessary to ensure good adhesion of the primer coat.

I strongly advise against applying primer filler or surfacer directly to a fibre glass surface, as these materials do not have the adhesive properties of an oil base primer and tend to crack and peel.

As primer is the most important coating of any paint system, it is recommended that Belco S/R primer surfacer or similar material is applied. The first coat is brushed and after overnight drying, two coats of cellulose primer surfacer is then applied. When dry, cellulose stopper may be applied as required. In the event of rubbing through during the flatting operation, spot prime with the oil-based S/R primer surfacer and proceed as for metal bodies.

(At no time should a sanding machine or a paint stripper be used, as it will destroy the glass fibre.)

Polyester resin – glass fibre lay-up operation

1. Preparation:
Clean and degrease the mould to be used.
Apply one coat of Wax type Release Agent.
Allow to dry 10 minutes.
Apply one coat of Water type Release Agent.
Allow to dry for 15 minutes.

2 Gel Coat
Mix Polyester Resin/Activator in the recommended proportions together wih Polyester Colour paste if required. The resin should be of the necessary thixotropy for the job in hand.
Apply one coat by brush and allow to gel for 20 minutes (until slightly tacky).

3. Lay-up
Mix a further quantity of Polyester Resin/Activator and colour paste if required.
Apply a heavy coat by brush. Lay on a sheet of Glass Fibre mat and roll down with a serrated roller until impregnation is complete. Allow to cure for 12 hours before removing from the mould.

4. Parting
Remove the lay-up from the mould. Trim edges and

Fibre glass Lotus Elan body is lowered onto the chassis following restoration. Colin Chapman's Elan was the first volume production 'plastic' car. (Photo: Duncan Wherrett)

remove all release agents from surfaces to be painted by washing with water or solvent.

Fibre glass reinforced plastic resins

Thermosetting resins
Polyester
Epoxide
Furane

Thermoplastic resins
Polystyrene is hard/brittle
Polythene and plasticized polyvinyl chloride are soft and tough, and widely used to ease fabrication, and has a limit temperature of about 75°C.

Polypropylene
Belongs to the polyolefine class of polymers and has a higher rigidity and temperature resistance than polyethylene. Its melting point is about 170°C.

Catalysts
Organic peroxides.

Accelerators
Those based on cobalt soap or those based on tertiary amine.

Fillers
Thixotropic fillers.

Moulds
Wood, steel, aluminium, polyester resin/glass fibre and plaster of Paris.

Release agents
These may be either water-soluble, film forming compounds or wax compounds.
Polyvinyl alcohol is applied as a solution by cloth, sponge or spray. It is diluted with 2–3 pints water to 1 pint of solution.
Wax emulsions e.g. carnauba or silicone lubricant.

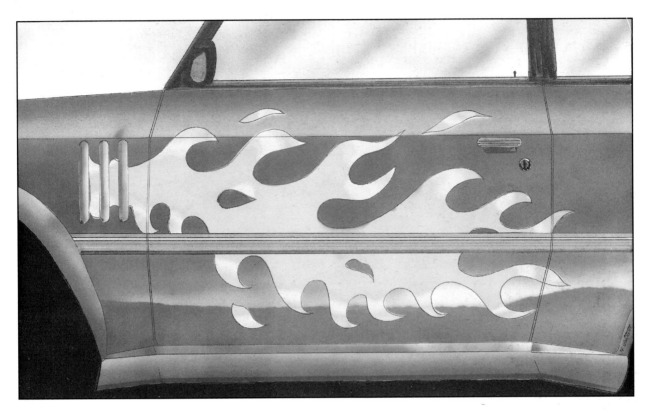

CUSTOM DECORATING A VEHICLE

Various special effects from card masking are often used on customised vehicles.

Custom painting

There are no set rules when custom painting a vehicle body: it is all up to the imagination. Most custom painting is done with pigmented or clear acrylic lacquers readily available in small quantities from art shops. Acrylics are especially easy to brush or spray. Each coat must be given time to flash off (surface-harden) before the next coat is applied. A very high durable gloss is achieved by polishing the final coat of clear acrylic lacquer.

An alternative is synthetic enamel, which is also available in small quantities, and which dries to a high gloss that needs no extra burnishing. But it takes a long time to dry, and this in turn means a long delay between the application of successive coats.

Preparation

The area to be custom painted must be examined very closely. For this it will need washing down thoroughly with a solvent-based water-miscible cleaning solution, a mild detergent, or a mixture of methylated spirit and water, in order to remove contaminants such as grease and silicon wax polish.

If the metal is then confirmed to be in good condition – with no rust spots, dents or scratches – wet-flat with P600-grade wet or dry abrasive paper, using hard soap as a lubricant, to remove the surface gloss. Mask off the surrounding area.

If, on the other hand, there are some rust spots, the recommended procedure is:
1 Sand out the rust.
2 Wet-flat with P320-grade wet or dry abrasive paper, using a cork or rubber block, and soap. The final effect should be that the paint tapers back so gradually from the bare metal to the sound paint surface that the gradation cannot be distinguished with the fingertips.
3 Clean all bare metal with a phosphoric acid metal cleaner.
4 After 10 minutes wash off thoroughly. Dry off.

Flamed 1955 Chevrolet: the result of card masking. (Photo: Colin Burnham).

5 Etch-prime the bare metal.
6 Apply two coats of primer-surfacer.
7 Apply cellulose stopper (filler) in thin layers, as required.
8 Flat the stopper, using P400-grade wet or dry abrasive paper. Wash off. Dry off.
9 Apply two more coats of primer-surfacer.
10 Flat the primer-surfacer, using P600-grade wet or dry abrasive paper. Wash off. Dry off. Blow out the seams with compressed air.
11 Spirit wipe the whole panel. Tack-rag wipe.
12 Apply the colour coats. Allow to dry overnight.
13 Remove masking. Wet-flat with P600-grade wet or dry abrasive paper and soap, to remove surface gloss.
14 Wash off. Dry off.
15 Remask surrounding areas to be custom painted.

Masking and stencilling
To mask off areas that should not be painted, especially windows and their rubbers, most refinishers use masking-tape 3/4 inch (19 mm) wide. But in the custom painting of straight or curving lines, the tape used is generally only 1/8 inch (3 mm) wide, and can itself be curved in two planes. This is

the narrowest stock width of tape, but can nonetheless be cut even narrower if 'spaghetti' stripes and swirls are desired. The narrower the tape, the smaller the radius that can be negotiated before the tape ruckles up.

It pays to use the better quality of masking-tape that comes away cleanly after use.

A stencil is a more elaborate mask. Stencils can be cut from any kind of paper, but the best for the purpose is the sort that is very thin, transparent, and adhesive on one side, with a backing sheet that can be peeled off after the design has been drawn and cut out.

With both masking and stencilling it is advisable first to try out the design on card or lining-paper, using the method of paint application intended for the final product. Better to make a mistake in such a trial than on the vehicle!

The same mask or stencil can be moved along the bodywork to produce repeat or symmetrical patterns. Large and elaborate designs may require a separate stencil for each colour. In these circumstances it is all too easy to spray the wrong colour or the wrong area, so it is advisable to label all stencils clearly and distinctly both for colour and area.

If a stencil is held a short distance away from the actual work surface, the stencil pattern is given soft edges: this is an ideal effect for metallic finishes (which are common in aerosol paint sprays).

But paint tends to build up on the edge of a mask or stencil – so beware drips.

● Fish scale pattern. The template for fish scales consists of a straight edge of cardboard on which a series of circular adhesive patches have been stuck to overlap tangentially. The mask is placed on the base coat, and the area around the edge of the line of patches is 'fogged' with an airbrush or aerosol. Then the mask is moved half a patch diameter back and half a diameter to one side, and the fogging repeated to give the effect of overlapping scales.

BELOW Arrow paint effects achieved by card masking. The possibilities are almost endless with this simple technique.

● Card masking. A similar fogging effect is put to use around a pack of old playing-cards or business cards, arranged in a fan-like shape. The fan as a whole is rotated or moved after each pass of the airbrush or aerosol.

● Lacework (silhouette) pattern. Another form of masking is lace painting. Any kind of lace fabric can be used as a stencil – only of course the pattern is in the negative. Stretch the lace as tightly as possible over the base coat, and stick it down with masking-tape. An airbrush, aerosol or spray gun can be used, only be sure to use a succession of thin mist coats rather than one wet coat, for the lace may not pull away cleanly if it becomes saturated.

● Flames. Flames have long been a popular design on car bodies. The most simple method is to draw the flame pattern on transparent adhesive paper, cutting it out, sticking it down on a red or orange base coat, and spraying around with a contrasting colour. If a black outline to the flame is required, the base coat should be black, and the outline of the flame masked off in very narrow masking-tape. The area inside the tape outline should then be sprayed orange or red, and the area outside the tape outline should be

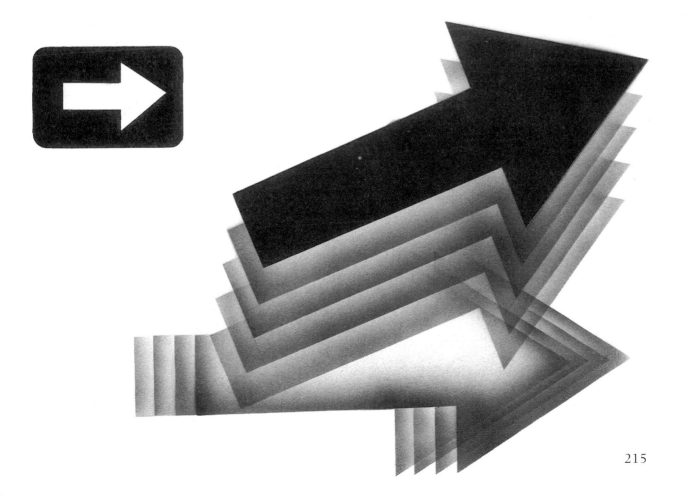

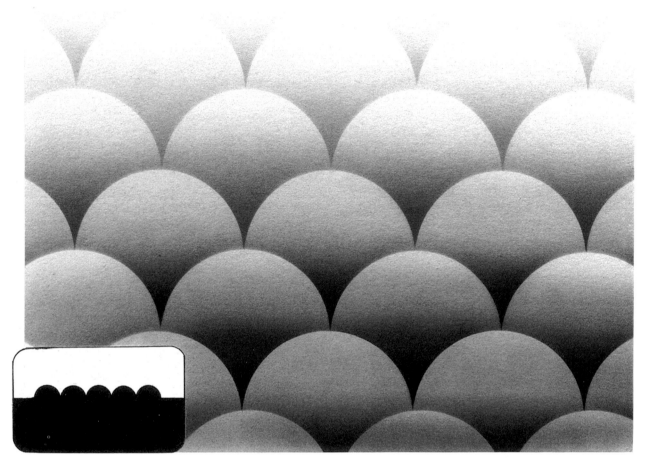

sprayed with a contrasting colour. Removing the mask reveals a black outline to an orange or red flame.

Fish scale paint effect from card masking.

Aerosol spraying

First attempts at decorating vehicles in a personal fashion were with chequered tape, and served a dual purpose: they were ideal for covering over patches of rust. The arrival of aerosol paints and the immediate introduction of new techniques with which to apply them greatly increased both the interest in car decoration on the part of the general public and the range of possible decorative forms. A whole new industry has grown up to supply the enthusiast with a host of different finishes, some of them exotic (to say the least).

The aerosol contains a mixture of fluid paint and a liquid propellant gas largely in vapour form above it, giving sufficient pressure to eject a stream of paint through the top nozzle when the valve is released by being depressed. The liquid gas acts as thinner to the paint, and vaporizes rapidly on emergence into the atmosphere, so atomizing the paint.

Shake the can well before use, perhaps for a couple of minutes or more, to disperse any pigment that may have settled in storage. (Settling is more likely to occur in an aerosol than in an ordinary paint tin because of the viscosity of the paint-gas mixture.) Apply the paint in an arc motion, holding the can about 25 cm (10 in) from the work surface.

Spraying with an aerosol must not be continuous over any period of time – application must be intermittent in order to allow some of the gas inside the container to vaporize and fill the space vacated by the paint.

Do not throw 'empty' aerosol cans away anywhere that they may come in contact with heat: they may explode.

Ripple paint effect accomplished by card masking. Drawn by Neil Watkins.

Airbrush spraying

For fine work, the artists' airbrush is used. The airbrush is a miniature spray gun, and the double-action type is very suitable for use in carrying out minor repairs on car body paintwork and for customizing. The ordinary variety has an adjustable spray, a 21-gramme (3/4-ounce) paint jar and a 1·9-metre (6-foot) hose. It is powered by an air compressor or a 370-gramme (13-ounce) can of aerosol propellant. Another type of airbrush is available that is much smaller still, not much larger than a fountain-pen. It is operated by a foot-pump or small electric compressor.

The double action is of the finger on the airbrush trigger: pressing down, the air valve is opened; pullling back starts the flow of colour into the air stream for atomization. The further the finger on the button is pulled back, the greater the volume of colour sprayed. The closer the airbrush is held to the work surface, the sharper the definition, and for really fine lines the airbrush is lightly rested at an angle on the work surface itself.

Airbrushwork should be covered with several coats of clear acrylic, which is left for two weeks or so before rubbing down with P1200-grade abrasive paper, used wet, followed bu burnishing with fine rubbing compound and liquid polishing.

● Freak drops. The effect of freak drops is obtained using the double-action airbrush. The paint is made watery by adding thinners. Then the brush is held 5 cm (2 in) away from the work surface, and a single short burst deposits a spider-shaped splotch on it. The shorter, more instant the burst, the larger the nucleus of the splotch; a longer burst tends to increase the spread of the spidery tentacles. But a burst of air (without any paint) from the airbrush can in any case spread the drops out once they are there. Too long a burst will deposit too much paint, which will

217

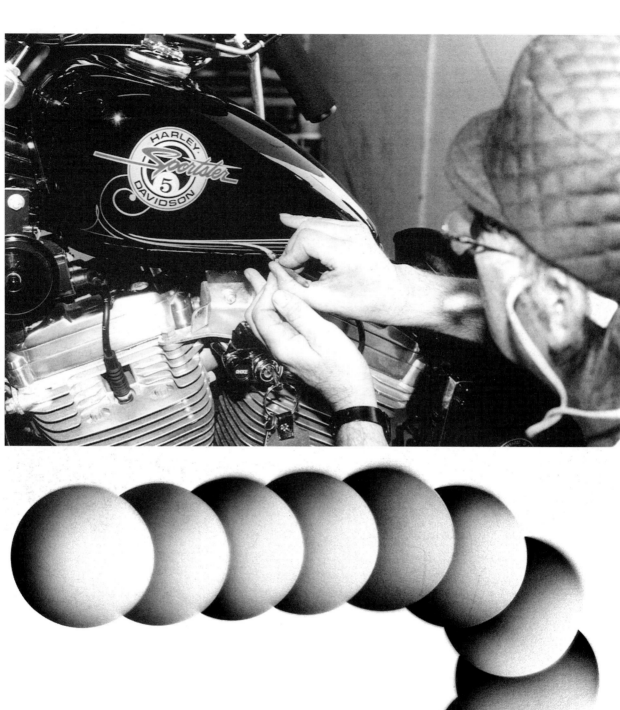

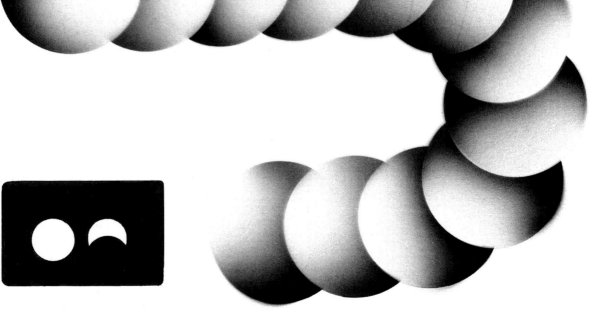

ABOVE LEFT *Running a line freehand using a lining brush. See The restoration of the horsedrawn carriage, page 177: certain effects owe very little to technological innovation!*

LEFT *Circular point effects achieved by card masking. Drawn by Neil Watkins.*

ABOVE *1986 Toyota sports truck. Paint makeovers like this for Ford and Chevy pickups, displaying fine lining and masking technique, are a common sight in the US. (Photo: David Fetherston)*

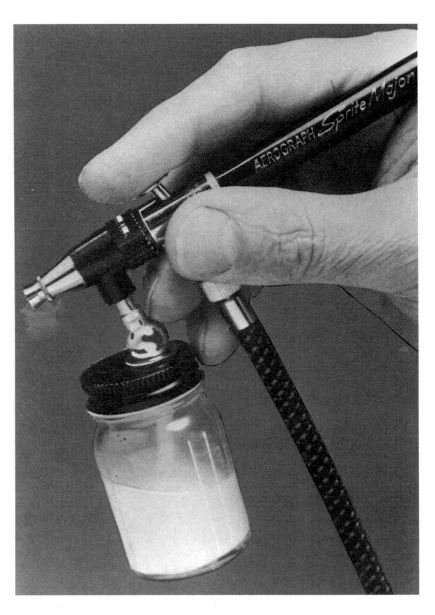

DeVilbiss air brush which can be used to produce the correct design effect when customising.

then simply run down the work surface.

Spray gun paints and their effects
● Metallic finishes. Metallic finishes need a thick layer of clear acrylic lacquer to protect them, especially in areas where they have to be petrol-proof. Spray seven to nine medium-wet coats, allowing 10 minutes drying time between each coat. Then leave the surface to dry for 12 hours before applying five more topcoats. After two days of air-drying, wet-flat with P600-grade abrasive paper until the 'orange-peel' disappears, but do not expose any metal flake. Wash and dry thoroughly. Tack-rag the lot. Apply three more coats of clear lacquer. After two weeks, wet-flat again with P600-grade abrasive paper, and spray a light coating of very thin lacquer. Allow to dry for 12 hours before burnishing with a fine

rubbing compound and finishing off with a liquid polish. Finally remove the masking.
● Pearlescent finishes. Acrylics loaded with pearlescents give an iridescent effect that in some cases changes with the point of view. Apply in three thin coats at 45–55 pounds per square inch (3·1–3·8 kg/cm^2) pressure, allowing 10 minutes flash-off time between each coat, and spraying alternate coats at right-angles to each other, to prevent streaking. Constant stirring is required.

Pearlescent paints are supplied in various tints and are sprayed over a coloured base, usually white. The tint may be enhanced or slightly darkened by the addition of further coats of translucent acrylic paint.
● Cobwebbing. A cobweb effect is obtained by blowing unthinned paint through the spray gun. Too viscous to atomize, the paint leaves the gun in long

filaments. The gun should be held just less than a metre (about 3 feet) away from the work surface. Extensive masking is necessary because the viscous paint emerges fairly wildly from the spray gun. When it is dry, protect the cobwebbing with clear acrylic lacquer coats.

● Patina mosaic. A finish that seems to have a network of tiny cracks in it can be achieved using a paint specially manufactured without the constituent that usually inhibits shrinkage. The paint is sprayed in the same way as other acrylics. The size of the cracking can be controlled: a thin coat gives an intricate pattern of small cracks, a heavy coat gives a more disparate pattern. The largest network pattern is obtained by spraying a second heavy coat before the first has even started to dry. The cracked surface should then be covered and filled with 8 to 10 coats of clear acrylic.

Flock spraying

From time to time a refinisher may be called upon to apply a flock finish to the interior compartments of vehicles. The technique consists of coating the substrate with an adhesive and then blowing flock uniformly over the surface so that the fibres embed themselves.

The vehicle manufacture industry uses flock in window channelling, glove and boot compartments, and sometimes in place of interior carpeting. Main advantages of flock coatings are toughness and durability of wear, the improvement in thermal insulation, and the reduction in condensation.

● The flock. Flock fibres can be of nylon or rayon. There are three forms for spraying:
a) cut flock, in which the fibres are of constant length;
b) random flock, in which the fibres are of different lengths; and
c) ground flock, which is powdered.
Some 30 colours of flock are commercially available, but manufacturers state that special shades can be supplied on request.
Sold by weight (in kilogrammes), flock covers an area proportional to its fibre length.

    1 kg flock 0·5 mm long covers approx. 8·4 m²
    (90 sq ft)
    1 kg   1·0 mm
    7·4 m² (80 sq ft)
    1 kg   2·0 mm
    4·2 m² (45 sq ft)

● The flock gun. The flock gun is similar to the conventional paint spray gun, although the nozzle and ports may be very much larger. Inside the gun, the flock fibres as a mass supported by an air current act just like fluid paint. Once the flock is ejected through the gun nozzle, it meets the air from the ports and is blown out in a cloud, again just like atomized paint.

Some guns come with applicators of different sizes for different types of flock or areas of application. But the use of several applicators with different flock colours in any case enables an easy and quick change from one colour to another.

● The adhesive. There are four main categories:

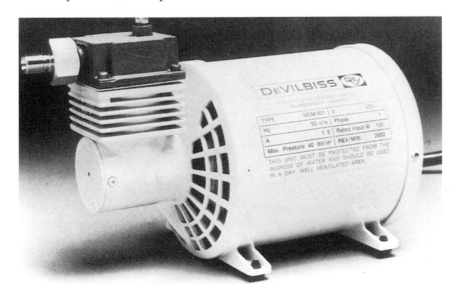

Miniature compressor used for the air brush when customising.

polyvinyl acetates (PVAs), acrylics, pigmented white-spirit-based (usually medium-oil alkyds), and epoxy resins.

Operational procedure

- Surface preparation. Walls and surfaces must be thoroughly cleaned and free from all contaminants. If the surface is porous it is advisable to seal it either with a good-quality emulsion or, even better in some circumstances, with good-quality bright aluminium.
- Adhesive application. To apply the adhesive, a roller is most often used for the flatter areas in conjunction with a brush for rounded areas or corners. But the adhesive may equally well be applied by screen printing or spray.
- Using the flock gun. The air supply should have a

LEFT *Spraytex 'miser' flock gun from Spray Technique.*

BELOW *Electrostatic flock applicator from Spray Technique.*

minimum pressure of 25 pounds per square inch (1.75 kg/cm^2). Too high a pressure results in excessive usage of materials. Adjust the fibre control to achieved density of fibre to flow into the air stream. Screwing it in decreases the flow; screwing it out increases it. The fibres should leave the gun in the form of a mist.

To ensure a good finish, do not hold the gun too close to the work surface, and apply the fibres from different angles, working up and down and from right to left, and releasing the trigger at the end of each stroke.

● Precautions. Some airborne fibres will escape during the process. Regular cleaning is important to avoid accumulation in the workshop of this 'fly', which in fact constitutes a fire hazard and may also be problematical to people who suffer from asthma or similar conditions. In critical areas, extraction fan systems should be fitted wherever practicable, with extra fire-fighting equipment ready to hand.

It is strongly advised that goggles are worn at all times when flock may present a danger to the eyes.

Window decoration

There are three major methods by which vehicle windows may be decorated:
  sand-blasting
  engraving
  acid embossing

● Sand-blasting. Sand-blasting is possible on toughened glass, through a paper stencil, if care and the right grade of sand are used.

● Engraving. Engraving is done with a revolving copper wheel. It is not possible on toughened glass, however, but is generally done on ordinary 5-mm glass which can then be taken to a safety-glass manufacturer for toughening.

Engraving with an electrically-operated engraving needle also requires the second toughening process, but the quality of finish is inferior to that produced by copper-wheel engraving.

● Acid embossing. Acid embossing is carried out only by firms who also undertake silvering and gilding on glass.

223

ACKNOWLEDGEMENTS

I wish to acknowledge my gratitude and express my appreciation for the assistance given to me by the personnel and their companies listed below. Their cooperation has made my task very much easier than it might otherwise have been, and in addition should enable craftsmen, apprentices and young people just coming into vehicle refinishing to benefit greatly from the information they have so generously provided.

The names are in alphabetical order of (the first) surname, and no other categorization is intended.

Mr Clive Bew, Technical Services, 3M (UK) plc.

Mr I. C. Bunker, Manager, Market Development, European Marketing, The DeVilbiss Company Limited.

Mrs Sue Calver, The Furniture Industry Research Association.

C. D. Cuckow and Sarah Williams, ESAB Group (UK) Ltd (for information on Murex products).

C. J. Goulding, Product Manager, Chubb Fire Ltd.

Keith Hammond, author of *Automobile Finishing*, published by Robert Draper Ltd, 1971.

Peter Holdcroft and Robert John, authors of *Welding and Cutting*, published in association with the ESAB Group, 1988.

Mr Malcolm Holland, Barfields Advertising & Publicity Ltd (for information on behalf of Spraybake Ltd).

Nicki Hopcroft, British Oxygen Company Ltd.

Mr S. R. Howton, Professional Products Division, Black & Decker Ltd.

Gary Jordon, Marketing Manager, L. G. Harris & Co. Ltd.

Mike Lambourne, Publicity Officer, Compair Broomwade Ltd.

Paul Leete, Internal Sales Engineer, Atlas Copco Tools Ltd.

Joanne Milroy, Welbeck Golin/Harris Communications Ltd.

Mr H. Norton, Chesterfield Cylinders Ltd.

Mrs Beryl Olive, Director, Spraytechnique (Warrington) Ltd.

Mr D. R. Orrell, Manager, Technical Advisory Department, Joseph Mason Paints plc.

Rod Ousbey, Master Coachpainter and proprietor of Withybrook Carriages and Harness Room.

David Preston and Janet Green, Press Relations Officers, Rolls-Royce Motor Cars Ltd.

Mr Alan Routs, Director, Sheen Instruments Ltd.

W. H. Tatton and E. W. Drew, authors of *Industrial Paint Application*, published by Butterworth/Heinemann, 1971.

Neil Watkins, customising designer.

Christine Whitworth, Marketing Services Executive, Sykes-Pickavant Group plc.

Mr R. Whybro, Director, Desoutter Automotive Ltd.

CONVERSION TABLES

Equivalents and conversions

Linear measure

1 cm	=	0·3937 in	1 in	=	2·54 cm
5 cm	=	1·9685 in	2 in	=	5·08 cm
10 cm	=	3·937 in	6 in	=	15·24 cm
20 cm	=	7·874 in	12 in, 1 ft =		30·48 cm
50 cm	=	19·685 in	18 in	=	45·72 cm
1 m	=	3·281 ft (1·094 yd)	2 ft	=	60·96 cm
1·5 m	=	4·922 ft (1·641 yd)	2 ft 6 in =		76·20 cm
2·0 m	=	6·562 ft (2·187 yd)	3 ft, 1 yd =		91·44 cm
5·0 m	=	16·405 ft (5·468 yd)	6 ft, 2 yd =		1·83 m
10·0 m	=	32·810 ft (10·94 yd)	10 yd	=	9·144 m
20·0 m	=	65·620 ft (21·88 yd)	100 yd	=	91·44 m
100·0 m	=	328·1 ft (109·4 yd)	220 yd	=	201·17 m
1 km	=	1,094 yd (0·623 mile)	1 mile	=	1·609 km

Temperature

0°C	=	32°F	150°C	=	302°F	32°F	=	0°C	275°F	= 135°C
15°C	=	59°F	180°C	=	356°F	60°F	=	16°C	360°F	= 182°C
20°C	=	68°F	200°C	=	392°F	75°F	=	24°C	400°F	= 204°C
25°C	=	77°F	220°C	=	428°F	85°F	=	29°C	430°F	= 221°C
37°C	=	99°F	250°C	=	482°F	100°F	=	38°C	480°F	= 249°C
50°C	=	122°F	300°C	=	572°F	120°F	=	49°C	570°F	= 299°C
60°C	=	140°F	350°C	=	662°F	140°F	=	60°C	660°F	= 349°C
70°C	=	158°F	400°C	=	752°F	160°F	=	71°C	750°F	= 399°C
75°C	=	167°F	450°C	=	842°F	170°F	=	77°C	840°F	= 449°C
80°C	=	176°F	500°C	=	932°F	180°F	=	82°C	930°F	= 499°C
100°C	=	212°F	550°C	=	1·022°F	195°F	=	91°C	1,020°F	= 549°C
120°C	=	248°F				212°F	=	100°C		

Litres/Pints (8 pints = 1 imperial gallon

litres		pints	litres		pints
0·5682	1	1·7598	28·9805	51	89·7498
1·1365	2	3·5196	29·5488	52	91·5096
1·7047	3	5·2794	30·1170	53	93·2694
2·2730	4	7·0392	30·6853	54	95·0292
2·8412	5	8·7990	31·2535	55	96·7890
3·4095	6	10·5588	31·8217	56	98·5488
3·9777	7	12·3186	32·3900	57	100·3086
4·5460	8	14·0784	32·9582	58	102·0684
5·1142	9	15·8382	33·5265	59	103·8282
5·6825	10	17·5980	34·0947	60	105·5880
6·2507	11	19·3578	34·6630	61	107·3478
6·8189	12	21·1176	35·2312	62	109·1076
7·3872	13	22·8774	35·7995	63	110·8674
7·9554	14	24·6372	36·3677	64	112·6272
8·5237	15	26·3970	36·9360	65	114·3870
9·0919	16	28·1568	37·5042	66	116·1468
9·6602	17	29·9166	38·0724	67	117·9066
10·2284	18	31·6764	38·6407	68	119·6664
10·7967	19	33·4362	39·2089	69	121·4262
11·3649	20	35·1960	39·7772	70	123·1860
11·9332	21	36·9558	40·3435	71	124·9458
12·5014	22	38·7156	40·9137	72	126·7056
13·0696	23	40·4754	41·4819	73	128·4654
13·6379	24	42·2352	42·0502	74	130·2252
14·2061	25	43·9950	42·6184	75	131·9850
14·7744	26	45·7548	43·1867	76	133·7448
15·3426	27	47·5146	43·7549	77	135·5046
15·9109	28	49·2744	44·3231	78	137·2644
16·4791	29	51·0342	44·8914	79	139·0242
17·0474	30	52·7940	45·4596	80	140·7840
17·6156	31	54·5538	46·0279	81	142·5438
18·1839	32	56·3136	46·5961	82	144·3036
18·7521	33	58·0734	47·1644	83	146·0634
19·3203	34	59·8332	47·7326	84	147·8232
19·8886	35	61·5930	48·3009	85	149·5830
20·4568	36	63·3528	48·8691	86	151·3428
21·0251	37	65·1126	49·4373	87	153·1026
21·5933	38	66·8724	50·0056	88	154·8624
22·1616	39	68·6322	50·5738	89	156·6222
22·7298	40	70·3920	51·1421	90	158·3820
23·2981	41	72·1518	51·7103	91	160·1418
23·8663	42	73·9116	52·2786	92	161·9016
24·4346	43	75·6714	52·8468	93	163·6614
25·0028	44	77·4312	53·4151	94	165·4212
25·5710	45	79·1910	53·9833	95	167·1810
26·1392	46	80·9508	54·5516	96	168·9408
26·7075	47	82·7106	55·1198	97	170·7006
27·2758	48	84·4704	55·6880	98	172·4604
27·8440	49	86·2302	56·2563	99	174·2202
28·4123	50	87·9900	56·8245	100	175·9800

$0\cdot1\,m^2$ = $1\cdot076$ sq ft
$0\cdot5\,m^2$ = $5\cdot382$ sq ft
$1\cdot0\,m^2$ = $10\cdot764$ sq ft,
$\qquad\qquad$ $1\cdot196$ sq yd
$1\cdot5\,m^2$ = $16\cdot146$ sq ft,
$\qquad\qquad$ $1\cdot794$ sq yd
$2\cdot0\,m^2$ = $21\cdot528$ sq ft,
$\qquad\qquad$ $2\cdot392$ sq yd
$5\cdot0\,m^2$ = $53\cdot820$ sq ft,
$\qquad\qquad$ $5\cdot980$ sq yd
$10\cdot0\,m^2$ = $11\cdot96$ sq yd
$20\,m^2$ = $23\cdot92$ sq yd
$50\,m^2$ = $59\cdot80$ sq yd
$100\,m^2$ = $119\cdot60$ sq yd

1 sq ft = $929\,cm^2$, $0\cdot0929\,m^2$
3 sq ft = $0\cdot2787\,m^2$
6 sq ft = $0\cdot5574\,m^2$
9 sq ft, 1 sq yd = $0\cdot8361\,m^2$
2 sq yd = $1\cdot6722\,m^2$
10 sq yd = $8\cdot361\,m^2$
20 sq yd = $16\cdot722\,m^2$
30 sq yd = $25\cdot083\,m^2$
40 sq yd = $33\cdot444\,m^2$
50 sq yd = $41\cdot805\,m^2$
60 sq yd = $50\cdot166\,m^2$
70 sq yd = $58\cdot527\,m^2$
80 sq yd = $66\cdot888\,m^2$
100 sq yd = $83\cdot610\,m^2$

Volumetric measure

10 ml = $0\cdot0176$ UK pt, $0\cdot021$ US pt
100 ml = $0\cdot1760$ UK pt, $0\cdot211$ US pt
500 ml = $0\cdot8799$ UK pt, $1\cdot057$ US pt
$1\cdot0$ l = $1\cdot7599$ UK pt, $2\cdot114$ US pt
$1\cdot5$ l = $2\cdot6399$ UK pt, $3\cdot171$ US pt
$2\cdot0$ l = $3\cdot5198$ UK pt, $4\cdot228$ US pt
$5\cdot0$ l = $8\cdot799$ UK pt, $1\cdot099$ UK gal,
$\qquad\qquad$ $10\cdot57$ US pt, $1\cdot321$ US gal
$10\cdot0$ l = $17\cdot599$ UK pt, $2\cdot199$ UK gal,
$\qquad\qquad$ $21\cdot14$ US pt, $2\cdot642$ US gal
$25\cdot0$ l = $43\cdot995$ UK pt, $5\cdot499$ UK gal,
$\qquad\qquad$ $52\cdot85$ US pt, $6\cdot606$ US gal

$0\cdot5$ UK pt = 284 ml
$1\cdot0$ UK pt = 568 ml
$1\cdot5$ UK pt = 852 ml
$2\cdot0$ UK pt = $1\cdot136$ l
$3\cdot0$ UK pt = $1\cdot705$ l
$4\cdot0$ UK pt = $2\cdot272$ l
8 UK pt, 1 gal = $4\cdot546$ l
$1\cdot5$ UK gal = $6\cdot819$ l
$2\cdot0$ UK gal = $9\cdot092$ l
5 UK gal = $22\cdot730$ l
10 UK gal = $45\cdot460$ l
20 UK gal = $90\cdot920$ l

Pressure

1 kg per cm^2 = $14\cdot227$ lb/sq in
2 kg per cm^2 = $28\cdot454$ lb/sq in
3 kg per cm^2 = $42\cdot681$ lb/sq in
4 kg per cm^2 = $56\cdot908$ lb/sq in
5 kg per cm^2 = $71\cdot135$ lb/sq in
10 kg per cm^2 = $142\cdot270$ lb/sq in
15 kg per cm^2 = $213\cdot405$ lb/sq in
20 kg per cm^2 = $284\cdot540$ lb/sq in
40 kg per cm^2 = $569\cdot080$ lb/sq in
50 kg per cm^2 = $711\cdot350$ lb/sq in
70 kg per cm^2 = $995\cdot890$ lb/sq in
90 kg per cm^2 = $1,280\cdot43$ lb/sq in

1 lb/sq in = $0\cdot07$ kg per cm^2
10 lb/sq in = $0\cdot70$ kg per cm^2
50 lb/sq in = $3\cdot50$ kg per cm^2
60 lb/sq in = $4\cdot20$ kg per cm^2
70 lb/sq in = $4\cdot90$ kg per cm^2
100 lb/sq in = $7\cdot00$ kg per cm^2
200 lb/sq in = $14\cdot00$ kg per cm^2
300 lb/sq in = $21\cdot00$ kg per cm^2
500 lb/sq in = $35\cdot00$ kg per cm^2
750 lb/sq in = $52\cdot50$ kg per cm^2
1,000 lb/sq in = $70\cdot00$ kg per cm^2
1,200 lb/sq in = $84\cdot00$ kg per cm^2

INDEX

Page references in *italic* refer to illustrations.